The Confederacy on Trial

LANDMARK LAW CASES

AMERICAN SOCIETY

Peter Charles Hoffer
N. E. H. Hull
Series Editors

MARK A. WEITZ

The Confederacy on Trial

The Piracy and

Sequestration Cases

of 1861

UNIVERSITY PRESS OF KANSAS

Published by the University Press of Kansas (Lawrence, Kansas 66049), which was
organized by the Kansas Board of Regents and is operated and funded by
Emporia State University, Fort Hays State University, Kansas State University,
Pittsburg State University, the University of Kansas, and Wichita State University

Library of Congress Cataloging-in-Publication Data
Weitz, Mark A., 1957–
The Confederacy on trial : the piracy and sequestration cases of 1861
/ Mark A. Weitz.
p. cm. — (Landmark law cases & American society)
Includes bibliographical references and index.
ISBN 0-7006-1385-4 (cloth : alk. paper) — ISBN 0-7006-1386-2 (pbk. : alk. paper)
1. Trials (Piracy)—United States—History—19th century.
2. Hijacking of ships—United States—Cases. 3. Prize law—United
States—Cases. 4. Capture at sea—Cases. 5. Enemy property—Cases.
6. Effectiveness and validity of law—United States—History—19th century.
7. Effectiveness and validity of law—Confederate States of America—
History—19th century. 8. United States—History—Civil War,
1861–1865—Confiscations and contributions. 9. Confederate States of
America—Trials, litigation, etc. 10. Confederate States of
America—International status. I. Title. II. Series.
KF221.P57W45 2005
345.73′0264—dc22
2005000782

British Library Cataloguing-in-Publication Data is available.

Printed in the United States of America

10 9 8 7 6 5 4 3 2 1

MY THANKS TO GERRIT, STEVE, ANN, AND JASON

Hazards and costs to other persons are of no concern
to the lawyer, who must not regard alarm, the torments,
the destruction which he may bring others. . . .
He must go on reckless of the consequences,
though it may be his unhappy fate to involve
his country in the confusion.

—LORD BROUGHAM

CONTENTS

In terms of the enormous numbers of casualties, the catastrophic physical destruction of the land, and the tremendous transformation of the laws that govern us, which ended slavery and created the beginnings of a truly centralized nation-state, the Civil War surely remains the most important single episode in our nation's history since 1776. But unlike the Revolution, the Civil War has many names and, laid alongside one another, they hint at a legal puzzle.

Was it a War Between the States, a War for Southern Independence, a War against Northern Aggression, or the War of the Great Rebellion? As the ongoing debate over its name suggests, the war years witnessed struggles within the North and South to define secession, the legal status of the Confederate States, and the rights of persons and property in the Union and the Confederacy. While the victory of federal forces appeared to answer these questions with finality, things were hardly so clear during the conflict itself. Even as the war raged from the Atlantic to the Mississippi, from Canada to the Gulf, the United States Congress, federal courts, and the Confederate state courts were wrestling with the complex, confusing, and intransigent issues of sequestration, confiscation, and piracy.

As Mark Weitz reveals in his fascinating account of the key Northern piracy and Southern sequestration cases, the novelty of the secession ran smack into very old and well-established ideas of private property, due process of law, and prosecutorial fairness in the South. In the North judges faced a similarly perplexing array of legal questions. Were Southern raiders acting under the authority of a sovereign government, giving the raiders' assaults on Northern shipping the color of legality, or were they simply pirates? To make these cases and the questions they raised even more important, both sides had one eye on the other's handling of persons and property. If the Confederate States of America were no more than a "conspiracy," as Weitz puts it, composed of traitors waging war against their own country, what was the status of the Confederate courts' decisions in ordinary cases of domestic crime, contracts, tort liability, and commercial transactions? Was every decision these courts rendered thus null and void?

The Confederacy was supposedly created to protect private property against an invasive federal regime. Faced with the exigencies of war, the Confederate Congress and the state courts imposed a series of unique burdens on Southern property holders. Property held by people living in the North was "sequestered" and sold even when Southerners had an economic interest in it. Debts owed to Northern merchants were forcibly surrendered to the government, under pain of fines. A comprehensive inquisitorial system was imposed to ensure that no one hid such debts—a far more oppressive regime than any the Lincoln Republicans might have imposed on the South.

On the other hand, what was the legal status of acts taken by federal forces to suppress the rebellion? In international law, for example, a blockade of another nation's coastline was permissible in war—but if the Confederate states were not a nation at all, how could their coastlines be interdicted, their ships seized, their cargos confiscated, and their sailors imprisoned? The Emancipation Proclamation took property from Southern slave owners without compensation, a violation of the due process clause of the Fifth Amendment (until the passage of the Thirteenth Amendment at the end of the war). Confiscation of enemy property was legal in wartime, but the Lincoln administration was putting down a rebellion, not waging war upon the Confederacy, at least in theory.

Over and over, the necessities of waging a war seemed to trump the niceties of law, but judges and courts are loath to give away their authority, and in both North and South the traditions of a government of laws still held firm. Thus in the piracy cases and the sequestration cases one finds an elegant and dramatic tension between political demands made on courts and courts' insistence on their primary role of reasoned, precedent-bound adjudication. Lawyers on both sides of the Mason Dixon Line took their jobs seriously, defending persons and property against prosecution. In neither section of the country was the legal process suspended. None of the trials was held in secret, despite the respective governments' interest in their outcome. This, and the intense public interest, reflected in newspaper coverage and the publication of counsels' arguments, enables Weitz to track the cases from their inception to their sometimes entirely unexpected results.

{ *The Confederacy on Trial* }

Weitz's achievement in the pages that follow is noteworthy for many reasons–the clarity of his presentation; the masterly weaving together of factual detail and legal rule; the immense respect he has for the legal system; and the breadth of his synthesis of politics and law. He reminds us also of the humanity of the defendants and counsel, the integrity of the judges and jurors, and our past commitment to legal means even in the midst of a horrific war. This is an especially valuable lesson in these days of special tribunals and trials of suspected terrorists.

"It Was as If It Were Not"

In 1863 James Hickman of Huntsville, Alabama, was indicted for treason in the district court of the Confederate States of America for the Northern District of Alabama. He stood accused of engaging in a hostile enterprise against the Confederate States of America. Hickman aided the U.S. Army in one of its many expeditions into northern Alabama during the war. Arrested and imprisoned pending trial, he applied to the presiding judge for bail and was denied. He remained in jail until his trial, whereupon he was acquitted and released. Thereafter he sued the judge, the clerk, the district attorney, the deputy marshal, an editor and publisher of a newspaper, and several others for malicious prosecution. During the trial the judge instructed the jury that if Hickman had not aided the United States under some form of duress, then the defendants should prevail because their actions did not constitute malicious prosecution. In other words, without duress Hickman acted willingly and at least seemed to have committed treason against the Confederacy, making the actions of the Confederate judiciary and newspapers appropriate. As a result of the instruction, Hickman lost his suit. He appealed, and in 1869, four years after the end of the American Civil War, the U.S. Supreme Court had occasion to comment on the Confederate judiciary and in the process pass judgment on the legal existence of the Confederacy itself.

In an opinion delivered by Justice Noah Swayne, the Court asserted that the rebellion out of which the war grew was without any legal sanction. In the eyes of the United States it was no different than if a county or smaller political subdivision had rebelled against a state to which it belonged. The length and intensity of the struggle neither altered its nature nor elevated the legal status of the Confederacy. Its government was "never de facto," nor did it ever receive recognition by the national government or any foreign power. The Confederacy never seized the U.S. capital, nor did it for a moment displace the rightful government, which was always "in existence, always in the regular discharge of its functions, and constantly exercising all of its military power to put down resistance to its authority in the insurrectionary states." Any recognition of the Confederacy as a "belligerent" had been solely for the sake of humanity. The act of the Confederate Congress that created the Confederate district courts likewise grew out of the rebellion and as such had never existed. Confederate courts were a nullity, and persons acting under the laws of the Confederacy realized no protection for their acts. In short, Hickman stated a valid claim for malicious prosecution, and whether he acted under duress was irrelevant. His actions in aiding the United States during the war were legal, and the conduct of the defendants in prosecuting him or aiding in that prosecution exposed them to civil liability under the law. Swayne's opinion served as a convenient obituary for a government that had struggled from its inception for recognition and never rose to the level to which it aspired.

The unequivocal denial of the Confederacy's existence reflected the luxury afforded to the victor in a civil war. That Swayne wrote the opinion should have surprised no one. He was the weakest of Lincoln's five appointees to the Court, and his only claim to distinction was his unwavering commitment to the president's war measures. However, as much as the United States and its Supreme Court wanted to forget that the Confederacy had ever existed, certain realities could not be ignored. Four years after *Hickman v. Jones*, the Supreme Court conceded that at least some of the Confederate courts had existed and that their actions had endured. In voiding an executor's investment of trust funds in Confederate bonds, the Court in *Horn v. Lockhart* admitted that "no one . . . seriously questions the validity of judicial or legislative acts in the insurrection states . . . where they were not hostile in their purpose or mode of enforcement to the authority of the national government." Thus even if the United States felt more comfortable believing that the Confederacy and its courts never existed, those courts did exist. What they did during the four years of the Confederacy had substance, and sometimes their actions were clearly "hostile" to the national government and its authority. In the process, however, they also took steps that, if not hostile toward their own citizens, limited or infringed on rights the Confederacy purported to have gone to war to protect. Those were the instances in which the Confederacy revealed something about itself.

For an entity with such a short life span, the Confederacy raised legal issues that endured long after its armies had surrendered in April 1865. Two months after South Carolina's secession on December 20, 1860, six other states followed suit and formed a government. Two months later the Confederacy found itself at war, a war that brought four more Southern states into the fold. An internal struggle that decided the fate of the "American Experiment" took on international ramifications almost immediately. The American Civil War forced the international community to define more clearly the law of belligerency. A conflict that saw almost three million men under arms on land and in warfare on the high seas resulted in the rewriting of the laws of war applicable to civil wars. Swayne's opinion in *Hickman* notwithstanding, for four years U.S. laws and courts ceased to operate in eleven states and compelled a reevaluation of the status of domestic institutions during time of war. The resolution of some of these issues reshaped the law of internal rebellion.

When Rhodesia unilaterally declared its independence in November 1965, the British courts looked to the American Civil War and its legal precedents for answers. In *Madzimbamuto v. Lardner-Burke* (1969) the Royal Privy Council's efforts to resolve a modern-day issue using America's Civil War as precedent reveal both the enduring nature of some of the Civil War legal authority and its limitations in answering questions as to the nature of the Confederacy during the rebellion.

The Privy Council's analysis of the Civil War cases reveals the unique place they occupy in international jurisprudence. However, they offered little help in resolving the situation in Rhodesia. As the British court observed, "The peculiarities of the American Constitution are such that it is not safe to rely for guidance upon the post–Civil War American cases, when dealing with a British Colony." Whereas British colonies enjoyed a "common sovereignty," American states possessed some aspect of independent sovereignty and thus possessed a claim to some form of separateness that British colonies could not claim. That being said, the American Civil War cases served as authority that some acts by a government in rebellion that were made to create peace, order, and good government authority were valid and had to be recognized even after the rebellion had been suppressed. The *Madzimbamuto* opinion provided an excellent discussion of postwar Supreme Court decisions.

Using *Texas v. White* (1869) for the proposition that the courts gave recognition to some acts of the Confederacy and withheld it from others, the British court discussed a long list of postwar jurisprudence, including *Hickman v. Jones* (1869), *Horn v. Lockhart* (1873), *Thomas v. City of Richmond* (1870), *Keith v. Clark* (1878), *Baldy v. Hunter* (1898), and *Sprout v. United States* (1874). Ultimately, the court concluded that the Civil War cases could not help resolve the Rhodesian situation for three reasons. First, all of the cases were decided after the war and rested at least in part on the inequity of refusing to recognize transactions that had governed the day-to-day lives of citizens in the rebel states, the unraveling and nullifying of which would have been an impossibility. Marriages, land contracts, and probate matters adjudicated by Confederate courts were good examples of acts that had to be recognized. Second, in every instance the post–Civil War cases supported "private rights of individuals" and never recognized the Confederate government or any measure that aided or supported the rebellion. Finally, the cases limited recognition of Confederate judicial acts to state courts, and the United States refused to recognize in any sense measures of the Confederacy.

Thus, although the post–Civil War decisions endured beyond the war, they represented peacetime efforts to restore order without ever sanctioning the rebellion itself. The Confederate States of America had no existence except as a conspiracy, and its legislative, executive, and judicial acts were a complete nullity. However, even the Privy Council decision recognized a reality that the U.S. Supreme Court refused to concede in 1869: "In America for four years there had been no lawful courts," and U.S. justice did not reach into the Confederacy. Although the body of law that emerged during the Reconstruction era provides precedent for the identity and fate of an unsuccessful rebellion, it does nothing to enlighten

{ *The Confederacy on Trial* }

the question of the status and identity of a rebellion that is still inchoate. To answer that question, one must look at the Confederate legislative, executive, and judicial acts promulgated during the war and the actions of the Confederate judiciary that is least known and understood, its federal bench. How people and nations reacted to and conceptualized the Confederacy between 1861 and 1865 tells so much more about its true identity than the judgment passed by the nation's high court in the years that followed the end of the war.

The decision most associated with the identity of the Confederate states is the series of cases that reached the U.S. Supreme Court in 1863 collectively known as the *Prize Cases*. Those cases arose almost immediately after the war began and involved efforts by U.S. sea captains to claim the law of prize for ships captured attempting to run the Union blockade. The law of prize created a legal conundrum for the United States. How could the Union maintain a naval blockade, a war measure central to its plan to suppress the rebellion, without a formal declaration, or at least recognition, that a state of war existed? If there was no war, there could be no blockade, at least not one that other nations were obliged to recognize under international law. Equally troublesome was the idea that captured ships could not be deemed the property of enemies without the ability to identify them or the property on them as belonging to residents of an enemy territory.

By declaring a blockade, Lincoln placed the internal struggle onto the international stage. The individual prize cases that made up the body of the Supreme Court case demonstrated how difficult the answer would be. The lower court decisions grappled with the issue of the definition of war, using the war with Mexico as a precedent and referencing the secession of the Southern states, their organization into a government, and that government's subsequent attack on federal forts as proof that a state of war existed. However, in all these arguments, the Confederacy remained an abstraction. Without truly defining what it was in international law, the Confederacy had taken certain actions that forced the United States to respond and in the process created a state of war. That state of war justified the blockade and the subsequent seizure of ships as war prizes. Thus, the ultimate resolution of the *Prize Cases* facilitated the Union's war objectives without recognizing the Confederacy beyond the concept of a belligerent. However, in so doing it afforded the Confederacy certain rights that it had rejected earlier in the war, rights that redefined the Confederacy and gave it a status in 1863 that the United States had been unwilling to concede in 1861.

The problem with trying to define the nature of the Confederacy as an international entity through the prize courts is that neither side had any interest in really addressing the question. The United States needed to legitimize its blockade and the cooperation that naturally flowed from foreign nations under international law. It had to avoid at all costs anything that resembled conveying nation status on the rebellion. Foreign recognition of the American colonies by France during the American Revolution contributed significantly to America's success. British and French recognition of the Confederacy loomed as a possibility from the inception of the war up until 1863. Thus the focus of the United States in resolving the issues in the *Prize Cases* rested on abstract issues of war and how it is defined. The defendants in those cases likewise had compelling reasons not only to avoid the question of the Confederacy's standing in international law but also to disavow that it had any status at all. Defendants, whether Southern or foreign, went into court to secure possession and ownership of their property. They would do so by undermining any notion that a war existed and could accomplish this goal in part by denying that the Confederacy had any status sufficient to deem the property of its residents "enemy property."

In 1861 the legal focus of the Union prize cases fell on the legality of executive and judicial actions under the U.S. Constitution. Specifically, could the executive branch of the government declare a state of war sufficient to legitimize some of the tools of waging war under the law of nations? If not, the actions of U.S. prize courts would be unconstitutional. To be sure, certain attributes of the Confederacy, or at least life in the Confederate states after April 12, 1861, had to be mentioned. Not only had the Confederacy attacked U.S. installations, but also the imposition of its alleged government had usurped the U.S. legal system. Contrary to Noah Swayne's pronouncement in 1869, U.S. law and courts did not operate in the Southern Confederacy after its member states seceded. However, these points were not raised to demonstrate the status of the Confederacy or to legitimize the government as at least de facto, but rather to emphasize that a state of war existed sufficient to utilize war measures recognized under international law.

In the legal world, standing, the right to bring a suit or prosecute a claim, can exist only where that requisite adversity of interest exists between the parties such that it will illuminate the issues so as to define clearly the legal question or rights at stake. In the prize cases neither side had any interest in directing the court's attention to the character and legal status of the Confederacy. But, at the same time that Union ships captured prizes on the high seas and brought them before U.S. federal courts, Confederate ships also seized ships— Union ships—and instituted prize proceedings before Confederate district courts. Unlike its Union counterparts, the Confederate courts readily acknowledged that a state of war existed. The seizure of enemy property and Union merchant ships on the high seas comported with every aspect of international law. However, the Confederacy did not enjoy the luxury of legitimizing its own existence. It could not obtain nation status simply because it professed to be independent of the United States.

When the Union navy captured the crews of several Confederate privateers in 1861, the U.S. government put them on trial for piracy. The trials that followed had that requisite adversity between the litigants that helped illuminate the issues of what the Confederacy was, and the United States had much at stake. To acknowledge Confederate seamen as privateers might legitimize the letters of marque issued by Jefferson Davis, under whose authority they sailed and made war. To do so would validate the acts of the Confederate legislative and executive branches. It not only would elevate these men to the status of combatants but also might well define the Confederacy as a nation, if not de jure, at least de facto, and in the process pave the way for foreign recognition. At a minimum, conceding that these men were privateers conveyed belligerent status on the Confederacy, and although short of proclaiming it a nation, such an act took a significant step toward some form of foreign recognition on which other nations could rely. Thus the United States not only had to confront the issue of the Confederacy and define it in such a way as to deny it the right to use war-making tools such as letters of marque, it also had to do so while preserving its own abilities to wage war under international law.

While the United States tried to deconstruct the Confederacy as a legitimate government and nation, the defendants in the piracy cases found themselves in a position of having to present the best possible case for recognizing the legitimacy of the Confederate government; their very lives depended on the legitimacy of their letters of marque. Without letters of marque the act of seizing ships on the high seas had but one definition: piracy. Piracy in 1861 carried the death penalty. To escape the gallows, Confederate sailors had to demonstrate in a U.S. court that the Confederate government was legitimate and had cloaked them with the requisite authority and protection to wage war on the high seas without being deemed common robbers and thieves. Such a task was difficult under any circumstances, but the Confederate privateers faced an even greater struggle because the Northern juries would almost certainly be made up of men who were predisposed to view the Confederacy as the symbol of treason and to see its agents as traitors.

As Shakespeare's Prince Hamlet pointed out, it is in the play where we find "the conscience of the King." Three prominent piracy cases were held in 1861. In the fall of that year crew members of the *Petrel*, the *Savannah*, and the *Jeff Davis* all awaited trial in a federal district court for piracy, the *Petrel* and *Jeff Davis* in Philadelphia and the *Savannah* in New York. In a world where district court cases were seldom reported or preserved in their entirety, the piracy cases present the rare opportunity to follow the only two ever tried from jury selection to verdict. Not only did the trial transcripts survive, but also much of the newspaper print that covered the trials remains. The cases went to trial almost simultaneously in front of different juries in different states. Although the arguments on both sides were virtually identical, key differences in how the judiciary viewed each case affected each outcome. However, more than simply the outcome, the arguments and evidence mustered by the respective sides are what truly helped define what the Confederacy was in 1861.

The trials of these cases also played a role in the subsequent ruling in the *Prize Cases* two years later. Judge Robert Grier, who wrote the majority opinion in the *Prize Cases*, presided in the *Jeff Davis* case. Irrespective of the outcome in that case, the arguments seemed to remain with him long after the jury rendered its verdict. Likewise, Judge Samuel Nelson, who presided over the *Savannah* case, was also an associate justice on the U.S. Supreme Court, and he delivered the dissenting opinion in the *Prize Cases*. Thus, the *Jeff Davis* and *Savannah* cases served to define the issues of what the Confederacy really was in a way that cases involving the mere right to property could not. Of note, both sides seemed to understand the far-reaching implications of each case when they began.

While the Confederate government helped redefine the nature of rebellion in international law, its legal importance went much further. The Southern Confederacy offered a constitutional alternative to the United States, one based on state supremacy that purported to be free of corruption and faithful to the vision of the founding fathers. Alexander Stevens, Robert Barnwell Rhett, and a host of other Southern writers extolled the virtues of the purer, agriculturally based, Jeffersonian vision of liberty. Despite a record of suppression of speech and expression for almost three decades leading up to the war in an effort to squelch any opposition to its vital and peculiar institution, on the eve of the war the Confederacy claimed to be the protector of civil liberties. Whereas Jefferson Davis's letters of marque triggered the legal and intellectual debate over the status of the Confederacy as a nation, the Confederate legislature and judiciary sparked the debate in 1861 over what kind of a nation the Confederacy was and would become. Just as Jefferson Davis could not unilaterally confer nationhood on the Confederacy by exercising the prerogatives afforded to countries under international law, the act of claiming to be the cradle of constitutional liberty did not make it so. The proof came only after the Confederacy passed through the cauldron of the legal process, in this instance its own court.

Traditionally, historians have labeled Lincoln and the Union as the oppressors of constitutional rights during the war. Critics point to the suspension of the writ of habeas corpus in 1861, the imposition of martial law, the cases of military courts trying civilians, and a host of other wartime measures as evidence that the Union and its executive ignored the Constitution for much of the war. Recently, however, scholars have begun to pay closer attention to the Confederacy and its wartime measures that seemed to trample on the Confederate Constitution. The prevalence of a strict passport system throughout the war, the imposition of martial law, and the small but significant population of political prisoners gave indications that perhaps the importance of civil liberties in the Confederacy had been exaggerated. Despite these infringements on personal liberty, it seems that Southerners tolerated certain restrictions in the interest of preserving law and order.

However, certain measures pushed Southerners to question the Confederacy's commitment to civil liberties and the notion of states' rights. Conscription not only struck people as inconsistent with state sovereignty but also undermined the notion of equality among all white men by turning the war into a poor man's war. After the first year of conscription, courts throughout the South wrestled with disputes that questioned the legality of the draft. The draft became so unpopular that the Confederacy needed lawyers in virtually every congressional district where there was no district attorney just to represent the Conscription Bureau in exemption cases. When the Confederate Congress suspended the writ of habeas corpus in 1862, it tampered with what some considered the surest protection of the common man. Ironically, in the South the writ benefited the wealthy more than the poor, but that did not dampen the furor over its suspension. Conscription lasted from 1862 through 1864. The Confederate Congress suspended the writ of habeas corpus again in 1864. Although these instances of Confederate war making infringed on personal rights, no act of the Confederate Congress lasted longer, applied with greater uniformly across the nation, and caused more unrest than the Alien Enemies Act and Sequestration Act of August 1861.

Three months after Abraham Lincoln suspended the writ of habeas corpus in Maryland to prevent that state from slipping out of the Union, the Confederacy took steps to consolidate its control over the eleven states that made up the new nation. First, it declared anyone living in the Confederacy who claimed residency in any state in the United States to be an "alien enemy." The act gave such persons forty days to leave the Confederacy or suffer the consequences. Three weeks later the Confederate Congress passed the Sequestration Act, which allowed the property of any alien enemy to be seized by the Confederate government and sold and the proceeds given to Confederate citizens who lost property to the Union by destruction or confiscation. The process of discovery, seizure, and sale of alien enemy property fell under the exclusive jurisdiction of the Confederate federal district courts.

The Sequestration Act had an immediate effect on citizens both North and South. Northerners with property in the South stood to lose it immediately to the new law. Southerners, however, faced an equally troubling problem. Many had extensive business relationships in the North. Partnerships between Northerners and Southerners abounded, and under the sequestration law these business entities had to be dissolved and the property partitioned lest Southerners fall victim to the seizure and sale of partnership property. Perhaps the most troubling aspect of the new law made debts owed by Southerners to an alien enemy subject to seizure. Monetary obligations to Northerners became payable to the Confederacy, and the government purported to absolve any Southerner of liability for that debt on payment to the government. The law created so much confusion as to how far it reached and the steps necessary to assure compliance that Southerners flocked to their lawyers for help. In the fall of 1861, lawyers articulated the insidious nature of the law and challenged the Confederate Sequestration Act.

The Sequestration Act affected members of the legal profession beyond the mere interruption of business relationships. Court-appointed receivers in charge of the collection and seizure of alien enemy property could send written discovery to any person who might have knowledge of the character and whereabouts of alien enemy property, compelling them under the threat of criminal penalty to reveal that property and, if in actual possession thereof, to deliver it to the receiver. For attorneys this meant breaching confidences and violating the legal relationships at the core of their profession. Responding truthfully to the receiver's discovery potentially meant disclosing client communications. In some instances, turning property over to the receiver required lawyers to violate their duty as trustees.

The conflict went beyond the divided loyalty felt by all attorneys as they struggled between safeguarding clients they swore to protect and assisting the new nation that was now at war. It literally pitted the states against the Confederate government. The Confederate Sequestration Act required attorneys to violate the oath they had taken when they became licensed. Then, like now, lawyers were licensed on the state level. The provisions of the Sequestration Act ran contrary to the mandates of the state bar, and an attorney could not comply with both. The sequestration cases provided the first test case of the Confederacy's commitment to states' rights and individual civil liberties as five lawyers in Charleston, South Carolina, stepped up to challenge the Confederate law.

Thus the sequestration cases provided the opening chapter of a debate that engulfed the Confederacy for the remainder of the war: to what extent did the exigencies of war allow it to undermine or qualify its own constitution? The cases took center stage in Charleston at the same time the piracy cases unfolded in Philadelphia and New York. Like the piracy cases, the sequestration cases featured a judge whose contributions to the Confederacy did not end with the suits. Andrew G. Magrath, a staunch secessionist and future governor of South Carolina, presided over the sequestration cases. The attorneys involved were among Charleston's most prominent figures, and one, James Petigru, was a living legend at the end of an illustrious career. His commitment to the law was so uncompromising that he insisted to the day of his death that the American Revolution had been wrong and that Confederate secession had been illegal. On the opposing side for the Confederacy was the acting district attorney for Charleston, South Carolina, C. R. Miles. Little is known of the lead counsel for one of the most important cases ever tried in the Confederate states. Sitting next to him was South Carolina Attorney General Isaac W. Hayne, the grandson of Isaac Hayne, a martyred hero of the American Revolution who was hanged by the British in Charleston in 1779. His extended family included Robert Hayne, the eloquent opponent of Daniel Webster in the debates on the floor of the U.S. Congress in 1832.

Just as in the piracy cases, the litigants realized that much was at stake. The record represents one of the few (if not the only) recorded trials in a Confederate district court. The reporter who chronicled the proceedings, a J. Woodruff, stated that the cases had "created a deep and wide-spread interest" and that "the more immediate object of the publication is to preserve an interesting and valuable record of the opinions of distinguished jurists upon an act affecting nearly every citizen in the Confederate states." Although Woodruff's comments might have been a self-serving advertisement designed to sell copies of the record, his words rang true, both as to the public interest generated by sequestration and as to the long-term effect on Confederate citizens.

A landmark case is one that marks a turning point or a stage in the development of a people or a nation. Together, the piracy and sequestration cases not only are landmarks but also offer a unique opportunity to get "inside" the Confederacy. Unlike the post–Civil War cases that passed judgment on the Confederacy as a failed rebellion, the piracy and the sequestration cases addressed the Confederacy as a viable entity, with its future and that of the United States hanging very much in the balance. Unlike the 1861 prize cases that focused on the nature of the war, the piracy cases required the defendants to define the Confederacy in order to give it nation status or at least belligerent status. To the extent that the 1863 *Prize Cases* dealt with the Confederacy as anything other than an abstraction, the piracy cases helped to define those issues by clearly articulating the competing arguments and the legal authority on which they rested. Often both sides invoked the same legal authority to support their position.

The sequestration cases provided a similar defining stage or turning point in the short life of the Confederacy. After thirty years of sectional debate that saw the emergence and entrenchment of the states' rights doctrine, the Confederacy's commitment to that ideology came into question almost immediately after the war began. The alien enemy and sequestration laws clearly trod on the laws governing attorney conduct in all eleven Confederate states. They violated the sanctity of the contract on multiple levels and subjected Confederate citizens to criminal sanctions for in effect refusing to inform on their friends, neighbors, and business associates. These transgressions on the legal and ideological foundation of the new Confederacy would be justified in the name of war. Within the halls of a Confederate courthouse, a place that Noah Swayne later claimed never existed, these issues played out and not only resolved the debate over this law but also defined the nature of the debate for other Confederate war measures that followed. The piracy and sequestration cases belong together not only because they provide insight into both the international definition of the Confederacy as well as its own self-image but also because they occur almost simultaneously, with each proceeding aware of the existence and progress of the other. The defense in the *Jeff Davis* case pointed directly to the Sequestration Act and the Confederate Militia Act as proof of the Confederacy's de facto status as a government to support its contention that the men on trial for piracy had taken the only course available by acquiescing to the only authority in existence in the Confederacy. At the same time, Judge Magrath pointed to the piracy cases and exhorted his fellow citizens on the grand jury that heard the sequestration evidence for the first time to punish and retaliate against the North's efforts to try soldiers as common robbers. At one point, William Whaley, one of the defendant lawyers in the sequestration cases, pointed to the hypocrisy of a Confederate position that sought recognition under international law, yet passed an act that in effect violated that very law. It was Whaley who articulated the effect of sequestering debts in a nineteenth-century international economic system that used evidences of debt as legal tender. Thus not only were the cases reverse sides of the same coin insofar as defining the Confederacy, but also the issues in each case intertwined, and to at least a limited extent the litigants knew this to be the case.

These cases merit landmark status for one other reason. More than just helping to define the Confederacy and the legal issues that swirled around it, the cases provide a defining moment in the development of the American legal profession. The American Civil War put lawyers in both the North and the South in the position of having to balance a conflict between personal and professional integrity and to manage the pressure exerted by their respective nations to compromise their professional duties in favor of national interest. Patriotism in effect became contrary to professionalism. The conflict surfaced in the sequestration cases as attorneys became defendants and ran the risk of criminal liability in order to assert their position. In the North the pressure was more subtle, but nevertheless present. Criminal trials in the United States work because no matter how heinous the crime or how abhorrent the defendant might seem to the general public, defense attorneys understand that their duty is to give that person the best possible defense. Just like their brethren in the South, the Northern bar had to be willing to put the Constitution and civil liberties above the national interest and undertake an unpopular cause. Members of the Northern bar did step up to represent the rebels and in the process helped define the Confederacy.

In 1869, Justice Swayne had the luxury of declaring that the Confederate judiciary and the nation that spawned it had not existed. In 1861 people in both the North and the South knew that was not true. Whereas the *Savannah*'s career ended almost as quickly as it began, the *Jeff Davis* enjoyed amazing success during the Confederacy's first summer as the privateer terrorized Northern shipping from New England to the Caribbean. Likewise, the Confederate Sequestration Act proved to be more than some obscure law; it had both teeth and endurance. During the act's existence, Confederate receivers seized and sold millions of dollars in "alien" property, affecting citizens in every Confederate state. The Confederacy did exist, and the battles that unfolded in courtrooms in both the North and the South attested to its substance. The fight began in 1861, almost immediately after the war began, as the new nation took steps to preserve its existence in the face of Northern efforts to preserve the Union.

CHAPTER I

"And the Fame of the Dane Revive Again / Ye Vikings of the South"

On April 12, 1861, the Confederacy opened fire on the Union garrison at Fort Sumter, South Carolina. Any chance the new Southern government had of quietly assuming all of the mantles of nationhood disappeared. When Major Robert Anderson surrendered twenty-four hours later, the Confederates had won a victory and in the process entered a war that would challenge the Confederacy's legal existence and test its commitment to civil liberties and the sanctity of its constitution. The Confederacy had to earn its place among the family of nations, and doing so severely tested its principles. The process began almost immediately. On April 15, 1861, President Abraham Lincoln issued a call for 75,000 men to put down the rebellion. Two days later, on April 17, 1861, Confederate president Jefferson Davis put out a call for privateers. That act moved the American Civil War from a mere internal dispute into the realm of international law.

Privateering derived its name from the original use of letters of marque, the document that created the legal authority that distinguished the practice from piracy. Prior to the eighteenth century, letters of marque served as a means to right a private wrong. Citizens who had been wronged or lost their property in another country could appeal to their sovereign for satisfaction on their return home. If the claim was legitimate, diplomatic efforts between the two nations were used to rectify the wrong. If such measures failed, the sovereign granted the citizen a letter of marque against a specific

The chapter title is taken from Edward C. Bruce, "Sea-Kings of the South" (1863).

country, allowing that person to capture the shipping of the other nation in satisfaction of the debt or grievance. The key language within the letter of marque, or letter of "reprisal," was the limitation to the shipping of a specific nation. This limitation distinguished a privateer from a pirate, one who was an enemy of all nations and subject to being tried and punished by any country that caught him.

By the eighteenth century, letters of marque had ceased to be remedies for private wrongs and had become instruments of state. Governments could supplement, and in some cases even create, a naval force by using private ships to meet the needs of the country. Although the practice served as the primary tool to destroy the commerce of an enemy, many nations still thought privateers to be little better than pirates. The lure of money more than the zeal of patriotism motivated most privateers, and foreigners routinely intervened in a war for the opportunity to loot the shipping of one of the warring nations. However, selfish motives aside, the ability to quickly raise a naval force proved too alluring to abandon the practice. In 1761, during the Seven Years' War, Louis XV, his naval forces exhausted, turned to privateers, and they rewarded his grant of power by taking more than 800 British trading vessels. Facing the world's most formidable navy with virtually no fleet of its own, the United States relied on privateers during both the American Revolution and the War of 1812. Some believe that, more than the battles at Saratoga and Yorktown, the attack on Britain's commerce struck the most severe blow to British supremacy in America. Likewise, in the War of 1812, as one of its first acts the United States developed a privateer fleet to attack British shipping.

Despite its utility, by the early nineteenth century a groundswell of support to abolish privateering had developed in Europe, culminating in 1856 in the Declaration of Paris. The declaration came out of European efforts to settle the Crimean War. The first article stated, "Privateering is and remains abolished." But the prohibition applied only to the nations that signed, and although invited to do so, the United States refused. Thus Jefferson Davis believed the Confederacy did not have to abide by the Declaration of Paris because the nation with whom it was at war had expressly rejected the treaty five years before the Civil War began.

President Lincoln did not stand by idly as the Confederacy

threatened to invoke this outdated, disfavored, but still acceptable form of naval warfare. On April 19, 1861, Lincoln took steps to make naval warfare under Confederate authority a dangerous proposition. Citing the commencement of hostilities and the threat of persons preying on U.S. shipping under the authority of Confederate letters of marque, Lincoln proclaimed that "if any person, under the pretended authority of said States [The Confederacy], or under any pretense, shall molest a vessel of the United States, or the person or cargo on board of her, such persons will be held amenable to the laws of the United States for the prevention and punishment of piracy." On April 24, 1861, the Lincoln administration tried to enlist European assistance in quashing the Confederate privateering threat before it materialized. In a circular issued to the ministers of Great Britain, France, Russia, Prussia, Austria, Belgium, Italy, and Denmark, the United States offered to abide unconditionally by the 1856 Declaration of Paris, and it submitted a specific agreement, or convention, to Great Britain purporting to bind the two nations.

However, the post hoc offer by the United States to sign the Paris declaration proved too transparent. Great Britain refused U.S. entreaties, as did the rest of Europe. By May 3, 1861, the international community knew the Union intended to blockade the South, and to embrace the Union's offer to "abolish privateering" would have looked like an endorsement of the United States and forced the Europeans to treat Confederate privateers as pirates. This they were unwilling to do. Britain expressed its intent to send a naval force to protect its own ships, and it refused to allow the Confederacy to bring prizes into its ports. Initially, the British government did not address U.S. prizes because it did not anticipate that the United States would issue letters of marque. However, by late June 1861, it seemed clear that neither side would be allowed to bring prizes into British ports, an early indication that Britain would not get actively involved in the American conflict.

Amid the whirlwind of diplomatic activity, the Confederacy pressed its efforts to wage war on the high seas. On May 6, 1861, the Confederate Congress passed "An Act recognizing the existence of war between the United States and the Confederate States, and concerning Letters of Marque, Prizes and Prize Goods." Jefferson Davis received authorization to use all land and naval forces of the

Confederacy to meet the needs of the war and to issue letters of marque and reprisal. The law carefully avoided inflaming foreign nations by exempting enemy property carried on neutral ships and by providing a grace period of thirty days to allow ships in the service of the United States to leave Southern ports and reach their destinations. The remainder of the act established procedures for obtaining letters of marque and claiming prizes. Confederate district courts in Southern port cities had exclusive jurisdiction over prize cases. Although the law required applicants to post a bond with two reliable sureties, Confederate prize procedures became streamlined, with certain taxes and duties reduced so as to make privateering as lucrative as possible to potential captains and shipowners. The Confederacy kept 5 percent of the net amount of the prize and placed those monies into a fund for the widows of men killed and for the support of men wounded serving on a Confederate privateer. This provision, although seemingly innocuous, served an important function in legitimizing Confederate privateering. The U.S. privateering act of June 26, 1812, made no provision for any portion of a prize to go to the government, a feature that cast a suspicious eye on American sea captains sailing under U.S. letters of marque. A man or ship who owed nothing to the nation from whom his authority was derived looked more like a pirate than a patriot. On June 5, 1813, the law was amended to provide a pension for naval veterans or their families if the men were killed or wounded in engagements while serving on a privateer.

Jefferson Davis issued a set of instructions requiring that ships sailing under Confederate letters of marque "pay the strictest regard to the rights of neutral powers and the usages of civilized nations." Toward enemy vessels and their crews, "you are to proceed in exercising the rights of war, with all the justice and humanity which characterize this Government and its citizens." On May 21, 1861, the Confederate Congress amended the May 6 law by adding to the bounty paid to privateer captains. In addition to prizes taken to Confederate ports, the Confederate government offered to pay 20 percent of the value of any U.S. ship sunk or destroyed. Although the allure of money motivated individuals, the Confederacy intended to use its privateer fleet to wage war, and paying captains for destroying Union ships drove that point home.

Whether fueled by patriotism, profit, or both, the Southern maritime community responded immediately. On April 18, 1861, the day after Jefferson Davis announced his intention to issue letters of marque, the collector of Savannah, Georgia, forwarded the application of a W. Howe for letters of marque and reprisal for the schooner *Gallatin*. The same day a B. S. Sanchez applied for letters for the brig *Hallie Jackson*. Almost every day from April 18 until May 6, someone either applied for a letter of marque or wrote the State Department inquiring as to how to apply. One man, W. R. Miles, wanted twenty to thirty letters with instructions sent to him with the name of the ship and captain left blank. Another man wanted to privateer on the Mississippi River, and consistent with prior wars, non-Confederates looked to take advantage of the opportunities privateering offered. Among the requests for letters of marque or information on how to obtain one came an inquiry from citizens of New England who expressed an interest in privateering if "inducements will be made for them to engage in that type of warfare."

Although applicants of all descriptions came calling on the Confederate State Department in April and May of 1861, two ships in particular would play the most significant role in the debate over Confederate identity. One became the most successful of the Confederate privateers; the other's voyage ended almost as soon as it began. Although the seafaring exploits of both contributed to the Confederacy's naval efforts, the subsequent trial of all or part of their crews tested the commitment of each side to follow through on the verbal threats that began almost immediately after the commencement of hostilities.

———

Charleston residents watched with almost childlike curiosity as the renovations on pilot boat No. 7 got under way in early May 1861. Soon christened CSS *Savannah*, the first Confederate ship to receive letters of marque evolved out of the dreams of two members of the Virginia Rifles, who, while drilling with the state volunteer unit on Morris Island, found themselves drawn to the sea. With ten other investors, T. Harrison Baker and John Harleston were among the first applicants to appear at the Confederate State Department for a commission to sail under arms for the Confederacy, and the commission was granted on May 18. Baker had experience as a sea captain and would command the privateer. Harleston had no seafaring experience and no qualifications other than an understanding of navigation. He had dismissed his discussions with Baker as the idle chatter of bored militiamen, and when the unit returned to civilian life, Harleston forgot the plan. Baker, however, did not, and by June 1, 1861, the *Savannah* prepared to depart Charleston harbor with Harleston an investor and a reluctant crew member. He should have followed his instincts.

By early June the Union blockade was in place. Over the next several months, military and civilian observers (foreign and domestic) questioned its effectiveness. But on May 10, 1861, when USS *Niagara* appeared off Charleston harbor, a clear Union threat existed to ships leaving the harbor. After announcing the blockade, the *Niagara* remained four days and then departed. On May 28 USS *Minnesota* took up blockade duty outside the harbor, joined shortly thereafter by USS *Perry*. Despite the blockade, everything began well as the *Savannah* slipped out to sea. Within two days the little privateer had claimed its first prize, the *Joseph*. However, the elation of both captain and crew would be short lived. No sooner had Baker chosen his prize crew, put it in place, and gotten the *Joseph* under way than lookouts spotted another ship.

The lookouts quickly saw that the other vessel was a man-of-war, and Baker decided they should try to run. Despite those efforts, however, the two ships closed to within a half mile, at which time the unidentified ship ran up the Stars and Stripes. Baker then ran up his flag, and as darkness settled in, the two ships entered into a sharp but brief fight. After twenty minutes Baker knew the *Savannah* could not hold its own, and although the attacker did not initially see what it had done, Baker dropped his sails in an act of capitulation. Within a short time the *Savannah* became the prize of USS *Perry*. Transferred twice, the crew found itself in irons, and on arriving in New York harbor the men were marched in chains to the Tombs, where they remained in prison until their trial.

The *Savannah* experience revealed a potential weakness in the Confederacy's use of letters of marque. Although the lure of wealth and the passions of patriotism might bring sailors to the cause, neither guaranteed that the sailors would also be warriors. When the *Perry* opened up on the *Savannah*, all but one crew member and the four officers ducked for cover. Under the best of circumstances the privateer could never have outgunned the Union warship, but had its crew remained calm, the *Savannah* might have outrun the *Perry* or at least found sanctuary in the shallow water and large reefs that dominated the Confederate coastline from Virginia to Corpus Christi. The captain and crew paid for their collective lack of martial skills and loss of composure. Their survival now depended on different skills, those of the advocate and the willingness of Northern lawyers to embrace their plight.

For this story the most significant request for a privateering commission came on April 23, 1861. Almost two full weeks before the Confederate Congress authorized Davis to issue letters of marque, a Mr. J. Gordon asked for letters of marque for the brig *Putnam*. The *Putnam* had been built in Baltimore, Maryland, in 1846. In August 1858 it was captured off the coast of Cuba by USS *Dolphin* for running slaves under the name *Echo* in violation of both U.S. and international law. Forfeited to the United States, the *Putnam* was sold at auction in 1859 to Captain Robert Hunter of Charleston, South Carolina.

When the war broke out Hunter assembled an investment group of twenty-seven shareholders and applied to the Confederate government for a letter of marque. On May 21, 1861, the investors petitioned the Confederacy to change the name of the *Putnam* to the *Jefferson Davis* (also called the *Jeff Davis*). On June 18, 1861, the Confederate State Department approved the application and granted the commission to the *Jefferson Davis*. Armed with five British iron guns, two 24-pounders, two 32-pounders, and an 18-pound swivel gun and sailing under the command of forty-three-year-old Louis M. Coxetter, the *Jeff Davis* enjoyed a festive send-off on June 28, 1861. Sailing out of Charleston harbor, the vessel slipped through Maffitt's Channel past the Union blockade and headed out to sea. The career of the Confederacy's most notorious and successful privateer had begun.

Among the ninety men who made up the crew and company of the *Jeff Davis* was a young Savannah pilot named William Wallace Smith. Smith left a wife and small child in Georgia when he made his way by train in late June to Charleston, South Carolina, and boarded the *Jeff Davis*. Smith's pilot skills made him a prime candidate to serve as prize master in the event that the *Jeff Davis* successfully carried out its mission and seized a Union merchant ship. Although Smith could expect to take charge of a Union prize at some point in the journey, he could never have anticipated becoming the lead defendant in a piracy case, a case that not only decided his own fate but also in the process helped to define the new nation under whose flag he sailed and made war.

The events that eventually took him to U.S. District Court in Philadelphia, Pennsylvania, did not take long to unfold. Almost immediately after clearing the Union blockade and reaching the high seas, the *Jeff Davis* found its first prey. A sighting on July 4 proved to be a British ship, the *Grace Worthington*, and consistent with President Davis's instructions, Coxetter allowed it to proceed on its way. Two days later, however, the *Jeff Davis* took its first two prizes, and one of them changed the course of the war for William Smith.

The first victim, the *John Welsh*, a three-year-old Philadelphia brig en route from Trinidad to Falmouth, England, carried a cargo of sugar and proved to be a fine prize after being condemned and sold at auction in Charleston. The *Jeff Davis*'s luck continued into the afternoon when the Confederate privateer came on the *Enchantress*. Under the command of Captain John Devereaux of Newburyport, Massachusetts, the schooner had left Boston bound for Santiago, Cuba. At roughly two o'clock in the afternoon the crew of the *Enchantress* saw what it believed to be a French flag. When the *Jeff Davis* approached, it lowered a boat, boarded the defenseless merchant ship, and claimed its second prize of the day. After evacuating the crew to the privateer, Coxetter put a prize crew on board the schooner under the command of William Smith. Smith's orders were to bring the prize to Charleston, and perhaps all would have proceeded as planned had it not been for a decision Coxetter made just before the *Enchantress* set sail.

Among the ship's company on the *Enchantress* was a black cook named Jacob Garrick. At first Garrick was transferred to the *Jeff Davis* along with the rest of the crew. At the last minute, however, Coxetter reconsidered and ordered Garrick back to the *Enchantress* to accompany the prize crew to Charleston, where he would be sold.

Ultimately, Coxetter's decision cost him his prize and put the lives of Smith and his prize crew in jeopardy. As much as Coxetter's decision, the words the captain said would haunt Smith in the months to come: "He will fetch fifteen hundred dollars when we get him back to Charleston." In the eyes of the Union, Smith and his crew became more than merely pirates; they became the nineteenth-century equivalents of the agents of Egyptian pharaoh Ramses II returning the Israelites to bondage.

All proceeded as planned until the *Enchantress* reached the coast of North Carolina. Off Cape Hatteras, Smith and his crew encountered USS *Albatross*. As the two ships came within hailing distance, Jacob Garrick took one last chance at freedom and jumped overboard. Once in the water he pointed to the ship and shouted, "A captured vessel of the privateer *Jeff Davis*, and they are taking her into Charleston." Garrick's bold move saved him and doomed Smith. Alerted to the true identity of the *Enchantress*, the Union steamer moved to board the schooner. Smith's small crew and unarmed ship proved no match for a warship, and soon he, his crew, and his prize were under the control of the Union gunboat. Smith and his crew went first to Fort Monroe and then north to Philadelphia to stand trial for piracy.

From almost the beginning of the war, Northern papers had followed the exploits of the Confederate "marauders." Beginning in April 1861 and running through the end of that year, Northern newspapers obsessed over the Confederacy's resort to letters of marque and the activity of its privateers. On April 23, 1861, the *New York Times* condemned the Southern promise to issue letters of marque by claiming that "the Slave Confederation could not have possibly taken a more direct road to cut themselves off from the sympathy of mankind, than by their new crusade against private property on the seas." The article conceded that the privateers could do damage but argued that it would pale in comparison to the harm they would cause the South. Still, the newspaper insisted that precautions be taken in Northern seaport towns to guard against suspicious vessels and insisted that the government arm merchant vessels. The piece concluded that every privateer caught should be summarily executed. Some observers feared that the privateers might form flotillas, as people flocked to take advantage of the potential for financial gain. The newspapers demanded that the blockade be more than simply paper, that is, that the blockade be active, not a mere declaration, and warned that the privateer threat to the blockade should not be underestimated.

In an effort to educate the public and shape opinion, newspaper editorials chronicled the development of privateering and the rejection of the concept in the fifty years preceding the Civil War. On June 10, 1861, the *New York Times* published the entire record of a debate over privateering in the French Academy of Moral and Political Science. Thus, even before the first prize had been taken, the American press manifested a keen interest in the subject and in the process put the American public on edge. Of note, the Northern papers did acknowledge that the United States refused to sign the Declaration of Paris in 1856 but blamed that failure on Jefferson Davis and other Southerners who allegedly were in control of Franklin Pierce's administration. A full narrative appeared on June 16, 1861, when the *Savannah* arrived in New York harbor after its capture by the *Perry*. People immediately feared that despite Lincoln's proclamation, the crew of the captured privateer would be exchanged as prisoners of war and returned to Charleston, notwithstanding Northern sentiment that cried for their execution as pirates.

While Smith and his comrades wasted away in jail in Philadelphia and T. Harrison Baker and his crew languished in New York, Coxetter and the *Jeff Davis* continued to make life miserable for Union merchants. In the process Coxetter struck fear into the hearts and minds of the Northern public and steeled public sentiment against the captured Confederate seamen. Northern papers reported the seizure of both the *John Welsh* and the *Enchantress*. Within days the *Jeff Davis* took two more prizes. Less than twenty-four hours after taking the *Enchantress*, the privateer captured the *S. J. Waring*, and two days later Coxetter's ship seized the *Mary Goodell*. After taking on water and five crewmen, Coxetter paroled the ship and remaining crew and company on the condition they resume their journey to Montevideo. The captain disobeyed and made for Portland, Maine, to spread the word that Confederate privateers were operating off the New England coast.

Northern papers tracked all of this activity, carefully describing the prizes and providing information on the *Jeff Davis* and its crew.

Newspapers began reporting that in addition to the harm to Northern shipping, the Confederate privateer activity demonstrated the weakness of the Northern blockade. This issue became important because under international law neutral nations must respect a blockade only if it is "efficient," that is, only if it effectively prevents the ingress and egress of all maritime vessels. By mid-July 1861 not only did the *Jeff Davis* wreak havoc but also a new menace, the *Sumter*, put to sea from New Orleans and slipped past the Union blockade. A converted mail steamer, the *Sumter* was the most heavily armed of all Confederate privateers. The vessel set up outside Cienfuegos, Cuba, where it immediately captured eight prizes as they left the harbor. When the privateer attempted to claim them in Cienfuegos, the Spanish authorities refused to do so, and the prizes were forfeited. However, even without its prizes the *Sumter* undermined the efficiency of the blockade and escalated Northern fears. By July 16, 1861, four Confederate privateers had taken twenty-three prizes, and the threat to the Aspinwall steamers carrying millions of dollars in California gold loomed large. Jefferson Davis's gamble paid early dividends. From nothing the Confederacy raised a navy that made the first significant military impression in the war. Not only had this small fleet compromised the blockade and brought victory on the high seas, but also it brought substance to the Confederacy's claim of nationhood. Notwithstanding Lincoln's threats to treat Confederate sailors as pirates, in the summer of 1861 the Confederacy certainly acted like a nation, and its sea captains made it look like one.

Despite the successes, certain aspects of Confederate privateering revealed the early boundaries of Confederate sovereignty. As neutrals, Britain, France, and most certainly Spain, as the *Sumter* quickly learned, did not allow Confederate prizes in their ports and reclaimed prizes captured in their waters and brought into their ports. The Confederacy enjoyed the status of a belligerent, but it would have to demonstrate more to achieve recognition and the benefits that accompanied that status. The early months of the war also revealed something about the nature of Confederate privateering. Although the Confederate law provided compensation for sinking Union ships, some captains seemed unwilling to do so. As noted earlier, Coxetter had taken prisoners and provisions off the *Mary*

Goodell and then released it on the verbal promise from the captain that he continue the voyage. Almost immediately after sending the *Goodell* on its way, the *Jeff Davis* came on the *Mary E. Thompson*, which was carrying lumber south from Searsport, Maine. Coxetter did not think it valuable enough to warrant a prize crew. He placed the nine prisoners he took from the *Goodell* on the *Mary Thompson* and let it continue on its way. Coxetter could have sunk both ships and chose not to do so. Thus, although the Confederacy realized clear benefits from its privateer fleet, there were limitations on the extent to which some of them would wage war against the Union.

The Northern newspapers painted a dark picture of the privateers, but the experiences of the captors revealed that Southern sea captains ran a tight ship. The Southerners not only treated the captured crews humanely but also made every effort to make those crews as comfortable as possible. Some of the crew of the *Enchantress* later testified that they slept in the same quarters as their captors, received more than ample rations, and, except for limitations on their movement aboard ship, were in all respects well treated. Captain Smith of the *Waring* told the *New York Herald*, "We expected from the statements made in the New York papers, that we would be stripped of everything and treated with the greatest severity; but our treatment was entirely different from that which we expected. Each officer did all in his power to make us comfortable." Bartlett Jones, a mate on the prize *Santa Clara*, gave Captain Coxetter high marks for his treatment of the captured crew.

Coxetter's conduct toward Union ships and crew, although consistently good, produced mixed results. His humane treatment of the Union crews followed Jefferson Davis's instructions, and in a war where questions still existed as to the treatment of prisoners, the Confederacy set a good example, one it hoped the Union would follow. However, Coxetter's decision not to destroy ships that held insufficient value to warrant a prize crew undermined the purpose of putting privateers on the seas. In at least one instance Coxetter allowed a Union merchant to pass unmolested because he deemed it not "worth the powder and shot" to capture it. The profit motive tended to obscure the more important objective of winning the war by reducing the Union merchant fleet. Still, before the land armies ever faced off on the fields of northern Virginia, Confederate privateers struck a significant blow for the fledgling nation that had begun to stake its claim for recognition.

Perhaps the most troubling aspect of the Confederate approach to naval warfare came with the realization that the Union would not reciprocate. On July 6, 1861, Jefferson Davis wrote Abraham Lincoln concerning the captain and crew of the *Savannah*. On June 19, 1861, shortly after the capture of the *Savannah*, Davis had sent a proposal to the commanding officer of the blockading squadron responsible for the privateer's capture. Davis proposed an exchange of prisoners, swapping the crew of the *Savannah* for Union prisoners held by the Confederacy. Captain Mercer, the officer in command of the Union squadron, replied that the privateer's crew was not on board any ship under his command. Davis told Lincoln that according to confirmed reports in New York newspapers, the crew now languished in a New York prison not as prisoners of war but as criminals. Placed in irons, the Confederate seamen had been arraigned and charged with both treason and piracy. Davis could not believe that men who bore arms in defense of "the rights of their government and under authority of its commission" could be treated in such a manner. He would not have thought this possible if it were not for Lincoln's April 19, 1861, proclamation that privateers would be treated as pirates and traitors. In light of that edict, the Confederate president could only assume the reports were accurate.

Davis told Lincoln that the Confederacy had wished to "conduct the war . . . as to mitigate its horrors, as far as may be possible." Consistent with that desire the Confederacy treated Union prisoners "with the greatest humanity and leniency consistent with public obligation." Some had been permitted to return home on parole, and others had been allowed to remain at large under parole within the Confederacy. In light of Lincoln's edict and the Union's intent to follow through on that proclamation as evidenced by the treatment of the *Savannah*, Davis had withdrawn "such indulgences" and begun holding Union prisoners in strict confinement. From that point forward Davis proclaimed a Confederacy dictated by reciprocity and retaliation. Union prisoners would receive treatment identical to that afforded Confederate prisoners, including captured privateers. If the Union executed any crew member of the *Savannah*, Union prisoners would likewise be put to death. Davis closed his letter to Lincoln by renewing his offer to exchange prisoners.

Lincoln did not respond to Davis. He did not have to; he had drawn his line in the sand in April, and to the extent a response was necessary or appropriate, the Northern press took up the gauntlet. Davis's threats caused a degree of reflection tempered by an understanding of what was at stake in the treatment of Confederate privateers. Acknowledging that public sentiment would allow Lincoln the latitude to treat privateers as pirates and punish them accordingly, the press argued that it was "necessary to act with caution . . . and not augment greatly the horrors . . . of this civil war." The mere act of taking privateers and holding them could be construed as recognizing the Southern states as belligerents. But in taking and holding the privateers, the press insisted, "We do not thereby concede to them any civil rights, nor in the slightest degree commit ourselves to a recognition of their political existence." However, prisoners, including the privateers, might be entitled to the benefits of international law conveyed by all civilized nations, specifically the exchange of captives as prisoners of war and not as rebels. It remained unclear whether by doing so the Union risked recognizing the legitimacy of Confederate letters of marque, at least insofar as that license distinguished privateering from piracy. The Northern press had begun to define the conundrum that privateering caused. The question of the legal status of the Confederate sailors and to a great extent the government that sent them to war seemed headed to the courts for resolution. But at the same time the issue posed a political question to be decided not merely by the law but also on considerations of public policy. As both sides prepared to go to trial, everyone realized that much was at stake in the piracy cases. More than just the fate of men, the definition of the present conflict required defining the Confederacy.

As the debate over the status and treatment of Confederate privateers intensified, Captain Coxetter and the *Jeff Davis* continued their odyssey. After releasing the *Mary Thompson* on July 9, Coxetter sailed as far north as Narragansett Shoals before turning south again for the West Indies. For almost two weeks the crew sighted only foreign vessels, which Coxetter took great care to leave alone. On

July 21, 1861, the *Jeff Davis* came on the *Alvarado*. Captained by G. C. Whiting, the vessel was bound for Boston from South Africa and carried a cargo of wool, sheepskins, hides, and old copper and iron valued at $75,000. Coxetter placed a prize crew aboard the ship under Gilbert Hay, and the ship set sail for Fernandina, Florida. Unfortunately for Coxetter, the prize ship ran aground on a shoal south of the Amelia Island, South Carolina, lighthouse when Hay panicked at the sight of a Union sloop-of-war. Unlike William Smith, Hay and his crew got off the ship to safety, but after a duel between Confederate shore guns and the Union ship *Jamestown*, a Union boarding party set the beached prize afire, destroying the ship and its cargo.

The *Jeff Davis* continued south. After allowing another ship to pass that was carrying British cargo, Coxetter put in at San Juan, Puerto Rico, for water and provisions and then continued on his voyage. First he encountered the *Windward*, which, although promising, he decided to pass up when a more lucrative prize appeared. The *Santa Clara* carried a cargo valued at $65,000, made up of predominantly sugar and molasses. Coxetter brought the brig alongside and, after ascertaining the ship's value, put a prize crew on board whose ranking member was a helmsman. One of the detriments of success was that by August 5, 1861, Coxetter had used all of his ranking officers on other prize crews. Fortunately, this crew successfully brought its prize to port. Once he secured the *Santa Clara*, Coxetter ran down the *Windward*, put his prisoners from the *Alvarado* and the *Santa Clara* on board, and released the vessel as a cartel, in effect treating the ship and the captured crews as prisoners of war. Both ships and crews were free but bound by their oaths not to engage in hostilities against the Confederacy or in service to the Union until formally exchanged.

This last prize effectively ended the voyage of the *Jeff Davis* because it exhausted Coxetter's ability to place prize crews on captured Union vessels. With water and food running low, Coxetter set sail for home. As the *Jeff Davis* approached the Florida coast, yet another prize opportunity presented itself. The *John Carver*, a chartered transport carrying coal to the Union Gulf Squadron, quickly surrendered under the threat of Coxetter's guns. Fully loaded, the ship drew twenty-two feet, much too deep to enter any South

Atlantic port, thus eliminating the possibility that it could be claimed as a prize. Because of its clear military mission, Coxetter could not release the *John Carver* as he had done with the purely privately owned merchant vessels. He removed the crew and then scuttled the ship and set it ablaze.

On August 16, 1861, having spent seven weeks at sea, the *Jeff Davis* arrived off the port of St. Augustine, Florida. Wind and sea conditions made it dangerous to cross the bar that guarded the port, so Coxetter waited all day on the seventeenth and into the eighteenth before trying to enter the harbor. With the ship sitting dead in the water and vulnerable to any Union warship that might pass by, Coxetter finally tried to enter the port and ran aground. Unable to free the ship, he salvaged the stores and small arms and, with his crew, safely escaped to the city. Their exploits had made the captain and crew of the *Jeff Davis* national heroes, and the residents of St. Augustine quickly made the privateers forget the hardships of the cruise and the loss of their ship. Two weeks later Captain Coxetter arrived in Charleston to a cheering throng at the railway station, where he accepted not only the praise of the crowd but also several gifts, including a large gold watch. The Charleston papers extolled Coxetter's deeds, claiming that the *Jeff Davis* had become "a word of terror" to the Yankees. In its brief but illustrious lifetime, the *Jeff Davis* claimed ten prizes and had indeed become synonymous with terror on the high seas. The *Charleston Mercury* proudly claimed that the prizes and cargo seized by the *Jeff Davis* were more valuable than any since the days of the *Saucy Jack*, one of the most successful privateers of the War of 1812, which, like the *Jeff Davis*, was a Charleston vessel.

Although the Confederacy would liked to have seen Coxetter sink or destroy some of the prizes he released, the Southern government had to be pleased with the spectacular success of its makeshift privateer fleet. Even with the *Jeff Davis* gone, the *Sumter* still sailed, and it became the focus of Union naval efforts and drew the attention of Northern newspapers. Although Coxetter lost his ship, the man lived on, and he went from being a successful privateer to becoming a successful blockade runner. But the *Jeff Davis*'s success did not come without a price. William Wallace Smith and his *Enchantress* prize crew sat in jail in Philadelphia awaiting their fate in a

Northern federal district court. The prize crew of the *S. J. Waring*, another Coxetter victim, had not been so lucky.

Whereas the actions of Jacob Garrick led to the capture of Smith and his company, the deeds of another freeman of color, a Rhode Island cook named Tillman, who was being held on the *Waring*, cost Prize Master Montague Amiel and his crew their lives. On the tenth night of the prize voyage, with the *Waring* within 100 miles of Charleston and the five-man prize crew either asleep or relaxing, Tillman struck. With an axe he crushed the skulls of the captain and the two mates. The second mate awakened, and although the blow to his head mortally wounded him, Tillman took no chances and tossed the man overboard. Tillman then returned to the captain and first mate, finishing them with repeated blows to the head before casting their broken and mangled bodies overboard. The two remaining Confederate seamen, cowed by Tillman's size and fury, relinquished the prize. Although ignorant of navigation, Tillman made land and followed the shoreline north to safety.

Although the South's privateering polices had no material effect on either free blacks or slaves, Garrick's and Tillman's experiences foreshadowed an aspect of Confederate military policy that undermined its ability to fight later in the war. In late 1863 the prisoner exchange system collapsed. Part of its demise came when the Confederacy announced its refusal to treat black soldiers as combatants. Captured Union African American soldiers faced enslavement if captured. Like Garrick, Tillman remained on the prize ship destined for a Southern port. Coxetter intended to sell Garrick, and the same fate apparently awaited Tillman. Regardless of his status in the North, a black man taken by the Confederate military could expect to find himself enslaved. In 1861 this policy cost Confederate sailors their freedom or, worse, their lives. In 1863 the policy severely crippled an important source of manpower for the Confederate army.

The fate of the two *Jeff Davis* prize crews attests to the risks involved in privateering. The *Savannah* discovered just how quickly a voyage could end, falling victim to a Union blockader shortly after taking its first and only prize. The *Petrel*, the third ship whose crew found itself charged with piracy, never cleared its own territorial waters. Originally the U.S. revenue cutter *Aiken* seized in Charleston harbor in November 1860, the *Petrel* sailed out of Charleston in early August 1861 and immediately sighted the Union's *St. Lawrence*. Accounts differ slightly as to the details of the encounter, but the Confederate privateer mistook the Union frigate for a merchant ship. The *Petrel* defiantly fired two shots at the Yankee ship, hoping to bring it to, only to be greeted with a withering return fire. The first broadside from the *St. Lawrence* cut the smaller Confederate vessel in half. Five of the crew drowned before Union rescue boats could reach them; the remainder found themselves in irons and confined on board USS *Flag*. The *Petrel* was sunk before it ever got started, and its crew shared the fate of William Wallace Smith and his *Jeff Davis* prize crew: defendants charged with treason and piracy in a Northern court on trial for their lives.

The *Jeff Davis* and the *Sumter* were the best examples of how privateering aided the Confederate war effort. But even the ill-fated voyages, such as those by the *Savannah* and the *Petrel*, played an important part in helping to define the fledgling Southern nation. The Confederate privateering fleet represented the first tangible manifestation of Confederate nationalism in a structural sense. Building armies and navies, financing them, and placing them into combat are crucial parts of what modern nations do. A rebellion looking for international recognition could certainly point to its early naval success as some proof that it "existed." More than just forcing the North to resolve the question of the legal status of Confederate privateers, the pending trials and Northern newspaper coverage revealed the novelty of many of the legal questions and the existence and strength of the two competing arguments. The piracy trials also confirmed an important characteristic of American jurisprudence: the law is seldom the only, or even the most important, factor on which jury verdicts and judicial decisions turn. Historical context and public policy mean something, and as we pass judgment on others we say something significant about how we view them and ourselves.

The process of defining a nation had many components and did not depend solely on Northern courts and juries struggling to administer justice within the context of a civil war. As privateering demonstrated, the Confederacy took an active role in staking its claim to nationhood. A key aspect of nationhood lies in the way a government treats its own citizens and those of other nations. As its fledgling fleet battled the Union navy and staked the Confederacy's claim to independence, the Southern government took steps to assert control over its people and territory. That process involved determining Confederate citizenship and deciding how to treat people deemed aliens if found within Confederate boundaries.

CHAPTER 2

"If They Meet
It Is Only to Combat"

In late September 1861, Confederate Secretary of State Robert Hunter wrote James Mason, the Confederacy's ambassador to Great Britain, instructing Mason to go back to England. Hunter insisted that things had changed since Mason's earlier efforts to secure diplomatic recognition from the British and told the ambassador to explain to the British that the secession was not a rebellion. "Eleven sovereign states, bound together by a common social system and the sympathies of identical interests have instituted a new confederacy and a new government. . . . Never were any people so united than are those of the Confederate States in their purpose to maintain their independence at any cost of life and treasure." To emphasize the Confederacy's unity of belief and purpose, Hunter proudly proclaimed that no "political offenses" had occurred since the war began.

Strictly speaking, Hunter may have been correct. Little during the spring and summer of 1861 suggested widespread dissent. Although pockets of unrest existed, most notably in some of the South's mountain regions, clear resistance to Confederate law had not surfaced. However legitimate Hunter's claim might have been, though, the serenity among Southerners that he described did not continue, and even as he wrote to Mason, the seeds of serious unrest had already been sown. In August 1861, an effort to wage war at home by the Confederate government introduced a Pandora's box into the South, creating an entire class of potential political prisoners and turning Southerners first against themselves and then against the new government.

In his letter to Mason, Hunter boasted that the Confederacy "cover[s] seven hundred and thirty-three thousand, one hundred forty-seven square miles of territory and nine million two hundred and forty-four thousand people." However, the Confederate government feared that despite Hunter's claims of unity, some of the population spread across the vastness of the South remained either sympathetic to the North or, worse, loyal to the old Union. Acting on this fear and the need to consolidate the home front, on August 8, 1861, the Confederate Congress moved to purge the new nation of anyone sympathetic to the Northern cause. "An act respecting alien enemies" provided that any time a state of war existed between the Confederacy and any other nation, that is, either the president of the Confederacy by public proclamation affirmed that a state of war existed or Congress passed an act declaring war, "all natives, citizens, denizens or subjects of the hostile nation or government being males fourteen or older that are within the Confederate states and not a citizen thereof" could be "apprehended, restrained, or secured, and removed as an alien enemy."

Tailored for the present conflict, the act excluded persons from the border states, Washington D.C., the Arizona and New Mexico territories, and Indian territory south of Kansas. The act left the specific regulations for implementing the order to the discretion of the Confederate president, but section 3 directed Jefferson Davis to require all persons of U.S. citizenship to leave the Confederate states within forty days from the date of his proclamation. The act also stated that so long as such persons did not pose a direct threat to the public safety they would be allowed sufficient time to dispose of their property and effects beyond the forty days set out in the law, and the president could prescribe such additional time "consistent with public safety and in accord with the dictates of humanity and national hospitality."

Both Confederate district and state courts had jurisdiction to entertain complaints filed against any person accused of being an alien enemy. With the complaint clearly criminal in nature, the accused could be apprehended and forcibly brought before the court, where the act provided for a full examination and hearing. If the person was found to be an alien enemy, the marshal of the district where the alien was apprehended would execute any order rendered by the court. On August 14, 1861, Davis issued a proclamation setting the provisions of the Alien Enemies Act into motion. He also provided a short set of regulations directing the district attorney, marshals, and other officers of the Confederate states to make complaints against all alien enemies as defined within the act. He ordered marshals to apprehend and hold all persons accused of being alien enemies and to remove any person found to be an alien enemy. Any person so removed who returned to the Confederacy and was thereafter apprehended could be held in prison by the military and treated as either a prisoner of war or a spy.

The Confederate civilian and military authorities went to work almost immediately, posting notices of the regulations and providing directions for disaffected citizens to make their way out of the Confederacy. Although no legal duty existed that compelled Confederate citizens to report alien enemies to the authorities, in order for the act to work, Southerners had to be willing to report persons they suspected of being alien enemies, and thus the potential for disunity loomed. In some places Southerners began to question the wisdom of forcing neighbors and friends to inform on one another. Citizens were arrested for treason on the slimmest of suspicion. In late August 1861, Confederate authorities arrested Dr. Archibald A. McBryde in Randalsville, North Carolina, for treason, in part because a search revealed that he possessed a letter signed by a prominent New York politician. McBryde, an archaeologist and literary figure, seemed an unlikely traitor, but no one escaped Confederate efforts to purge the land of alien enemies. A month later the Charleston papers reported the arrest of two Richmond merchants, identified as Messrs. Turner and Gaynor, on their return from New York. After the two merchants were questioned, they had the choice of either swearing allegiance to the Confederacy or being considered alien enemies.

Despite the potential harm of tearing communities and neighborhoods apart and the appearance of witch hunting, the act made sense. The war would be fought in the South, and allowing persons loyal to the Union to remain in the Confederacy invited disaster. A civilian population loyal to the United States could become an organized fifth column as the federal army moved farther into the South. It seemed that most Southerners understood this, and although the Alien Enemies Act caused some discomfort, it did not generate significant unrest in 1861. However, the act served as the predicate for significant dissension and eventually open resistance.

On August 30, 1861, slightly more than three weeks after the passage of the Alien Enemies Act, the Confederate Congress passed "An Act for the sequestration of the estates, property, and effects of alien enemies and for the indemnity of citizens of the Confederate states and persons aiding the same in the existing war with the United States." Known thereafter as the Sequestration Act, this Confederate law represented one of the first efforts to extend the national government's control across the land through an exercise of its war-making powers. Whereas the Alien Enemies Act targeted Northern citizens and placed the official burden of enforcement on the Confederate judiciary and legal officers, the Sequestration Act imposed an affirmative legal duty on every Confederate citizen to report the existence and character of alien enemy property and, if in possession of that property, to turn it over promptly to the Confederate authorities. Failure to do so exposed the person to criminal sanctions. This law drew the ire of Southerners, and the reaction was both immediate and strong. The law fell particularly hard on attorneys, and members of the South Carolina bar voiced the first and most stringent objection to its mandates.

The short preamble to the Sequestration Act clearly stated its purpose: to retaliate. On August 6, 1861, two days before the passage of the Confederate Alien Enemies Act, the U.S. Congress passed the first of two confiscation acts, brought about in part by General Benjamin Butler's actions in May of 1861 of allowing fugitive slaves to seek refuge in Union lines as contrabands. The First Confiscation Act authorized Lincoln to seize any property used to aid the rebellion and to void the claims of any master whose slaves were employed in the service of the Confederate military. Union confiscation took place through judicial proceedings, with jurisdiction vested in the courts where the property lay or had been confiscated. By August 1861 most, if not all, property subject to confiscation under the act was situated inside the Confederacy. Although Lincoln did not authorize his attorney general to enforce the act until January 1863, Southern newspapers saw Union confiscation as the "last step in a programme of outrage and insolence." It was not enough that Southerners would have to defend their homes on the battlefield and that their prisoners of war (a clear reference to the men of the *Savannah* and the *Jeff Davis* prize crews) were "to be treated with every indignity and brutality. What the field of battle spared—what the dungeons and chains cannot reach—must likewise suffer." The initial reaction was "let them confiscate." Northern actions could only harden Southerners to the reality that this would not be, as the *Charleston Mercury* noted, a "rose-water affair," and the Confederate government responded quickly to the demands of war. A Northern war measure designed to strike at the heart of the South's most sacred social and economic institution begot the Sequestration Act, and all proceeds derived from the sale of alien enemy property were earmarked under the act for Confederate citizens who lost property to Union confiscation.

Notwithstanding the rhetoric in Southern newspapers, the Union confiscation acts arguably represented Northern reactions to Confederate property seizures that began in late 1860 and continued after the war began. U.S. military installations fell to Southern seizures beginning on December 27, 1860, with the seizure of Fort Moultrie and Castle Pickney in South Carolina, and federal installations in Georgia and Texas soon fell into Confederate hands. By February 1, 1861, only four U.S. properties remained in the seceding states: Forts Jefferson, Pickens, and Taylor in Florida and Fort Sumter in South Carolina. Although the seizure of government property clearly stirred the emotions of the Northern public, the sudden realization that secession brought severe economic ramifications really aroused the ire of the North. Not only did the seizure of federal forts seem like theft of what was considered jointly owned property, but the forts also maintained federal customs houses, key institutions of commerce and trade.

Months before passage of the First Confiscation Act, Northern citizens began calling for the government to attack the rebels' "lives, their wealth, their family comfort, their slaves and the property of their children." Demands even extended to the seizure of property in Virginia before that state ever seceded. When Jefferson Davis issued his proclamation in April 1861 announcing his intention to issue letters of marque, Northern fears seemed justified. Secession meant not only disunion but also an all-out assault on Northern property rights. Within this context the Confederate Sequestration Act represented the escalation of a "property" war that had seen both sides trading volleys since December 1860.

The Sequestration Act sequestered "all and every the lands, tenements and hereditaments, goods and chattels, rights and credits, within these Confederate States, and every right and interest thereon held, owned, possessed, or enjoyed by or for any alien enemy" since May 21, 1861. If another state joined the Confederacy after May 21, 1861, then the act applied to alien property within that state as of the day the state became a member of the Confederacy. The act exempted certain assets, specifically public securities of the Confederate government or any state therein and any debt owed by the Confederate government to an alien enemy. The act also exempted property held by an alien enemy in any border state, Washington D.C., the Arizona and New Mexico territories, and Indian territory south of Kansas.

To *sequester* means to seize or to set apart. By virtue of the statute the Confederacy legally seized all property belonging to alien enemies, including any debts owed them by Confederate citizens. However, in reality the seizure occurred in name only. In order to effect the seizure and sale of the property, the government had to locate it, and for that the law placed the duty to disclose and turn over such property squarely on the shoulders of the Confederate citizen. Section 2 of the act made it the duty of "each and every citizen of these Confederate states speedily to give information to the officers charged with the execution of the law" as to the whereabouts of any alien property. Section 3 went one step further and imposed a duty on "every attorney, agent, former partner, trustee, or other person holding or controlling" alien enemy property to give a full accounting and if possible deliver the property to the receiver appointed in the district where the property was located. Turning the property over to the receiver absolved the person of any further responsibility or obligation with regard to that property. However, any person willfully refusing to give an accounting or to give information could be convicted of a "high misdemeanor," fined up to $5,000, and imprisoned for up to six months. Thereafter, the Confederate government could sue the uncooperative citizen for a sum equal to double the value of the property held by the person or subject to the person's control. The Confederate district courts exercised exclusive jurisdiction over any proceeding under the Sequestration Act, and the law directed the judges in each district to convene a grand jury to inquire and report on the alien enemy property in its district.

In theory Confederate district court jurisdiction extended to all types of civil matters and admiralty, but after November 1861, sequestration cases came to dominate these courts. The courts had been U.S. federal district courts prior to secession, and the administrative records in each district continued almost unabated after secession. In many cases the Confederacy kept the identical federal forms in use prior to secession, with "United States" redacted and "Confederate" written in its place. The records maintained by the court clerks in several of these districts demonstrate the degree to which Confederate district courts became "sequestration courts."

The docket sheets in the Northern District of Alabama from May to November 1861 reflected a typical civil court with pending lawsuits between private citizens over a variety of matters. However, the court records after November 1861 show a drastic change in the nature and volume of the cases. The November docket showed 13 general civil cases followed by 290 sequestration cases, mostly violations of the writ of garnishment process. Slightly more than a year later, the sequestration caseload had almost doubled. The January 1863 docket for the same court showed 12 general civil cases and 588 garnishment cases or other proceedings under the Sequestration Act. As the numbers from just one district suggest, this early act of Confederate nationalism became a multimillion dollar business and touched citizens throughout the Confederacy.

Confederate citizens felt the impact of the law almost immediately as it spread to every state from Virginia to Texas. William Pitt Ballinger, one of the five receivers appointed under the act by Justice William Pinckney Hill of the Eastern District of Texas in October 1861, provides a good example. Ballinger's district encompassed nine east Texas counties, and his first official accounting to Judge Hill in late December 1861 underscored just how pervasive this new law and its effect on Confederate citizens would be. Ballinger identified 501 alien enemies and took 411 judgments. He sequestered $994,177 in money debts and seized 100,893 acres of land

and $2,000 in personal effects, all in two months. During the entire four years of the war, Hill presided over only eighteen admiralty prize cases, the second most prevalent legal matter in the Confederate district courts.

The Confederate secretary of the treasury became the ultimate custodian for sequestration accounting records. Not all of these records survived the end of the war, and therefore complete sequestration receipt numbers do not exist. However, even the partial reports are revealing. The report of the treasury secretary for the period January to September 1863 showed $1,862,550.21 received from sequestration seizures and sales. Thus, not only did the Confederacy seize property on a local level, but also it converted it to cash and passed it on to the Treasury Department. When five Charleston lawyers stepped to the bar to challenge the constitutionality of the Sequestration Act in October 1861, the success or failure of their efforts carried heavy consequences.

The process of locating, seizing, liquidating, accounting, and transferring the proceeds from the sale of alien property required constant effort. The receiver held the most important position within the sequestration system. Appointed by the district judge and required to post a bond, the receiver had the obligation of actually gathering property. This task included not only taking possession of property where either the location was disclosed to him or the property was actually turned over to him but also prosecuting all legal actions authorized under the act to enforce its provisions. Every six months the receiver accounted to the district court for all the property in his possession.

One of the receiver's most important powers was the authority to request writs of garnishment, issued by the Confederate district court, commanding persons to appear and to answer under oath as to the whereabouts of any alien enemy property under their control or that had been under their control. On the basis of those answers the court could condemn the property, effects, or debts identified by the responding party. The receiver had the authority to test the veracity of the garnishee's answers by filing a statement identifying the particular aspects of the answers that were untrue. If the receiver challenged a person's answers, the court then litigated the truth of the garnishee's answer in the same manner as any other disputed issue of fact. During that process the receiver could propound inter-rogatories, written questions sent to the garnishee, and if that per-son refused to answer, the court could imprison that individual until the questions were answered.

The closest modern-day equivalent to a Confederate sequestra-tion receiver is a bankruptcy trustee. Charged with gathering assets in the main bankruptcy proceeding, a bankruptcy trustee has au-thority to initiate "ancillary proceedings" or adversary actions against the debtor, third parties, and even creditors to gather, dis-cover, or preserve assets of the estate. The sequestration receiver possessed many of the same powers. However, whereas a bank-ruptcy trustee owes a duty both to the court and to the creditors of a debtor, the sequestration receiver owed an allegiance to one entity: the Confederate government. In theory receivers are impartial per-sons, holding property while a dispute is resolved between other parties. The Confederate sequestration receivers held no pretense of impartiality, however. When a receiver sued, he did so in the name of the Confederate States of America, and his duty to account ran solely to the government. As the plaintiff in a Confederate dis-trict court prosecuting actions on behalf of the Confederacy, the re-ceiver proved formidable. For example, the records of the Confed-erate District Court for the Northern District of Georgia, Atlanta Division, on one day in March 1863 show twenty-nine cases with the receiver as plaintiff, and he won every case. The same result oc-curred in almost every sequestration docket in that district; defen-dants rarely prevailed.

When the receiver indicted, or formally accused, a person of fail-ure to turn over property or to make an accounting, the allegations carried an ominous ring. Henry Ash, a South Carolinian, acted as the agent for a Mr. Leeds, a declared alien enemy. Ash refused to turn over the property of his principal, and in November 1861 his indict-ment read as follows: "To wit on the twenty-third day of November in the year of our Lord 1861, with force and arms at Charleston in the district aforesaid and within the jurisdiction of the court, unlaw-fully and willfully did fail to give information and render an account to the receiver of the sequestered estate duly appointed by the judge of the Confederate States for the district aforesaid."

Ash stood accused of refusing to turn over property he sold to Mr. Leeds of New York but had yet to deliver when the war began. Ash was the lone defendant in that case, but the property of one alien enemy routinely generated proceedings with multiple defendants. For example, a case involving a Northern company doing business in the South could have as defendants in the same garnishment proceeding every Southern debtor in the district who owed that company money. One South Carolina case had thirty-one defendants.

The amount of the alien enemy property in question seemed irrelevant, as did the gender of the defendant, as the receivers seized everything they could reach. In a culture where a woman's only right was the right to protection, Southern women seldom participated in antebellum judicial proceedings. However, the Sequestration Act made no distinction between men and women and abandoned any notion of protecting women. If a woman held property belonging to an alien enemy or came under suspicion of being an alien enemy, the law treated her in a manner no different from a man. A petition filed by the receiver in Savannah, Georgia, accused Maria A. Deloney of being an alien enemy and sought to seize her one slave and the $85.00 in wages she claimed were due her.

At the other extreme stood the case of the estate of John Butler. Butler, allegedly a resident of Pennsylvania, left his entire estate to his wife. After his death the district receiver learned of the estate and sued his widow. Discovering the whereabouts and extent of Butler's property proved easy. John Butler owned half of Butler's Island off the coast of McIntosh County, Georgia, including a sizeable rice plantation, more than 500 slaves, livestock, and 1,700 acres of unimproved swamp land. The task became much easier because Gabriella M. Butler, the decedent's wife and executrix, did not contest the proceeding and filed an accounting of everything. The court records indicate that Mrs. Butler's reaction to the seizure was common. Whether because they feared the wrath of the government or simply lacked the means to contest the proceedings, most people did not put up a fight. Mrs. Butler and Henry Ash actually filed answers, written responses to the government's lawsuit. The majority of files contained a petition, a return of service, and a judgment indicating the defendant had allowed the government to win by default.

A closer look at the identities of these alien enemies reveals just how connected the North and South had been prior to the war and the hardship experienced by Southerners when severing long-standing business relationships. The court sequestration records reveal almost every kind of person and entity as defendants, including lawyers, brokers, cotton factors, banks, and merchants of all types. The way in which many of these persons conducted business was more important than their identity or the nature of their businesses. Although corporations existed in antebellum America, particularly when such businesses conducted large-scale enterprises such as railroads and communications, the legal entity of choice seemed to be partnerships. In a partnership arrangement the entity, not the individual partners, owns the property, equipment, and other assets. Under the Sequestration Act partnerships had to be dissolved and the property partitioned so as to allow the Confederacy to seize the property of the alien enemies.

As the details of the Sequestration Act became known in the weeks prior to its passage, citizens flocked to their attorneys seeking advice as to how the law affected their business and how to comply. Some Southerners dissolved their partnerships on their own, cutting out the Northern partner and continuing the business, often under the same name. Others found it more difficult for either personal or professional reasons simply to cut people out of the business they helped build and make prosper. A partnership issue brought the first sequestration client into Mr. Edward McGrady's Charleston office, setting a chain of events into motion that made McGrady a defendant in *the* sequestration case, placing him at center of the debate two months later.

The partnership problem even caused the Charleston grand jury to reflect on the problems and inequities of the sequestration law. In a presentment made during the grand jury's October 1861 term, the citizens of Charleston charged with investigating and indicting offenders under the sequestration law pointed out one of the overriding realities of the war and the application of the law: "It becomes us to remember the intimate relations in which we lived with the people of the North. Until December 21, 1860, we have not lived near each other as separate nations, but as one people; and our free intercourse and absolute free trade with each other has drawn us closer to each other than has ever happened with partnerships, between different nationalities." This astute observation came in the context of the grand jury's challenge to the provisions of the Sequestration Act that required partners to put up security for the partnership property of alien enemies, including any debt that might have existed between partners. The grand jury pointed out that requiring men to put up security for what was in many cases large sums might bankrupt otherwise solvent men. The South, it argued, could ill afford to crush its own merchant class because credit, particularly in the South, depended on the life of the merchant. Requiring security as the government now demanded ignored the very nature of business. "Commercial truth was a point of honor." Men honored their debts because to do otherwise destroyed them in the community. The security requirement in effect punished Southern merchants for having been in business with Northerners and worked a greater hardship on the citizen than on the alien enemy.

Even the Confederate judiciary saw the potential harm. On October 3, 1861, before he appointed his first receiver, Justice Hill of Texas shared his thoughts on the new law with his close friend David G. Burnet. Burnet had apparently not seen the act, and in words echoing the concerns of the Charleston grand jury, Hill conceded, "Truly it is a comprehensive act, but must be administered in much discretion, or it will destroy some of our people while it benefits others." Hill tried to calm fears by publicly assuring the citizens in his district that he intended to administer the act so that the burden fell "upon our foes and not upon citizens." Hill not only saw the inherent danger in the sequestration law but also touched on yet another problem: the law might be proper in its enactment but fail to pass constitutional muster as to its application. It is important to keep in mind that attacking a law as overly broad, vague, or applied in an arbitrary and capricious manner did not find acceptance until almost the twentieth century. However, that does not mean that nineteenth-century men did not see the problems and that nineteenth-century citizens did not suffer the consequences of such shortcomings in the law.

Waging war, whether at home or on the battlefield, presented the risk of casualties from friendly fire. Hill's general concerns and the specific problems manifest in the partnership issue clearly fleshed out the problems inherent in separating alien enemies from loyal citizens and the need to protect the latter in its zealous pursuit of the former. The Confederacy soon discovered another problem with its seizure law aside from the potential civil liberty violations, and that problem demonstrated that the intimate closeness that characterized antebellum relations could not be so easily dissolved in the zeal to crush the enemy. In some cases sequestration ran aground not on moral or constitutional grounds but on the unwillingness of private enterprise to succumb to the law.

Much of the South's transportation and communications infrastructure flowed from the North. The nationwide telegraph system that linked both sections provides one of the best examples. Estimates vary, but almost 50,000 miles of telegraph wire crisscrossed the nation in 1860, easily exceeding the railroad mileage of 36,000 miles in 1866. Ten thousand employees operated the 1,400 stations that linked the United States. Prior to the war the South used this vast network without giving much thought to the identity of its ownership. But when the war broke out in 1861, the American Telegraph Company, a New York corporation, and Southwestern Telegraph Company, a New Jersey company created by a special act of that state's legislature, operated most of the telegraph wire in North America.

Southwestern Telegraph ran most of the telegraph system in the South through seven principal telegraph lines, the longest of which, the Washington and New Orleans Telegraph Company, extended 1,700 miles from Washington to New Orleans via Richmond, Charleston, Savannah, Montgomery, and Mobile. When the war began, both sides moved to seize the telegraph infrastructure within their geographical boundary.

The ownership of the Southwestern Telegraph Company clearly brought it under the provisions of the Confederate Sequestration Act because Northern stockholders exercised a controlling interest in its main line, the Washington to New Orleans. This communications giant demonstrated the limits of Confederate law. Northern and Southern stockholders came together to protect the company and prevent Confederate sequestration of the Southern lines. The lines ran effectively throughout the war, but the Confederacy never seized the company, in great part because private business protected its investment, and sequestration efforts ran into a roadblock because alien interests could not be identified. The primary discovery tool, a writ of garnishment, proved useless because Southern company officials did not have the corporate books. Those books resided at the home office in New Jersey, and without them no one could identify alien enemy stock ownership. Despite efforts to seize the company and notwithstanding the complaints concerning the quality of service, particularly from the military, Southern shareholders and executives, with assistance from their Northern counterparts, effectively established the Southern Telegraph Company. Although this company provided service to the Confederacy, it never came under Confederate government control, and at the end of the war the American Telegraph Company resumed control, completing wartime efforts to frustrate sequestration and preserve a substantial asset.

Although money, stocks, slaves, and real estate made up a significant portion of the "alien" property subject to sequestration, the most controversial seizures involved debts owed by Southern persons or entities to Northerners. Alex A. Allemong, a Charleston attorney, found himself a defendant in a sequestration case because he held assets assigned to a trustee by Stevens and Betts, a Charleston business, to cover the debts owed by that business to a New York company. Allemong represented the New Yorkers and contested the sequestration proceeding not because he questioned his clients' status as alien enemies or the propriety of the seizure but because he had expenses owed him by his clients that he wanted to offset with the property he held in trust. In fairness to Allemong, one should note that his case arose in 1862, after many of the constitutional issues had been raised and resolved, and thus his willingness to breach his trust relationship reflected the reality of the legal climate rather than a callous disregard for his legal obligations. However, his case revealed a significant problem with the Sequestration Act, a problem raised initially in the 1861 sequestration cases and not easily resolved by a simple ruling. Debts, particularly those evidenced by promissory notes, represented money in nineteenth-century America. A holder of a promissory note or other evidence of indebtedness often paid for goods or services by assigning that debt or note to another party. Promissory notes made by Southerners to

Northern companies not only changed hands throughout the United States in payment of other obligations; debtors often assigned them to foreigners in satisfaction of debts. Although the United States might have to accept the breakdown of commerce caused by the war, foreign creditors of Confederate citizens holding their debts through assignments from Northern persons or businesses had a right under international law to collect those debts. The Confederate Sequestration Act looked no further than the immediate creditor. Finding him, her, or it to be an alien enemy, the government seized the debt and absolved the Confederate debtor. By doing so the Confederate law sequestered and liquidated assets of persons and entities who were not alien enemies. A government seeking to establish its place in the community of nations, whose representatives actively courted both Britain and France for diplomatic recognition and whose sailors vehemently argued in Northern courts that the Confederacy had a legal status under international law, undermined both its efforts and its argument by seizing debts that did not belong to alien enemies.

———

Hardship and international law notwithstanding, the most zealous opposition to Confederate sequestration came from those questioning its moral and constitutional basis. The trial in October 1861 did not occur within an intellectual vacuum. The debate throughout the Confederacy began almost immediately after the war started. Early in the war it seemed that the Southern legal community might embrace Confederate property seizures. In the opinion of one Louisiana attorney, war changed everything, including commercial transactions. On June 5, 1861, Thomas Jenkins Semmes, the Louisiana attorney general, issued an opinion letter to the president of the Mechanics and Traders Bank in New Orleans as to the legality of the transfer of stock by an alien enemy in time of war. A Louisiana citizen holding a power of attorney from a New York citizen sought to transfer to himself thirty shares of the bank's stock held by the New York citizen. Semmes concluded that the power of attorney was a nullity, making the transfer illegal and void. Relying on Semmes's opinion, the bank refused to record the transfer.

Semmes asserted that under international law the declaration of war "arrests all intercourse between belligerents." Citing English international law cases, he told the bank, "In a state of war nation is known to nation only by their armed exterior, each threatening the other with conquest or annihilation. The individuals who compose the belligerent states exist, as to each other in a state of utter occlusion. If they meet it is only to combat." As a result, all communication between citizens of the belligerents ceases. To do otherwise might demoralize and undermine the need to have all citizens "reconcile to one common fate." Semmes concluded that the Southern citizen had no authority to act on behalf of the New Yorker who issued the power of attorney, that person clearly being an alien enemy. No intercourse between belligerent citizens could result in any legally binding contract or relationship.

Semmes's opinion letter came two months before passage of the Alien Enemies Act and almost three months before the Sequestration Act. Although he did not speak directly to the taking of alien enemy property, his analysis of international law made such seizures the next logical step in a sequence of events that began with the declaration of war. If belligerents existed only as enemies to one another, legally incapable of conducting any type of civilian intercourse, then any property of an alien enemy physically located within the borders of a belligerent nation at the outbreak of hostilities became subject to the same rules of international law that terminated ongoing commercial relations between citizens of a foreign nation.

The writings of Frenchman Emmerich de Vattel, whose principles of international law served as a textbook during the nineteenth century, seemed to support Semmes. According to Vattel, warring nations have the right to "deprive our enemy of his possession of every thing which may augment his strength and enable him to make war. This everyone endeavors to accomplish in the manner most suitable to him." Vattel concluded that "whenever we may have an opportunity, we seize on the enemy's property, and convert it to our own use, and thus, besides diminishing the enemy's power, augment our own, and obtain at least a partial indemnification or equivalent, either for what constitutes the subject of war, or for the expenses and losses incurred in its prosecution; in a word—we do ourselves justice." As the *Charleston Mercury* pointed out, that clause could not have been more applicable to the Confederacy if Vattel had written it specifically for the new nation.

The Sequestration Act seemed to embrace both the letter and the spirit of international law. From Vattel's writings one could easily discern that in war the object is to win, and if the object is "just and right," then the means cannot be wrong. Despite Justice Hill's concern that the law might be improperly "applied," the Confederate government could argue that a citizen had no right to protect and save an alien enemy's property. Doing so directly aided an enemy by preventing that citizen's country from augmenting its own strength and diminishing that of its adversary. In effect, secreting alien enemy property aided the Union cause. A citizen should not have to be compelled to identify and turn over alien enemy property; the demand of one's country alone should be sufficient to obtain one's willing obedience.

But what of the argument that sequestration violated the Confederate Constitution? Shortly after the Sequestration Act passed, the editor of the *Augusta Constitutionalist* enlisted the aid of his "intelligent correspondent 'Nemo'" to comment on the controversial Confederate legislation. Although conceding that the policy behind the act stood beyond reproach, given that the North had forced the South into retaliating, the editor nevertheless observed that the "constitutionality" of the act remained an open question headed to the courts for resolution. Hoping for resolution in the courts probably placed undue faith in the ability of the judiciary to decide the issue. Of the three branches the judiciary is the weakest, and the courts often fail to protect legal rights under assault by political and military decisions rendered by the executive and legislative branches. But, with the debate raging and the views of "able writers on each side" weighing in on the question, the editor offered his paper's opinion in the hope of receiving an "impartial judgment" from the courts.

"Nemo" wasted no time destroying any suspense as to where he stood on the issue. The act, passed in haste and with undue passion, should be repealed or significantly modified because it was unconstitutional as an ex post facto law that impaired the obligation of contracts. A contract, legal when made, suddenly becoming illegal if honored by virtue of legislative fiat seemed to Nemo like an obvious violation of the prohibition against ex post facto laws and the nullification of contracts. Both ex post facto laws and the nullification of contracts, according to Nemo, violated "all our State and Federal constitutions." Although Nemo conceded that alien enemies had no right to the protection of the courts during wartime, that fact mitigated in favor of protecting the sanctity of contracts. For support he pointed to the Spanish merchants who during war defied their own government and held firm in their insistence that contractual relations be honored. "We have been . . . great sticklers for strict construction of the Constitution." Now, he argued, the Confederacy had resorted to retroactive confiscation and sequestration when neither had been used since the United States achieved its independence.

Nemo argued that during the War of 1812 the United States might have benefitted by confiscating English debt, yet denied such a measure as a proper war-making power and did not "strike a heavy blow at the good faith of our merchants, equally injurious to the character of our young Republic." "I have heard," Nemo said, "the Marquis de Hastings 'stormed a fortress upon a promissory note:' but the framers of the Constitution never dreamed of mustering a regiment to capture an open account, for a note already paid." Nemo's objection went to the effect of the sequestration law making it a crime to have disposed of a debt in existence on May 21, 1861, by paying a Northern creditor prior to the enactment of the Sequestration Act on August 30, 1861. Such a law was simply "untenable."

Nemo's objections came in two letters to his editor styled "Thoughts on the Confiscation Act—No.1 and No.2." Most of his substantive legal argument came in the first letter. The second letter offered a detailed description of how England paid its immense war debt amassed during the Napoleonic Wars without resorting to the economically crippling measures the Confederacy implemented. According to Nemo, England paid off its debt by protecting the private property of all nations, alien enemy or otherwise. England, in arms on land and particularly on the ocean, had been one of the greatest robbers of all time, but it robbed by the sword, against belligerents, "and not against confiding merchants, and helpless women and children." Nemo saw only two alternatives: either repeal the law in its entirety or repeal the law insofar as it acted on commercial interests.

Nemo zealously argued his position, and although many of his points rang true, his legal argument contained conspicuous flaws. At one point Nemo referred to "our own new constitution" as being "emphatic in its object" by adding that "ex post facto laws, and laws impairing the obligation of contracts and retroactive legislation injuriously affecting the rights of citizens, are prohibited." At first glace it would seem that Nemo was referring to the Confederate Constitution, but that was not the case. He was actually referencing Georgia's amended constitution of March 23, 1861, and this reliance on the state law, coupled with his other arguments, points to a significant aspect of citizen resistance to the Sequestration Act: the inability to comprehend the difference between federal and state power and prohibition. The prohibition against impairment of contracts applied to the states, not the Confederate government, a situation no different prior to secession. Article 1, section 10 of the U.S. Constitution provides that no state "shall impair the obligation of contract." Constitutionally, the Confederate government could impair the obligation of contract at will. Although technically Nemo's ex post facto argument had merit, it ignored completely the effect of war on commerce and the considerable body of international law presented in part by Louisiana Attorney General Thomas Semmes. Nemo's argument reflected a gut-level reaction of the Confederate population who resisted aspects of the Sequestration Act that infringed on rights protected by the state constitutions.

Nemo's strongest argument lay in his insistence that sequestration made no economic sense. Just as Hill and others had feared, the Sequestration Act posed a legitimate threat to Southern economic interests. However, although his practical objections had merit, Nemo's historically based argument omitted certain aspects of the American experience that provided precedent for seizing alien enemy property. Nemo claimed that the United States had refrained from sequestration and confiscation in every war since American independence. But he neglected to point out that during America's war for independence, the colonials had used both tools as sources of income and as punishment for British loyalists.

American colonists in New York and Vermont initiated sequestration and property sales as means of raising military units. Vermont's sequestration program not only provided sufficient funds to raise regiments but also allowed a region still trying to separate itself from New York to operate its own government. As the American Revolution progressed, Vermont's sequestration program gradually evolved into a systematic way of finding, seizing, and liquidating all or part of the assets held by British loyalists. As Vermont's separatist movement grew in strength, it turned the threat of sequestration against New Yorkers living in the southeastern part of the state to force them to recognize Vermont as their legal government. Thus, Nemo's claim that sequestration had no American precedent ignored our historical experience.

Had he looked closer to home, Nemo could have pointed to other examples of colonial seizure of loyalist property during America's struggle for independence. The *Charleston Mercury* pointed out that South Carolina also used sequestration and confiscation during the American Revolution. As the debate intensified in the months preceding the sequestration trials, the *Mercury* stepped to the forefront as a proponent of sequestration. It argued that under international law the Confederacy could sequester property of its enemies and that nothing within the Confederate Constitution prohibited such a war-making act. The newspaper also argued that an alien enemy had no right to use the constitution of its enemy to protect its property rights. Consistent with the position taken by Thomas Semmes, the newspaper argued that the advent of war destroyed the property rights of belligerent citizens. Otherwise a person could be both an enemy and a citizen.

In an editorial that appeared less than two weeks before the trial of the five Charleston lawyers, the *Mercury* argued that trustees and attorneys ceased to operate in that capacity with regard to enemy property once war began. The state of war abolished any fiduciary relationship that existed. Thus, the only question was: could a government of a country at war with another country compel one of its citizens to give up the property of an enemy in that citizen's possession? The only logical answer was "yes." To suggest otherwise meant that a warring nation could never seize the property of an enemy, no matter where it might find that property. A blanket exemption of enemy property ran directly contrary to the law of nations. Thus, if a nation could seize enemy property in the actual possession of an enemy, no legal or constitutional argument existed to bar that nation from seizing enemy property held by an agent or trustee of the enemy.

The *Mercury* conceded that "able men will more elaborately consider" the issues, but its editor saw no grounds to nullify sequestration as unconstitutional. Indeed, the true test would come in the courtroom, but just as the piracy cases played out in the Northern press prior to trial, the sequestration cases had been tried in the court of public opinion almost since the inception of the act. In October 1861, as Confederate sailors stood trial in two U.S. federal courts for piracy, a handful of Charleston's finest and most prominent attorneys went to court not just to protect their clients but to defend their own conduct in opposing the Sequestration Act.

––––––––

The court battle to decide the constitutionality of the Sequestration Act loomed on the horizon. The Confederacy stood ready to enforce its law; all that remained was for someone to step forward and challenge the act. In order to challenge the act one had to be personally affected by its provisions. Although private citizens across the South became defendants every day, either because they were accused of being alien enemies or because they held alien enemy property, the average citizen posed an unlikely challenger to the authority of the Confederate government in the fall of 1861. Summer victories on battlefields in Virginia and Missouri and the exploits of its privateer fleet boded well for the success of the upstart nation. The civil unrest and signs of defeat that accompanied conscription, the suspension of the writ of habeas corpus, and other government measures later in the war had not surfaced in September 1861. Amid the spirit of the "Second American Revolution," anyone challenging the government's right, or the means it employed to defeat the Union, argued in the face of mainstream public opinion. Although such newspapers as the *Augusta Constitutionalist* argued against the act, much of the rhetoric focused on not injuring Confederate citizens in the zeal to crush the North. This spirit fought sequestration as contrary to the Confederacy's best interest. It would be a different story for anyone who resisted the law on the grounds that it violated constitutional rights of Southerners under circumstances where the effect would be to guard the property of the South's enemies. Challenging the Sequestration Act in open court required someone with both the means and the ability to push the debate to a higher plane and make people see the larger issues. It required lawyers who were not merely advocates but defendants.

No sane attorney went looking for a fight with the Confederate government in early 1861. However, in September 1861 the Confederacy took the initial steps to implement sequestration, steps that forced lawyers to act and in the process compelled them to choose between their obligations as lawyers and trustees and their duties as Confederate citizens. On September 12, 1861, the Confederate Department of Justice issued "Instructions to Receivers under the Act." Reprinted in newspapers across the South, including the *Charleston Mercury* on September 18, 1861, the instructions defined "alien enemies" and ordered receivers to seize their property. In addition, the Confederate Justice Department required receivers to "forthwith apply to the clerk of the court for writs of garnishment under Sec. 8 of the act." With specific persons still unidentified, the writs went out to certain classes of people most likely to be in possession of property or to know where such property might be located. The first group named "Attorneys and Counselors practicing law within your district." Within a short time every attorney in the Confederacy received such a writ, including every lawyer in Charleston, South Carolina. When those writs found their way to the offices of James Petigru, William Whaley, Edward McGrady, James Wilkinson, and Nelson Mitchell, the Confederacy had unsuspectingly found the defendants to step forward and challenge the Sequestration Act.

CHAPTER 3

"We Shall Have No More Peace Forever"

Even before the Sequestration Act passed, Charleston citizens streamed into the offices of the city's attorneys to seek legal advice on their status and that of their businesses under the new Alien Enemies Act. Some found their way into the office of Edward McGrady Sr. By the summer of 1861 Edward McGrady stood among the elite of Charleston's bar. Born in 1802, McGrady belonged to a prominent Charleston family and had served in the South Carolina legislature during the 1850s. In the years following the war he worked zealously alongside his son, Edward Jr., to restore white rule in the South. In 1861 McGrady not only had a thriving commercial legal practice but also owned land outside Charleston and at least fifteen slaves. An opponent of the nullification movement in the 1830s, McGrady supported secession not only in spirit but also by example. His son left the family practice in 1861 to join Maxcy Gregg's First South Carolina Volunteers, where he saw extensive combat and received wounds at both Second Manassas and Fredericksburg. In terms of wealth, position, and social philosophy, Edward McGrady stood as a living example of everything the Southern Confederacy represented. His role in the sequestration cases exemplified the degree to which the Confederacy's wartime legislation alienated even its most loyal citizens.

A meticulous record keeper, McGrady maintained daily journals from 1844 through 1875, identifying every client matter he engaged in, the time he spent in that matter, and the general nature of the work or meeting. At the end of each year's diary he provided an alphabetical listing of his client base for that year. Among his ninety clients in 1861 he listed the Planters and Mechanics Bank of South Carolina, the same bank in Louisiana that presented the state attorney general with the alien enemy transfer problem in June 1861.

Such businessmen as Hyatt McBurney, of Hyatt McBurney and Company, made up the remainder of McGrady's clients. Most merchants in a large port city did business with Northern companies and individuals, and McBurney was no exception. He entered McGrady's office on August 16, 1861, with his connection to the North clearly on his mind.

McBurney voiced immediate concerns about his own status. In his first meeting with McGrady, he raised the possibility of becoming a naturalized Confederate citizen. Within the week he returned, and the two discussed plans for him to make Charleston his home. McGrady apparently made arrangements for McBurney to appear before Judge Andrew Magrath on August 21, 1861, to take the oath of allegiance to the Confederacy. With the passage of the Sequestration Act only days away, McBurney and others brought questions about how to treat Northern assets and debts owed to alien enemies.

McGrady and McBurney discussed the possibility of paying debts due to Northerners into the Confederate treasury. The Charleston firm of Jennings and Thomlinson wanted advice on the legal ownership of an attachment suit in Florida against two Northern citizens. By September McGrady had begun taking a harder line against complying with the Confederate confiscation law. When the district receivers of Charleston sent out their writs of garnishment, the list of McGrady's clients grew. Dunham Taft and Company, Waldron Eageston and Company, Sundry Merchants of Hayne, South Carolina, the agent of a Miss Charlotte C. Kelsey, and Mr. J. W. Harrell all wanted to know how to respond to the receiver. McGrady drafted a petition for Thomlinson, told Miss Kelsey's agent not to respond at all, and came into contact with the Charleston firm of Campbell and Mitchell, specifically Nelson Mitchell, in his consultation with the Sundry Merchants of Hayne. This common client and the writs of garnishment served on Mitchell and McGrady made both men defendants in criminal proceedings brought by the Confederate States of America.

Little is known of Nelson Mitchell. He had been in practice at least twenty years when the sequestration matter arose. He was predominately a probate attorney, and his legal records showed the type of diversity common to a general practitioner of the era. He handled runaway slave cases, insurance matters, disputes between citizens and banks, and disagreements between banks themselves. His most unusual case involved a trial over a duel. Like McGrady, Mitchell belonged to the upper end of Southern society, part of the social and political base that made secession a reality. In addition to his thriving legal practice, Mitchell owned a plantation on Daniels Island and had slaves who worked his cotton and cattle business. However, like McGrady, he saw the Sequestration Act as a threat that struck at the heart of his legal business, and like McGrady, he opposed the government's confiscation efforts, which placed him at odds with measures that in theory helped preserve the very social and economic structure in which he thrived. The effect of the act on Mitchell proved more long lasting than on any of the other defendants in the sequestration cases. When the cases ended in October 1861, Mitchell resolved to carry on the battle. One of his clients kept Mitchell actively fighting sequestration well into 1863.

The receiver's writs of garnishment brought two other men into the fray. When fifty-four-year-old William Whaley defended himself in October 1861, he held as prominent a place in Charleston society as both McGrady and Mitchell. Whaley's family moved among the upper crust of Charleston society and could trace its ancestry to early American colonists all along the Atlantic seaboard. One branch of the family claimed ancestors with close connections to Oliver Cromwell. By 1860 William Whaley occupied the same status as his codefendants, a prominent member of a community who stood to profit most from secession yet now opposed the new government. The background of James W. Wilkinson, the fourth of the five defendants, is the most obscure. The Wilkinson family had a strong presence in the Charleston community, with parts of the family connected to the Whaleys, but direct references to James are almost nonexistent.

Without question James Louis Petigru was the most important man caught in the wide garnishment net cast by the Charleston receiver. Born in 1789 near Abbeville, South Carolina, Petigru grew up in the household of a relative on a moderately successful backcountry farm complete with a complement of slaves. Intellectually driven from a young age, he went to college at age seventeen and began his law practice six years later. Two contradictory themes dominated Petigru's life: the belief that the federal union provided the best guarantee of individual liberty and his position on slavery.

Although never an abolitionist, Petigru considered the South's peculiar institution a human injustice and strongly opposed its expansion into the territories. At the same time he accepted slavery in the South and even owned slaves throughout his life. But despite owning slaves he worked consistently over the course of his career to facilitate the legal emancipation of slaves in contravention of South Carolina's ban on private emancipation. In one case he not only secured the freedom of a slave but also helped raise the money to purchase two slaves within the same family who had been improperly sold and sent the entire emancipated family to Liberia. During his second term in the South Carolina legislature, he spearheaded an effort to pass special legislation for the emancipation of family members of freed blacks. His effort to codify state law regarding freed blacks and slaves seemed too lenient to most South Carolinians and never passed. Yet despite these efforts Petigru never used his position as one of South Carolina's most respected jurists to challenge the onerous criminal justice system that applied to blacks in South Carolina.

Petigru's stance on slavery at times appeared inconsistent, but it was also progressive, considering the times and the place he lived. However, his position on the Union never wavered and often seemed impractical. He was a Whig in a staunchly Democratic state, but his political persuasion only partly explains his commitment to the Union. In a state that stood at the forefront of antebellum resistance to the Union, Petigru steadfastly maintained his allegiance to the United States. In 1832 Petigru led South Carolina Unionists in opposition to nullification. After the crisis passed, most Unionists left South Carolina, but not James Petigru. He remained to become one of the giants of the nineteenth-century American bar, and despite the growing division between North and South, Petigru preached the merits of the Union at every opportunity. On June 28, 1844, he gave a speech at Fort Moultrie, South Carolina, wherein he extolled the virtues of the U.S. Constitution as a product of both great skill on the part of the founding fathers and "the goodness of providence, which placed in our hands an instrument of peace and order which human ingenuity could not have devised."

Until the day of his death Petigru held the deep conviction that "on the union of the states . . . laid the foundation of national defense and the guard of civil liberties." In Petigru's estimation the U.S. Constitution represented the greatest plan of government ever devised.

When South Carolina seceded in 1860, Petigru stood as literally the only man in South Carolina opposed to secession. On secession day his friend John Pope recalled passing Petigru on the street.

"Where's the fire?'" Petigru asked.

"There is no fire. Those are the joy bells ringing in honor of the passage of the secession ordinance," replied Pope.

"I tell you there is a fire. They have this day set a blazing torch to the temple of constitutional liberty, and, please God, we shall have no more peace forever."

Petigru added that he had "seen the last happy day" of his life and publicly referred to his native state as "a very large insane asylum."

Described in his youth as having great muscular power that seemed to make him larger than he was, Petigru had a "rather low but broad forehead, . . . a strong and massive chin, and dark and magnificent gray eyes [that] gave a dignity of character . . . that would otherwise have been homely." His voice added to his imposing physical presence and became his singular defining physical attribute to those who ever heard him speak. Petigru's appearance and oratory skills, combined with his intellect and deep love for the law, had served him well throughout his career. By the fall of 1861 Petigru had come to the end of a long life, and his physical attributes remained but a shadow of what they had been. As he prepared for the last great fight of his life, he had to summon up one last time all of the skills that made him South Carolina's greatest living orator and jurist. Opposing him and his four codefendants was the overwhelming weight of public opinion and patriotic sentiment then raging through South Carolina and a legal team with its own deep connections to South Carolina determined to squelch this opposition to the Confederate war effort.

The least known member of the prosecution, at least historically, was the Confederate district attorney, Charles Richardson Miles. Thirty-two years old in the fall of 1861, Miles had represented the Confederate government in all proceedings filed under the Sequestration Act. Although his life exists only in obscurity today, Miles zealously defended the Confederacy and prosecuted those who opposed its will. If his correspondence is accurate, his zeal transcended the law itself. For example, he reported the arrest of two men in July 1861, supposedly under the "act of 1798." Unless he was referring to some state act of South Carolina, only the 1798 Alien Act could have supported the arrest of the two U.S. citizens in July 1861. Although never formally repealed, the 1798 Alien Act had expired and in 1861 provided no legal basis for arresting anyone. Miles had the two New Yorkers arrested because he feared they might be carrying intelligence to the enemy. His report went to Judah Benjamin, the attorney general of the Confederacy, with an urgent request that President Davis issue a proclamation as to how to deal with alien enemies.

Isaac W. Hayne joined Miles at the counsel table. As mentioned earlier, Hayne was the grandson of Colonel Isaac Hayne, an American martyr executed by the British in 1779, and a relative of Robert Hayne, who eloquently defended the South against Daniel Webster in the famous Hayne-Webster debates. Born in 1809 and educated at South Carolina College in Columbia, Hayne passed the bar in 1831 and became the editor of a political newspaper. His position on slavery and states' rights proved as uncompromising as Petigru's defense of the Union. Hayne moved to the Beaufort district of South Carolina in 1832, where he was elected clerk of the Nullification Convention. Thereafter he served for six years as the secretary to Governors Robert Hayne and George McDuffie before moving in 1838 to Montgomery, Alabama, where he went into private practice. For eight years he practiced in the Alabama capital and routinely crossed paths with the best lawyers in the state, acquiring a reputation as an earnest, skillful, and successful advocate.

In 1846 Hayne returned to Charleston and stepped into a formidable legal community that included such men as B. F. Hunt, C. G. Memminger, Henry Baily, Richard Yeardon, and, of course, James Louis Petigru. The transition proved difficult not so much because of the quality of the legal community but because of the difference in the law. Unlike Alabama's land courts, by 1846 the common law of South Carolina had become heavily laden with statute, and Hayne's trial experience could not immediately overcome his lack of familiarity with the law. However, Hayne adapted well, and the records of his years of private practice in Charleston reflect a strong commercial practice with a good mix of probate, real estate, admiralty, and insurance. But Isaac Hayne was not destined to remain a private practitioner. In 1848 the South Carolina General Assembly elected him attorney general of South Carolina. When he took his place alongside Charles Miles in October 1861, he brought with him all of the power and prestige that came with being the official legal representative of the people of South Carolina.

Even with the strength of public opinion and the considerable skill and prestige that Isaac Hayne brought to the prosecution, the defenders of the Sequestration Act seemed outmatched. However, any advantage the defendants enjoyed disappeared in the shadow cast by the one person who in theory acted as an unbiased arbiter—the presiding judge, Andrew Gordon Magrath. Born in Charleston in 1813, Magrath, the son of an Irish merchant, graduated from South Carolina College in 1831 and briefly attended Harvard Law School before returning to Charleston and reading the law under the tutelage of none other than James Petigru. Admitted to the bar in 1835, Magrath established a lucrative law practice and raised his family in Charleston. In 1856 Franklin Pierce appointed Magrath the U.S. district judge for South Carolina.

Early in life Magrath had been a cooperationist, but by 1860 he completely embraced secession. Although personally opposed to the slave trade, Magrath used his judicial position to hand proslavery and states' rights advocates a clear victory in early 1860. Magrath presided over the trials of the *Echo* and the *Wanderer*, two ships seized for engaging in the African slave trade. The ships' captains and crews faced charges of piracy under the 1820 federal piracy law, the same law that the *Jeff Davis* and *Savannah* defendants stood accused of violating. Magrath ruled that trading in slaves did not constitute piracy, rejecting the imposition of the death penalty under the piracy law in favor of the more lenient punishment provided under the anti–slave trade statute. The case came back to haunt the North because, as noted earlier, in 1861 the *Echo*, sold at auction in 1859, returned as the Confederate privateer *Jeff Davis*.

Any doubt as to where Magrath stood on secession and states' rights disappeared almost immediately following Lincoln's election.

On November 7, 1860, the day after the election, Magrath dramatically tore off his judicial robes and closed his court "before its altar has been desecrated with sacrifices to tyranny." President Buchanan called the act more disturbing than anything in the South except the occupation of Fort Sumter by federal troops. Posters of Magrath tearing off his ropes and firing a cannon at a law library appeared all over Charleston. Magrath quickly assumed the mantle as one of Charleston's most ardent secessionists, and after sitting in the state's secession convention, he accepted a position as South Carolina's secretary of state. His tenure in South Carolina's executive branch lasted less than a year. In the summer of 1861 he returned to his former courtroom as the judge of the Confederate District Court in Charleston, where one of his first tasks would be presiding over the sequestration cases.

While the four other attorney defendants mulled over their options, James Petigru forced the issue to a head and in so doing provided a preview of what to expect when the cases went to trial. On October 7, 1861, he appeared in Confederate district court and filed a general demurrer, or formal objection, to the writs of garnishment. This initial objection raised so many issues and garnered so much attention that Magrath set Petigru's motion for a full trial the next week and consolidated the objection cases of the other four attorneys.

Petigru received a writ requiring him to disclose the existence and location of alien enemy property. The writ cited an impressive and diverse list of clients, including Major Rawlins Lowndes, William Lowndes, and Mrs. Abraham Van Buren of New York, the daughter of a Colonel John Singleton of Wateree, South Carolina; the funds of the Mount Vernon Association held by a Miss A. Parmelee Cunningham; and, finally, a group of free people of color from Philadelphia who were the beneficiaries of the estate of a Mrs. Kohn. Each person had some connection to property deemed alien enemy property under the act. The interrogatories that accompanied the writ served on Petigru required him to breach his attorney-client relationship with each of these people and in some cases to violate his duties as a trustee. His objection was that "no human authority had the right to put these questions to me or any one in the same circumstances."

What was void as to one was void as to all. Petigru put the validity of the entire act into question and raised as one of the cornerstones of his argument that morning a position no one could have imagined he would take: states' rights. The man who spent his entire life defending the power of the federal government in the face of the most ardent proponents of state sovereignty now argued that although South Carolina might legally compel him to reveal client secrets, the Confederate government could not.

Petigru's argument began with the premise that the source of all governmental power in the Confederacy flowed from the states. "He [Petigru] might recognize the authority of the State of South Carolina to do as proposed by that Act, because in a State like South Carolina a sufferer has no security or remedy against those in power, unless from some guarantee in the Constitution of the State. For a State may do whatever it is not forbidden to do by the fundamental law of the State." But, Petigru argued, the "Confederate States" have no such general power. Their authority is "confined" to the constitution that confers it and the "powers delegated to them." As Petigru saw it, a sovereign is within its rights to act absent a specific constitutional prohibition. The Confederacy, however, had no such "sovereignty," and in order to act it needed to demonstrate a clear grant of power or authority from the states. In short, Petigru could find no authority within the Confederate Constitution that allowed it to set up an "inquisition," which is how he described the garnishment process under the act.

Petigru's opening assault surely warmed the hearts of the South's most ardent states' rights proponents. Power flowed up from the states, and the Confederate government existed as a political subdivision under a limited grant of authority. The states made no specific grant of authority to confiscate property, and by arguing for a strict interpretation of the Confederate Constitution, Petigru tried to cut off any counterargument that the central government could sequester and garnish based on an implied power. For at least one man in the room the irony of Petigru's position proved impossible to overlook. Charles Miles called the oddity of Petigru's position to the attention of those gathered in the courtroom, calling it "the singular position which the eminent respondent today for the first time occupied." Miles conceded that Petigru's defense of alien enemies, people he still called his "fellow citizens," was consistent with many of his prior stands. However, "[it was a] remarkable metamorphosis" that a man who stood fearlessly and alone against the actions of South Carolina should now advocate the "strictest and sternest construction of states' rights that had ever been contended for even in South Carolina."

At first glance Petigru's states' rights argument might well have been his weakest. Virtually every state constitution in the Confederacy, including South Carolina's, contained a provision precluding the state from passing any bill of attainder, ex post facto law, or law impairing the obligation of contracts. As noted in the last chapter, Nemo, the correspondent from the *Augusta Constitutionalist*, had vehemently denounced the Sequestration Act as both an ex post facto law and a law impairing contractual obligations but overlooked the fact that the Confederate Constitution contained no such prohibition against the central government. Modeled after the U.S. Constitution, article 1, section 8 set out the enumerated powers of the Confederate Congress that included regulating commerce with foreign nations, raising and supporting an army, and declaring war. Like the U.S. Constitution, the Confederate document contained a "necessary and proper clause," and the "test" applied to the propriety and constitutionality of legislative acts was the famous "ends-means" test set out by John Marshall in *McCulloch v. Maryland*. So long as the end was "legitimate" and the means "not specifically prohibited" by the Constitution, a law of Congress passed scrutiny under the Constitution. But Petigru argued that in the Union the federal government reigned as the highest political subdivision. It, not the states, possessed superior "sovereignty" and, consistent with Marshall's landmark test, could do as it wished so long as its actions were not specifically prohibited. In the Confederacy the relationship was inverted, and Marshall's test did not apply.

Although interesting, Petigru's invoking of states' rights proved peripheral to his main argument. At the core of his resistance to the Confederate Sequestration Act lay a belief that in its application the act authorized an inquisition. He referred directly to Hudson's treatise on the Star Chamber in the *Second Collectanea Judica* for proof that the methods prescribed in the Sequestration Act mirrored precisely those used by the Star Chamber. The writ of garnishment and interrogatories that accompanied it required the recipient to answer all questions. With no lawsuit on file, no plaintiff, and no specific defendant, the questions became a written "general inquisition."

Confronting the argument that the act fell within the warmaking power of the Confederate Congress, Petigru insisted that there had never been a similar law cloaked as a war-making power. No English monarch or parliament ever sanctioned such an act. The war power did not extend to this act because war allows the sovereign to do what is usual and necessary to wage war. This act was neither. Many other wars in human history developed welldefined laws of war. The Sequestration Act had no legal precedent. If the Confederacy wished to confiscate property, Petigru said, then he would encourage it to do so; he rebelled at having to betray confidences of friends, neighbors, and clients. Confiscation seized enemy property, but the interrogatories, directed at loyal citizens, did not touch any alien enemy. Referring to Torquemada, the head of the Spanish Inquisition, Petigru contended that he "might have burnt Jews and Protestants without calling upon their best friends to inform against them, and making it penal not to do so."

The way the law turned neighbor against neighbor clearly bothered Petigru, and this concern in turn revealed something about the Confederacy. When the South seceded and subsequently passed laws declaring Northerners alien enemies and seizing their property, such laws differed from actions of a country such as France declaring war and forcing all persons of English, Austrian, or Russian citizenship to leave the country. Englishmen and Austrians had been "aliens" before hostilities ever broke out; they traveled and did business in a foreign country at the pleasure of that nation's government. When the South seceded and war followed, the Confederacy took steps to dissolve relationships between people that in many cases had existed for decades. But legally calling someone an enemy did not automatically dissolve the emotional and communal ties between people. From the moment of its creation the Confederacy became a place with clouded loyalties. The elimination of the U.S. courts and other incidents of government and replacing them with

Confederate infrastructure proved easy. Convincing people that fidelity to the Confederacy required them to subordinate their duty to friends and community ran against the grain of Southern culture, and Petigru aimed to hammer away at that conflict.

For Petigru the debate transcended the legality of the Sequestration Act. The resolution of the case said something about the Confederacy as a nation and its citizens as a people. The law represented an "extraordinary stretch of power" at precisely the moment when "we are endeavoring to make good before the world our right to its respect as an enlightened people; a people capable of self government, and of governing themselves in a manner worthy of the civilization and the light of the age." Petigru could not believe that the Confederacy had resorted to a law "borrowed from the darkest periods of tyranny . . . [and] dug up from the very quarters of despotism" and held it out to the world as "our sentiments." They were not his sentiments, and he would be "sorry" if in this sentiment "he was solitary and alone." Everyone knew at this point that Confederate privateers awaited trial in the North for piracy and that the crux of their defense rested on establishing the Confederacy as a nation, or at the least as a belligerent, entitled to the rights afforded such a status under international law. Petigru argued that the "appearance" of nationhood had no meaning unless the people and their laws evidenced the kind of morals and sense of justice that gave nationhood real substance.

This case continued to be tried in the Southern court of public opinion, and Petigru understood the importance of swaying the people, even if he could not prevail in court. The sanctity of the attorney-client relationship and the duty owed by trustees had real legal significance, but the idea of neighbors and friends turning on one another resonated with the common man. Petigru played to that fear as best he could. His comments on October 7, 1861, targeted the general public as much as the court. He told the court that he would answer every interrogatory put to him in the negative. Insofar as breaching confidences not covered by his duty as an attorney, Petigru demanded to be "better instructed" by the court. As he sat down he told everyone listening that day, "There are cases when it is dishonor or death, death will certainly be chosen by every man who deserves the name." Petigru had thrown down the gauntlet. Magrath set the demurrer for a full hearing on October 14, 1861, one week away.

Petigru certainly got his message out. The next day, Alfred Huger, one of Petigru's oldest friends, wrote him regarding his plea to the court. Huger supported secession, but once it came he held the North responsible. However, he agreed with his friend as to the Sequestration Act and the Confederate efforts to enforce the law. "The miserable idea of suppressing truth in the name of public opinion is no less Jacobinical on this side of the Atlantic than it had been on the other," he said. Huger insisted that "heaven has provided men like yourself to resist such aggression wherever and whenever it appears; the defense of the weak and the absent is your peculiar province," he told Petigru. "Mine is to look on with admiration."

Although Huger's words must have provided some comfort, James Petigru knew what to expect when he entered Andrew Magrath's courtroom. Prior affiliations and relationships meant nothing now, and Petigru conceded, "I have no hope of touching Magrath's conscience." Petigru could only hope that the debate itself might convince the Southern public of the injustice of the law and bring about its repeal. Forty-five days after the Sequestration Act passed, the two sides stood poised for trial. On October 14, 1861, not a seat or a place to stand could be found in Magrath's courtroom when the sequestration cases got under way.

CHAPTER 4

"A Fair and Impartial Trial"

Seven hundred miles north of Charleston, the two Confederate privateer crews awaited their fate. The crew of the *Savannah* languished in a New York City jail for more than four months in the Tombs. The five-member prize crew of the *Jeff Davis* who had been captured on the *Enchantress* spent more than three months in a Philadelphia jail prior to trial. While the men waited, the legal teams formed for both sides. Whereas in Charleston little doubt existed as to the quality of the defendants' representation, Union war sentiment put pressure on the Northern bar almost immediately after the war began. If the Confederate "pirates" were to have any chance, Northern attorneys had to cross the line and take on a very unpopular position as the defense counsel for the privateers. The patriotic fever that swept the North in the wake of Fort Sumter made crossing the line a difficult proposition.

On April 23, 1861, a column appeared on the front page of the *New York Times* titled "The Bar and the Union: Law and Loyalty." The piece reported on a special meeting of the New York City Bar Association and several resolutions adopted relating to the war and the conduct of the legal profession. The preface to the resolutions stated that in "all periods of the history of our people, the lawyers have been preeminently true to the cause of civil liberty, the supremacy of the law, and the integrity of the constitution." The members acknowledged their "high obligation of fidelity to the Union and the Constitution," and they implored all lawyers, whether judges, practitioners, clerks, or law students, to "rally to the defense of our dearly cherished institutions, against the felonious assaults now made upon them." The association acknowledged the obvious, that the present contest had no parallels in history, and "where the wisdom of the past can afford us no adequate guide, it becomes the lawyer, regardless of the obscurity which so often settles upon moral courage, amid the blaze of material renown, to be firm, true, calm and active in every emergency, and by a generous self-sacrifice evince at once the ardor and the purity of his patriotism." The clear message in New York City demanded that lawyers forsake work or representation that might compromise the national goals of suppressing the rebellion. However, in order to show moral courage and preserve both civil liberty and the Constitution, lawyers would have to undertake unpopular causes even at the risk of appearing unpatriotic.

Although the sequestration cases provided for criminal penalties, everyone understood that none of the defendants risked prison or other severe criminal sanctions. Despite Magrath's grand jury instruction equating the failure to cooperate with sequestration to treason, the real issue remained the validity of the law. Prior to the trial the five attorney defendants moved freely about Charleston, and their lives and legal practices continued unabated. McGrady even met with Judge Magrath on several occasions prior to the trial. In Philadelphia and New York, however, such was not the case. *United States v. Baker* and *United States v. Smith*, as the *Savannah* and *Jeff Davis* cases became officially known, carried the heaviest of criminal sanctions: the death penalty. As a result, both cases proceeded with all the formalities surrounding criminal trials.

On July 16, 1861, the grand jury finally indicted the crew of the *Savannah* on the charge of piracy, and the next day the court arraigned the Confederates before a packed courtroom in New York City. The main purpose of the arraignment was to take the plea of the defendants, set a date for trial, and attend to any other pretrial matters. Despite the pleas to patriotism and defense of the Union made by the New York City bar in April 1861, as the arraignment proceeded it became clear that some of New York's finest lawyers had stepped forward to defend the Confederate privateers. The willingness of New York City's attorneys to undertake an unpopular defense not only spoke to the conviction of some of the city's elite lawyers that the system required a zealous defense regardless of public opinion but also demonstrated the strength of personal connections even during time of war.

Daniel Lord Jr., the founder of Lord, Day and Lord, one of the city's most prominent firms, stood up to defend John Harleston, T. Harrison Baker's partner and reluctant seaman. Why would Lord decide to defend Harleston? Harleston's father had been Lord's classmate at Yale University. Although seventy years old, Lord remained one of the heads of the New York City bar. He was universally regarded as a top-flight attorney with a reputation for integrity beyond reproach. The Confederate government hired Algernon S. Sullivan, the founder of the New York firm of Sullivan and Cromwell, to represent all defendants in the case and to act as counsel for any other privateers who might come to New York as prisoners. Sullivan, described as "a tall, thin, distinguished looking man," was an Ohio native and had a reputation as a fine lawyer and an eloquent speaker. He used his connections to bring a third lawyer into the case, James T. Brady. Brady, the leading criminal lawyer in New York City and former district attorney, represented T. Harrison Baker, the captain of the *Savannah*. Brady was described by Harleston as having a "medium build, square shoulders, a big head and plenty of brains," and his prowess in the courtroom made him the most celebrated lawyer in the city. E. Delafield Smith, the U.S. district attorney and professor of law at City University, drew the assignment of prosecuting the privateers.

From the outset Smith believed the success of his case depended on speed, and thus he insisted that the case be tried as soon as possible. At the arraignment, defense counsel objected to having to enter a plea on the grounds that the indictment had just been entered and that they had insufficient time to examine it in detail before responding. The defense also argued that the case could not be tried during the court's present term. To prepare adequately, the defense needed to take testimony in the South. More important, because the case carried the death penalty, two judges had to preside. Judge William D. Shipman, the U.S. district judge for the District of Connecticut, sat on the case by designation. The defense wanted Circuit Justice Samuel Nelson to join Shipman, but Nelson could not attend because of an injury sustained when he fell from his horse. Shipman listened to both sides, but the only ruling he made that day was to reset the arraignment for July 23, 1861.

Faced with a formidable defense team, Smith went about his job with admirable zeal and showed a willingness to use everything at his disposal to gain an advantage. In late July, either by accident or by design, Smith took advantage of the media attention that already surrounded the case. William Smith and the other members of the *Jeff Davis* prize crew captured on July 22, 1861, had finally arrived in the North and were being held by the U.S. marshal's office in New York. Delafield Smith appeared at the marshal's office amid a throng of reporters from the *New York Times*. Mr. Tillman, the black cook on the *S. J. Waring* who had single-handedly recaptured the prize from its Confederate crew and successfully navigated the ship back to New York, also appeared. Tillman described his ordeal as the newspaper reporters flocked around him. The picture of a black man held captive and being returned to slavery did not escape the crowd.

"I am glad to see you," said one bystander. "You deserve to have your liberty."

"Yes," yelled another man, "If all the colored people were like you, we would not have all of this trouble."

"I did the best I could," said Tillman; "I couldn't see any other way to get my liberty."

After being introduced to the crowd, Smith wasted no time in taking advantage of the opportunity. Shaking Tillman's hand with vigor, he said, "I am glad to see you, sir, and shake you by the hand." From the crowd someone shouted, "He saved you a great deal of trouble!" Smith laughed and told Tillman he wanted him to stay in New York under pay and intended to use him as a witness. Tillman agreed to remain in New York. Tillman displayed the axe he used to slay his oppressors, along with the bloodstained secession flag that the privateers had made from the American banner. The privateer crews stood almost emotionless for public inspection, powerful images of rebellion and the slave power that brought it about, images Smith hoped would be inconsistent with the defense's portrayal of the privateers as Confederate seafaring warriors.

It is unclear whether Smith intended to use Tillman in the *Savannah* trial or whether he thought he would also be trying the *Jeff Davis* crew. In either case Smith clearly understood that the privateer cases would be tried as much in the court of public opinion as in a court of law. As far as he was concerned, anything he could do to play on existing Northern fears of Confederate privateers served to advance his cause in both courts. The privateers from the *Savannah* would be tried by a New York City jury, and notwithstanding their disclaimers and assurances that they could be fair, Smith counted on people's inability to block certain images from their minds.

The next day the arraignment of the *Savannah* defendants reconvened, and Smith continued his efforts to depict these men as pirates. In a courtroom once again filled to capacity with reporters and onlookers, the defense waived the reading of the indictment in open court. Smith nevertheless insisted it be read so that everyone could hear the crimes the men stood accused of committing. Then he launched into his argument for the fastest trial date possible. In Smith's opinion the case required little preparation because the evidence, narrow in scope and easily attainable, left no doubt as to the defendants' guilt. In view of the events that transpired daily on the high seas, Smith wanted these men tried and convicted as quickly as possible so as to set an example "to those who pursue [this] . . . species of marauding," and he requested a trial date of July 31, 1861, just eight days away.

The defense watched Smith but could do little to stop him. One member of the team remarked that "his [Smith's] ends were already attained." Smith made his speech in front of a large body of spectators, including reporters, who took down his every word. The public would now know the prosecution thought the case should go quickly because the Confederates were undoubtedly guilty. The defense reminded the court that all men are innocent until proved guilty, that Smith could not possibly know what evidence the defense intended to offer, and that when the case came to trial, Smith would find the case more complicated than he now believed. From a practical standpoint the defense needed documents and witnesses that lay beyond the court's jurisdiction and required time to secure, and they could not be ready for trial before the fall. The defendants could not control whatever transpired on the high seas in the meantime. The defense also reminded the court that Judge Nelson had expressed a desire to assist in the trial of the case.

Smith reasserted his demand for an early setting and offered to stipulate to certain facts to avoid the delay in gathering evidence. Shipman stopped the debate. He told the defense that Justice

Nelson could communicate his intentions to the court personally and did not need counsel's assistance. Then, addressing the prosecution's motion, he stated that rules did not change based on the class or classes of defendants and that stipulating to facts in a criminal case led to "no good." Shipman had already made his decision. Capital cases required two judges because only if a difference of opinion existed between them could a defendant appeal to the U.S. Supreme Court. The laws of the United States punished piracy by death, and two judges had to preside. In addition, fundamental fairness required that the defense have adequate time to prepare, and Shipman saw no reason for an exception in this case. Judge Nelson had indeed told the court that he wished to be present but could not return to work at that time because of his accident. Shipman therefore set the case for the third week of the October term at eleven o'clock in the morning.

Of the two judges presiding in the *Savannah* case, Shipman was by far the least known. He was born in Chester, Connecticut, in 1818, and his early years hardly held the promise of legal notoriety. A manual laborer and a factory worker until he was twenty-four, Shipman began his career as a teacher, a vocation he practiced until he was thirty. He devoted his leisure time to studying a wide range of subjects, and during his last three years of teaching he studied the law on his own. In 1849 he began reading the law under a local attorney, Moses Culver, and passed the bar in Middlesex County, Connecticut, in 1850. From 1854 until 1860 Shipman served as the U.S. district attorney for the District of Connecticut, and in the spring of 1860 President Buchanan appointed him the U.S. district judge for the District of Connecticut. Shipman had been on the bench a little over a year when the *Savannah* trial began. Although he had virtually no experience, Shipman had made one thing plainly clear in the way he handled the preliminary matters during the arraignment: regardless of his personal views or public opinion, these Confederate prisoners would receive a fair trial.

Justice Samuel Nelson presided over the case with Shipman. Referred to in the court records and newspapers as a circuit judge, Nelson had been a sitting member of the U.S. Supreme Court for more than fifteen years. Until 1891 Supreme Court justices rode circuit as the intermediate level of appeal between the district courts and the Supreme Court, and Nelson's circuit court duties allowed him to sit at the district court level in certain situations. Born in 1792 in upstate New York, he had planned to enter the ministry, but on graduating from Middlebury College in Vermont, he chose to study the law instead. Licensed in New York in 1817, Nelson developed a successful civil practice that he maintained until 1823. Over the next twenty-two years he held a variety of judicial commissions before his elevation to the U.S. Supreme Court in 1845.

Nelson had been nominated by John Tyler as a compromise candidate after the Democrats had defeated two earlier attempts to fill the vacancy of Justice Smith Thompson. Nelson's career spanned twenty-seven years on the high court. His expertise lay in admiralty and patent law, and his written opinions reflected an attempt to reach commonsense results within the boundaries of established law. His concurrence in *Scott v. Sanford* deferred to the state law as to Scott's citizenship and completely avoided the issue of the constitutionality of the Missouri Compromise. In 1860 he joined the unsuccessful efforts of Justice John A. Campbell to negotiate a compromise between the North and South. When compromise failed, Nelson waited like everyone else in the United States for the conflict that followed. As he recuperated from his riding accident in the late summer of 1861, the lawyers on each side hurriedly prepared to try the case.

The defense team began preparing for trial almost immediately after the arraignment. Renown for his expertise in business matters, Daniel Lord actually conceived the *Savannah*'s legal defense before the ship ever set sail. Northern businessmen shared the same concerns and uncertainties voiced by their Southern counterparts as to how hostilities affected commerce. On May 21, 1861, Lord circulated a six-page opinion letter to his commercial clients, many of whom were involved in international trade. In the letter titled "The Legal Effect of the Secession Troubles on the Commercial Relations of the Country," Lord questioned the legality of the blockade absent an official declaration of war, but unequivocally stated that active participation in the war effort by citizens in the seceding states constituted treason against the United States. In Lord's opinion, privateering constituted treason because President Lincoln's proclamation in April 1861 rejected any notion that the Confederacy possessed the attributes of an independent nation sufficient to allow it to issue letters of marque or engage in any other act of war. As such, the Confederate commissions could not change the character of captured property, could not protect subsequent purchasers of seized property, and could not shield anyone from harm who, acting under such commissions, seized property on the high seas.

However, Lord believed that whether such acts could be deemed piracy depended on "considerations somewhat varying from those commonly proposed . . . [and] the color of authority" under which a privateer sailed, and the publicity that followed the capture of such men might actually reduce the offense from piracy to something less onerous. The key, however, lay in avoiding the notion that regardless of whether one believed he was acting under a duly constituted authority, an act of aggression against the United States was treason. Therein lay the heart of the defense in the *Savannah*. The prosecution's indictment had missed the connection between privateering and treason. The charges in the indictment limited themselves to the seizure of the *Joseph*, the *Savannah*'s lone prize. Lord believed if he could show that the men believed they had authority to act and if he could exclude any evidence or testimony of treason, he could build a defense predicated on good faith that could survive a legal attack and avoid the taint of treason in the court of public opinion.

Encouraged by the presence of Judge Nelson and determined to prove the men sailed under the color of legitimate authority, the defense went to work amid the continuing and sometimes bizarre publicity that attended the case. For example, an unrelated proceeding drew a Mrs. Buckley to President Lincoln's office in July 1861. The only record of her visit is a letter dated July 24, 1861, and published in the *Boston Journal*. Reprinted a week later in the *New York Times*, the letter contained no addressee, nor did it identify its author. However, the writer believed the story demonstrated the leniency that might be expected from President Lincoln if a jury found the crew members of the *Savannah* guilty and sentenced them to death.

The letter described how Mrs. Buckley, "a lady of position residing in Fifth Avenue," went to Mr. Lincoln to intercede on behalf of "young Collins, Featherston and Dunleavy," three men convicted of murdering the captain of the *General Parkhill*, a Confederate steamer captured by USS *Niagara* in May 1861. When Mrs. Buckley referred to "the case of the unfortunate men imprisoned in the Tombs in New York," Lincoln politely but firmly cut her off. He told her not to waste her time, "as his mind was made up to let the law take its course." When Mrs. Buckley again tried to urge her case, Lincoln again interjected that it was enough that these men were captured on the *Savannah*, and he refused to intervene on their behalf. Buckley then realized Lincoln had been misled by her reference to the men in the Tombs. She cleared up the misunderstanding, proceeded with her plea, and as a result Lincoln delayed the executions set for July 26 until November 29, 1861, to review the case on the grounds that an examination of the testimony at trial revealed it to be vague and contradictory. The anonymous author of the letter feared that even if convicted, these pirates might not hang. In a case where public sentiment seemed to matter, this letter served as a warning to the prosecution that winning would not be enough; it had to do so cleanly. To an extent, the writer sought to pressure Mr. Lincoln with a subtle tone to the letter, implying his leniency might be construed as a sign of weakness.

What President Lincoln might do in the event the *Savannah* crew lost did not matter. Lord, Sullivan, and Brady intended to keep the case out of the president's hands. In an effort to acquire the evidence necessary to prove their case, Algernon Sullivan wrote to J. R. Tucker, the attorney general of Virginia, requesting documents on secession, the formation of the Confederate government, the adherence of South Carolina to that government, the letters of marque issued to the *Savannah*, and any records that showed the disposition of the *Joseph* in a Confederate prize court. These last two documents were to support the defense that these men did not make war on all nations, but conducted themselves as "soldiers" whose acts of aggression were aimed at only one enemy. Sullivan told Tucker that the defense intended to argue in open court that on the day the *Savannah* seized the *Joseph* the defendants were not U.S. citizens.

Sullivan's letter not only made it through the mail but also found its way to Confederate Attorney General Judah Benjamin. Benjamin wrote Tucker, offering "gladly" to do everything in his power to assist the men defending the *Savannah* and its crew, but questioned whether he could do anything to help their cause. In Benjamin's estimation the case presented a political question, not a legal one. If the U.S. government refused to recognize the Confederacy as even a belligerent, the proof Sullivan requested meant nothing. Benjamin had struck on a key problem for the defense. Everything rested on how the Union defined the Confederacy.

The North understood the connection between the piracy cases and the Confederacy's evolving place in the community of nations. While the Northern press worked hard to stir up public sentiment against the "pirates," the U.S. government reacted as the defense team zealously worked to prepare for trial. Gathering evidence required communicating with the Confederate government, and on September 7, 1861, less than seven weeks before the trial, the police arrested Algernon Sullivan at his residence and threw him into prison at Fort Lafayette, a fortress on a rocky shoal in the narrows of New York harbor.

Sullivan had not been indicted by any court, nor had he been arrested in the act of committing a crime. His arrest and incarceration came on the strength of a one-sentence telegram from Secretary of State William Seward to John A. Kennedy, the police commissioner of New York City, which stated: "Your letter of yesterday received, arrest Algernon S. Sullivan, No. 59 Williams Street and deliver him to Colonel Martin Burke, Fort Lafayette." Seward wielded tremendous power in the early days of the war, and Sullivan's arrest testifies as to how quickly one could be divested of his freedom with no legal recourse. Lord wrote Seward a scathing letter of protest to which Seward replied that "this Department is possessed of treasonable correspondence of that person which no rights, or privileges of a lawyer or counsel can justify or excuse. The public safety will not admit of his being discharged."

Sullivan's efforts to gather evidence led to his arrest. The State Department had a dossier on him containing a reference to a letter from Sullivan to Robert Hunter, the Confederate secretary of state, requesting numerous documents for the defense of Baker and his crew. More than just his efforts to free Confederate sailors, apparently Sullivan's letters showed an unacceptable level of sympathy for the Confederacy. Although the letter that led to his arrest did not survive, notes in his file quoted Sullivan as saying, "I desire not to evade the high ground that the Confederate States are sovereign and that her citizens are not citizens of the United States." High ground, indeed. If the Confederacy was sovereign and her citizens were not U.S. citizens, not only could the "pirates" prevail, but also in the process the Confederacy could take a huge step in its efforts to secure international recognition.

The fact that Sullivan, a Northern attorney, represented Southern sailors on an ongoing basis lent credibility to the Confederacy's claim of legal existence. Sullivan had been hired by the Confederate government, and his willingness to have it as a client suggested that as to at least one Northern citizen the new Southern nation had legal substance. A closer look at Sullivan reveals why he may have undertaken the task of defending the privateers and why he became a target for a government trying just as hard to consolidate its wartime home front as its Southern adversary.

In addition to several other letters from Sullivan to Southern officials that reflected a clear sympathy for the Confederate cause, including one letter that expressed a "painful suspense" and "hope and anxiety" over the outcome of the battle of First Manassas, Sullivan married a Virginian. Described by John Harleston in his diary as a "genuine Confederate, very pretty and very smart," Mrs. Sullivan exerted strong influence on her husband. Harleston recalled conversations with her about the South and the Yankees and seeing her eyes "blaze." In the estimation of Union officials, Sullivan expressed a level of sympathy for the Confederate cause that had gone beyond emotional support and ethical duty and had become an active attempt to subvert Northern war aims. Everyone knew the issues at stake in the piracy trials. If it could have done so, the Lincoln administration might have locked up the entire legal defense team of the *Savannah*. As can be seen by Seward's incarceration of Sullivan, the government certainly possessed the means. However, to a certain extent the piracy cases put the federal government before the court of public opinion as much as the Confederate privateers, and only Sullivan had provided sufficient justification for an action that in peacetime would have drawn condemnation from virtually every sector of Northern society.

Sullivan's arrest and incarceration had done more than cripple the defense team by removing one of its key members; it had chilled the ability of those who remained to gather crucial evidence. While Sullivan worked diligently through his Southern contacts to obtain the documentary proof necessary to establish the Confederacy's legal existence and thereby establish the color of authority needed to exonerate the privateers, the defense team explored other avenues of discovery. On the day of his arrest, Sullivan coauthored a letter with Lord and Brady, asking the prosecutor to support a defense request that the U.S. government provide "the necessary facilities" for obtaining authenticated Confederate government documents, the acts of the Confederate Prize Court in Charleston, and a promise of safe conduct for any witnesses the defense might bring from the South.

Delafield Smith did nothing with the letter until September 20, when his curt reply told the defense to take its request directly to Washington, D.C. With Sullivan in prison in part because of his efforts to secure discovery, Lord and Brady pressed the government for assistance. Tired of waiting for Smith, the defense wrote U.S. Attorney General Edward Bates on September 18. Bates responded on October 8 and apologized for the delay, but regrettably he still did not have an answer to their request. He added that like his Confederate counterpart, Judah Benjamin, he did not think the defense could prove the "existence" of the Confederacy by documentary evidence. The issue involved political questions, and both the president and U.S. Congress had already "determined against the nationality of the C.S.A." Four days later Lord and Brady got their answer. "The Government declines to take an active part in the aid of the accused" by helping to procure evidence and testimony. With the trial twelve days away and one of its counsel imprisoned without bail, the fate of the *Savannah* crew seemed all but fixed. Two days before trial Seward released Sullivan after the attorney swore an oath of allegiance to the Union and promised not to engage in treasonous correspondence.

Despite the numerous obstacles the defense encountered in preparing its case, on the eve of trial the prosecution believed it was overmatched. Smith already had the assistance of Assistant U.S. Attorney Ethan Allen, a descendant of the Vermont hero of the American Revolution, as well as Samuel Blatchford, compiler of *Blatchford's Reports*, the nineteenth-century predecessor to West Publishing Company's *National Reports*. Blatchford eventually served as a U.S. district judge and a U.S. circuit court judge and capped a remarkable career in 1882 with his appointment as an associate justice of the U.S. Supreme Court. Nevertheless, despite an able, if not spectacular, supporting cast, Smith felt outgunned.

On October 10, 1861, Smith wrote Edward Bates, saying that "in view of the magnitude of the cases of the pirates of the *Savannah* and other vessels; in consideration also of the extraordinary array of counsel for the defense, and the novelty of some of the questions which will be raised therein, I request authority to associate Mr. William M. Evarts." Evarts, regarded by many as the foremost trial lawyer in the United States, represented President Andrew Johnson in his impeachment proceedings in 1868, and before his death he served as U.S. attorney general, secretary of state, and U.S. senator from New York. In recognition of the case's importance, Bates approved Smith's request. Evarts joined the prosecution on the day before the trial began and later told Bates that he had been opposed by "the most numerous array of able counsel that I have ever known combined in any cause."

On July 22, 1861, the day before the rearraignment of the *Savannah* crew, USS *Albatross* captured William Smith and his small prize crew aboard the *Enchantress* off the coast of North Carolina. Contrary to Delafield Smith's belief that the *Jeff Davis* pirates might be tried in New York, the prisoners were removed to Philadelphia. During the first week of August 1861, U.S. Commissioner Hazlett conducted a preliminary hearing to determine whether William Smith and his crew should stand trial for piracy. The public attention that accompanied the proceedings surrounding the *Savannah* in New York had not abated when the *Jeff Davis* case got under way. A crowd had gathered outside the courthouse at Fifth and Chestnut streets, and when the doors opened the people filed in, filling every corner of the hearing room. Some confusion arose because people had come thinking they would see the thirty-six members of the Confederate privateer *Petrel*, captured on August 7, 1861. What they saw were five members of the *Jeff Davis* crew. After taking testimony, Hazlett ordered the hearing reconvened for August 8.

The purpose of the preliminary hearing was to determine whether probable cause existed to try the defendants. Perhaps the most damning testimony came from the black steward of the *Enchantress*, Jacob Garrick, who, as mentioned earlier, had been left on the prize vessel because he would "fetch fifteen hundred dollars [in] Charleston." Garrick described in great detail the capture of the *Enchantress* by the *Albatross*. When the hearing reconvened on August 8, the prosecution called Julius Wendell, the master's mate on the *Albatross*. He testified to the removal of Smith and crew after their capture, and with that the hearing ended. Without hesitation Commissioner Hazlett bound the prisoners over for trial on the charge of piracy at the next term of the circuit court. The prisoners remained in jail without bail. The next term of the U.S. District Court for Philadelphia would be the third week of October. Despite being captured almost seven weeks after the *Savannah*, the crew of the *Jeff Davis* would be tried at the same time in a different court.

Just as the New York defense bar had stepped up to defend the *Savannah*, the Philadelphia bar rose to the occasion on behalf of the crew of the *Jeff Davis*, and an unknown lawyer named Nathaniel Harrison crossed the line first. Perhaps more than any other attorney involved in the piracy cases, Harrison exemplified the tragedy of the Civil War on a personal level. He eventually became a man trapped between two worlds, not fully accepted in either and destined to be shunned by both. His early years are shrouded in obscurity. Originally from Mercer County, Virginia, Harrison held strong Unionist feelings and moved from Virginia to Philadelphia in 1859. Admitted to the Pennsylvania bar that same year, Harrison traveled frequently between his new home and his old one, continuing to take on legal cases in Virginia. Early in the war he represented Mr. George Rucker, a Virginia Unionist arrested in Mercer County and charged with multiple offenses, including murder.

The taint of his wartime sentiments and exploits followed Harrison for the rest of his life. Following the piracy trial and the negative publicity that attended defending the privateers, Harrison, Confederate records show, went to Richmond in 1862, where authorities there suspected him of being a Union spy. In 1865 he returned to Mercer County and served as a county court judge. However, the local citizenry, most of whom supported the Confederate cause and saw their county burned for it, refused to allow him to hold court in Princeton, the site of the former county seat, because he had left the Confederacy and had gone north.

Harrison stood alone until August 14, 1861, when Mr. John P. O'Neill, a prominent lawyer from New York City, came down to help Harrison defend the crew of the *Petrel*. Harrison had volunteered to defend Captain Perry and the thirty-five members of his crew captured by the *St. Lawrence*. O'Neill joined him and agreed to help defend the *Jeff Davis* crew as well. Little is known of O'Neill. *Martin's Bench and Bar of Philadelphia* shows that he was admitted to practice in 1851 and that he died in 1883 at the age of fifty-seven. When the piracy cases came to trial he would have been thirty-five years old, hardly a novice, but clearly nowhere near the caliber of the defense team assembled in New York. However, with Harrison being licensed in Pennsylvania less than two years, O'Neill brought experience that Harrison did not have and may have had a role in Harrison's first defense strategy.

Harrison had already become painfully aware of the effect any public hearing would have on the defense of the privateers. A courtroom packed with onlookers watched the *Jeff Davis* preliminary hearing, and every time the newspapers reported on the piracy cases they seemed to drive another nail in the coffin of the Confederate seamen. Algernon Sullivan admitted in his correspondence with Robert Hunter that the publicity hurt his efforts. Sullivan expressed concern over the constant reports of the damage other privateers had done to the U.S. merchant marine. The exploits of the Southern Vikings made the papers almost daily, "exasperating" the public and influencing the government. Harrison and O'Neill seemed more concerned with the negative publicity attendant to the repeated testimony of their own clients' exploits. Facing trial in October on the *Jeff Davis*, the lawyers went to court on August 14 for the *Petrel* preliminary hearing knowing how the negative publicity had already affected the trial of the *Jeff Davis*.

The district attorney stood up, prepared to move forward, when Harrison interrupted and told Commissioner Hazlett that his clients agreed to waive the preliminary hearing and proceed directly to trial. Obviously surprised by the defense motion, Hazlett questioned whether the defendants could waive the hearing. Harrison insisted that because the hearing had but one purpose, to determine whether probable cause existed to try the defendants, waiving the hearing and going directly to trial accomplished that goal. Harrison remembered the two days of testimony and the publicity that followed during the *Jeff Davis* preliminary hearing and flatly told Hazlett that he and O'Neill wanted to avoid the "prejudice of the community before the trial." All his clients wanted or expected to receive from a Philadelphia jury was a "fair and impartial trial." If the hearing went forward, the evidence presented would appear in the newspapers, where every man, woman, and child could read the testimony, thereby prejudicing them prior to trial. Hazlett remained uncertain, but defense counsel insisted they could provide authority if necessary. Hazlett recessed the hearing, bound the crew of the *Petrel* over for trial, and Harrison and O'Neill had won a small victory.

Although controlling public opinion would be crucial, the case still had to be tried on the evidence. As demonstrated in the preliminary hearing, the *Jeff Davis* defense team faced the same logistical nightmare that their New York counterparts grappled with: how to defend their clients when the evidence and witnesses crucial to their case lay behind enemy lines in the South. Any connections Harrison had in the South may have been tainted by his Unionist sentiments, notwithstanding his willingness to represent the Confederacy's seamen. But he still had Southern connections that gave him at least a chance to secure the documentary evidence needed to defend the *Jeff Davis* privateers. On the day of Algernon Sullivan's arrest in New York City, a Mrs. Virginia McNeill penned a letter to a Mr. John Lyons of Nashville, Tennessee. Mrs. McNeill lived in Macon, Georgia, and had just left Philadelphia. She wrote on Harrison's behalf, requesting that Mr. Lyons call on either Jefferson Davis or Mr. Memminger, a prominent attorney in Charleston, and ask either man to send Harrison the letters of marque under which the *Jefferson Davis* sailed. McNeill explained that Harrison "was using every effort . . . and was confident of success," but clearly Harrison needed help not only to prepare his defense but also to provide even bare necessities for the imprisoned sailors. Apparently Harrison had written Memminger already, but had received no reply. He had also written Mr. William Grayson of Charleston and none other than James Petigru, trying desperately to get clothing and money for his clients, who were suffering in prison. Mrs. McNeill requested that any correspondence be sent directly to Mr. Harrison's Philadelphia address. In light of Algernon Sullivan's experience, correspondence flowing directly to a Northern attorney from Confederate officials might prove dangerous, but Harrison had no choice.

Despite their zeal and ingenuity, Harrison and O'Neill needed help to defend Smith and his crew. Public opinion fueled both by the activities of the Confederate privateers still at large and by the attention the pretrial proceedings had drawn made the job more difficult. The defense needed a skilled attorney with strong community ties, and it got both in the person of George Mifflin Wharton.

Born the day after Christmas in 1806, Wharton attended the University of Pennsylvania in 1823 and on graduation went into the law. By 1861 he had an impeccable reputation as a skilled attorney and was one of Philadelphia's most distinguished citizens. During James Buchanan's administration, he served for a year as the U.S. district attorney for the Eastern District of Pennsylvania and had been back in private practice less than a week when the *Jeff Davis* case arose. A strong proponent of public education, Wharton worked closely with the Philadelphia school system, work that gave him strong local ties. He had married Maria Markoe, the daughter of one of Philadelphia's most distinguished families, and together they raised eight children in the community. A former Whig, Wharton gravitated toward the northern Democratic Party after the Whigs disintegrated in the 1850s, and by 1860 he counted himself among the staunchest of Democrats and worked zealously for a peaceful resolution to the conflict. Politically, socially, and professionally, Wharton made a perfect addition to a legal team that for all its efforts seemed overmatched as the trial date grew nearer.

U.S. District Attorney George Alexander Coffey drew the task of prosecuting the *Jeff Davis* defendants. Commissioned on July 22, 1861, the day before the *Savannah* crew's rearraignment in New York, and just in time to handle the preliminary hearing for the *Jeff Davis* case, Coffey had a reputation as an able lawyer and a tireless worker. Consistent with his character he set out to make himself an expert on matters of privateering and international law, and assisted by George H. Earle, Coffey went to work preparing to prosecute the privateers. Throughout the trial his abilities and knowledge of the law drew praise from both sides, not because of his performance but because of his absence. Between the preliminary hearing and the trial, Coffey became ill, and his condition became so severe that although he survived, he withdrew as counsel in the *Jeff Davis* trial. That job then fell on the young shoulders of J. Hubley Ashton.

Born in 1836, the twenty-five-year-old Ashton had just graduated from the University of Pennsylvania Law School when he became U.S. assistant district attorney under Coffey. In time Ashton became a prominent attorney and legal scholar. When Ashton was twenty-eight Lincoln named him U.S. assistant attorney general, and he helped represent the government in the *Prize Cases*. In 1869 he resigned his government position to join the first faculty of Georgetown Law School. He became one of the founding members of the American Bar Association and served as counsel for Chinese aliens in the Chinese Exclusion Act cases in 1890. However, in the fall of 1861 all of this lay ahead of young Ashton. As the *Jeff Davis* trial approached, the balance of power at the counsel table had shifted. The prosecution had a man at the helm licensed less than three years. On the basis of experience, Ashton and George Earle, his co-counsel, could not match either O'Neill or Harrison. With the addition of Wharton the defense held an impressive advantage not only at the bar but also in the court of public opinion. The prosecution needed help.

Help arrived in the form of Philadelphia's most influential and powerful figure in 1861, William Darrah Kelley. Kelley was born in Philadelphia in 1814, and his father died when he was two years old. Quitting school at age eleven to help support his mother and three siblings, he worked odd jobs until apprenticing as a jeweler for seven years in Philadelphia. After working four years in Boston, Kelley returned home, took up the study of law, and at age twenty-seven passed the Pennsylvania Bar. He was already active in politics as a Jacksonian Democrat, and his efforts in Francis Shunk's successful run for governor brought him an appointment as prosecuting attorney for Philadelphia County in 1845. Two years later he became judge of the Court of Common Pleas, where he served until 1856, when he relinquished his post to run for the House of Representatives. One of the founding members of the Republican Party, Kelley lost in his first attempt to win Pennsylvania's Fourth District congressional seat, but in 1860 he claimed the seat that he would hold for almost three decades. Known by colleagues and constituents alike as "Judge," Kelley served as a delegate to the famous "Wigwam Convention" that nominated Lincoln for president. Thereafter he enjoyed an active correspondence with the new president. A staunch Unionist, a zealous supporter of the war, and an abolitionist, Kelley exemplified many of the things the war embodied in the North. More the politician than the litigator, he brought a formidable presence to the table when he agreed to assist Earle and Ashton in trying the crew of the *Jeff Davis*. Every juror on the panel knew and respected Kelley. In a case that rested as much on how people felt as what they believed the evidence showed, Kelley's addition to the prosecution did not bode well for the defense.

With the death penalty looming as a possibility, two judges presided over the trial of William Smith and his prize crew. Shouldered with the responsibility would be the able tandem of Judge John Cadwalader and Justice Robert Grier. Cadwalader, the junior member of the panel in both age and experience on the federal bench, was born in Philadelphia in 1805 and graduated from the University of Pennsylvania in 1821. After reading the law he passed the bar in 1825 and began a career in private practice that spanned thirty years, during which time he served as the solicitor for the Philadelphia branch of the Bank of the United States and for twenty years acted as the vice provost for the Law Academy of Pennsylvania. In 1855 Cadwalader left private practice, never to return. He served one term in the U.S. Congress, and on April 19, 1858, he became judge of the U.S. District Court for the Eastern District of Pennsylvania, a position he held until his death in 1879.

Associate Justice of the U.S. Supreme Court Robert Grier made up the other half of the panel. Grier was born in Cumberland County, Pennsylvania, in 1794, one of eleven children. He was the son of a Presbyterian minister, and his early education came in his father's school. Grier graduated from Dickinson College in 1812, and when his father died in 1815, Grier assumed the reins of his academy and began studying law. Licensed in 1817 he went into private practice, supporting his mother and providing for the education of his ten brothers and sisters. In 1833 he became the judge of the Allegheny County State District Court, a position he retained until Henry Baldwin, the Pennsylvanian on the U.S. Supreme Court, died in 1844. President Tyler and his successor, James Polk, struggled to find an acceptable replacement until Polk nominated the uncontroversial and virtually unknown Grier.

Over the course of his twenty-three-year career on the high court, Grier usually found the middle ground. In the slave cases he sided with the Southern wing of the court. Although he played only a minor role in *Scott v. Sanford*, at Buchanan's insistence he threw his full support to Taney's decision and then revealed the outcome of the opinion to the president-elect. When Buchanan actually mentioned the opinion in his inaugural address, everyone blamed Taney when Grier was the guilty party. By 1861 Grier had the reputation as a "doughface," a Northern man with Southern principles. As the trial of the *Jeff Davis* approached, Harrison, O'Neill, and Wharton could only hope the critics were right. They needed all the help they could muster.

In the months leading up to trial, the political nature of the piracy cases got lost amid the legal maneuvering. The severe schisms and partial destruction of the political party system in the decades before the Civil War contributed to the rebellion. The slavery issue split the Democratic Party and destroyed the Whigs and its immediate successor, the American Party. The Republican Party won the election in 1860 in great part due to the Democratic split. However, in the North, party relationships remained strained even after secession. A peace movement within the Democratic Party existed for most for the war, and Democratic support of the war effort fluctuated throughout. Although there is no indication that politics dictated how the judges tried the cases, the political affiliations of the participants clearly played a part in the story and may have provided at least some of the motivation for defending the Confederates.

In Philadelphia George Wharton played a major role in the local Democratic Party and was the first speaker at the Philadelphia Democratic Peace Rally on January 18, 1861. Nathaniel Harrison's party affiliation is uncertain, but being from West Virginia, he was most likely a nonaffiliated ex-Whig or gravitated to the Democratic Party. Both men's backgrounds and political beliefs made them ideal candidates to defend the rebels. For the prosecution Hubley Ashton and William Kelley clearly sided with the Lincoln administration.

On the bench, Grier was a Democrat, and Cadwalader's appointment came from Pennsylvania Democrat James Buchanan. Grier's affiliation had to be encouraging for the defense, but Cadwalader's potential Democratic leanings may have been tempered by the fact that he had spent the better part of the war enforcing the Lincoln administration's prize policy.

In New York the party affiliations mirrored those of Philadelphia. The prosecutors, Smith and Evarts, firmly resided in the Republican camp. The defense, on the other hand, belonged to the Democratic Party. Daniel Lord and James Brady, both Democrats, enlisted Jeremiah Larocque of Bowdoin, Larocque and Barlow when Sullivan was arrested. Larocque's party affiliation is unclear, but his partner, Samuel Barlow, was a prominent Democrat with a reputation for receiving extraordinary fees. Barlow's firm had made exceptional money since its formation in 1852, and Barlow's Democratic affiliation might explain in part how this high-powered defense team could financially afford to take on a case that held little hope of financial gain. Algernon S. Sullivan had Southern connections sufficient to see him retained directly by the Confederate government. Whether the Confederacy ever paid him remains unclear, but his affiliation with the Democratic Party seems almost certain. The New York bench looked much like its Philadelphia counterpart. Like Grier, Samuel Nelson was a Democrat. Judge Shipman received his appointment to the federal bench from Buchanan, just as Cadwalader had, but just like Cadwalader, Shipman had already seen his share of prize cases.

The lawyers in both cases clearly split down party lines, and the zeal of their representation may well have been tied to their opinions of Lincoln's administration. The judges seemed clearly Democrat, and as members of the federal bench they enjoyed a certain insulation from political pressure that came with a lifetime appointment. Whether their party affiliation or their experience with the prize cases biased them toward either side is impossible to determine. However, on the eve of trial in the piracy cases, the political turmoil that dominated American politics for at least the preceding ten years had found its way into the courtroom, and the affiliation of the participants contributed yet another ingredient to an already volatile situation.

On October 23, 1861, jury selection began in the case of the *Savannah* and took all of half a day. In selecting or *voirdiring* a jury, attorneys choose the panel by excluding potential members. The process is called "challenging," and lawyers can do so in one of two ways. They may challenge a juror for cause, usually bias or some other form of predisposition that makes the person unqualified to serve. The best examples in this case would be so much exposure to media coverage that a person had already formed an opinion as to guilt or innocence or did not have the ability to find the defendants guilty if the facts demonstrated their guilt because such a verdict carried the death penalty. The second challenge is called peremptory and requires no reason whatsoever. Peremptory challenges are limited, usually anywhere from four to six per side. Challenges for cause, on the other hand, are unlimited, because there can be no restriction on the ability of either side to disqualify a person who cannot fairly judge the case.

Seventeen names made up the initial jury pool from which to impanel a twelve-man jury. The questions put to potential jurors went to issues of bias, and neither side struck anyone for cause, although the attorneys initially challenged every juror. One question by the defense did create some controversy. The legal existence of the Confederacy made up a crucial component of the defense's argument that these men had acted under the color of authority and could therefore not be guilty of piracy. Defense counsel asked juror 1 whether he had formed an opinion whether "acting under a commission from President Davis, or the Confederate government, constitutes piracy?" Mr. Evarts objected, claiming the question was one of pure law and therefore inappropriate. The defense actually cited legal authority for disqualifying a juror where that juror had already determined that the conduct at issue constituted treason. Judge Nelson distinguished that case, however, by stating that in *United States v. Wilson*, the question put to the juror was of the crime. In other words, the juror had read an account of the occurrence and had formed an opinion based on both the law and the facts. The defense's question went solely to the law. The defense then rephrased the question to ask whether the juror had formed or expressed an opinion as to "whether the acts charged, if proved, constitute treason." This the court found acceptable.

The defense used four peremptory strikes, and one man, Thomas Dugan, literally disqualified himself. The first question asked by Delafield Smith inquired as to whether Mr. Dugan had "any conscientious scruples that would interfere with rendering a verdict of guilty, if you deem the prisoner guilty upon the evidence." Dugan responded he had "strong conscientious scruples." Smith moved to strike, and the defense objected. In the longest questioning of the morning, Dugan claimed that despite his feelings, he could put aside his sympathies and render a proper verdict. Evarts argued that the juror had disqualified himself, but Brady disagreed, saying that a juror should not be disqualified just because the juror had insisted guilt would have to be beyond any shadow of a doubt. This is what everyone should want in a juror. The rule for disqualification required that to disqualify a juror, his scruples must be of such a character that even if the evidence were clear and convincing beyond a shadow of a doubt, the juror expressed the opinion that he could not render a guilty verdict.

Judge Nelson pushed Dugan to be more specific as to his reservations and his willingness to render a guilty verdict. Dugan expressed the same concerns that jurors face today. He had read of men convicted and then subsequently found to be innocent, and he would rather go to the gallows himself than send an innocent man to his death. Dugan told Nelson he could not "trust himself." Nelson believed he had to disqualify Dugan, but gave the defense one last chance to save him. But when asked if his conscience prevented him from finding a defendant guilty if the evidence demonstrated guilt, Dugan responded, "It would not now. It might in the jury room." That was all Nelson needed, and he disqualified Dugan. The remainder of the process proceeded without incident, and by late morning the lawyers had chosen a jury panel.

As fate would have it, despite being captured seven weeks after the *Savannah* crew, the trial of William Smith and his prize crew started a day before that of Baker, Harleston, and their men. On October 22, 1861, the trial of the *Jeff Davis* privateers began in Philadelphia as both sides went about picking a jury. Either the jury selection was not recorded, or the records did not survive, but by the end of the morning a twelve-man panel had been selected, consisting of five "gentlemen," a clerk, a machinist, a varnisher, a lime dealer, an engineer, a trunk maker, and a collector. The clerk read the indictment in open court and then turned to William Smith and asked, "How will you be tried?" Smith replied, "By God and on the country." The trial of the Confederate privateers was about to begin.

CHAPTER 5

"Summon the Community
by Sound of Trumpet"

With the piracy trials poised to begin in the North, the sequestration cases got under way in Charleston. Unlike the *Jeff Davis* and the *Savannah* cases, the sequestration cases were a bench trial, with Judge Magrath as both judge and jury. Despite Petigru's fear that Magrath's bias made a fair trial impossible, given the nature of the cases a bench trial made perfect sense. The purpose of a jury is to hear and weigh disputed facts, apply the legal principles given by the judge in the instructions, and then combine the law and the facts to arrive at a verdict. In the sequestration cases everyone agreed on the facts; the only issues in dispute involved questions of law. Was the act unconstitutional or a violation of some other law, either in its creation or in its application? If not, then the issue became the nature of the offense committed by the defendants. Failure to comply with the Sequestration Act carried penalties clearly articulated within the act itself. But Magrath also charged the grand jury that certain conduct, although short of actually levying war against the Confederacy, could nevertheless be deemed treasonous if within the realm of giving aid and comfort to the enemy. Would treason become a relevant issue? None of the five attorney defendants had been indicted by a grand jury. They stood before the court for failing to respond to the writ of garnishment issued by the receiver. The fact that the writs did not come from the judge or the grand jury did not escape the defendants, and the receiver's broad garnishment power was but one aspect of the Sequestration Act that came under attack.

Under normal circumstances the prosecution presented its case, and the defense responded. However, the sequestration cases proceeded differently, with the defendants presenting their case first and the prosecution rebutting, or responding to, the arguments made by the defendants. In effect, the Confederacy defended its own law against the defendants' claim that it was invalid. But the burden clearly rested on the attorneys to establish the law's invalidity. With each defendant allowed to argue his case, it seemed unlikely anything could be overlooked.

The defendants needed to be thorough. When William Whaley opened the defense case on the morning of October 14, 1861, he stepped into the path of a storm. Magrath's courtroom had been the scene of almost constant litigation involving the Sequestration and Alien Enemies acts, and defendants fell like wheat to the scythe. On October 11, 1861, a jury found the Jones and Hanabergh Company to be an alien enemy. That afternoon the case of *Confederate States of America v. W. B. Bristoll* began and concluded the next day with the defendant adjudged a U.S. citizen and his property divested.

It is unclear from the record just how concerted an attack the five defendants made on the Sequestration Act. Petigru's correspondence and papers reveal no communication with any of the other defendants prior to trial. The only evidence that suggests the defendants consulted one another in preparation for trial is in Ed McGrady's 1861 journal. Ten days before trial McGrady received a retainer from several merchants in Charleston to consult with Nelson Mitchell's firm regarding the constitutionality of the Sequestration Act. McGrady sat in court on October 7 when Petigru presented his demurrer and made his initial argument. On returning to his office he had "a long consultation with Campbell & Mitchell" regarding the Sequestration Act. Over the next week McGrady and Mitchell worked together to prepare an answer to the writs served on Mitchell, and McGrady watched intently when William Whaley opened on the fourteenth.

———

William Whaley "stood before the court as one who had been served with a process which he believed before God was wrong, according to the dictates of his own conscience and according to the laws of the land." Petigru's demurrer a week earlier defined the legal issues and laid the groundwork for the arguments that followed. Acting on his "best judgment and a sincere conviction to do right," Whaley began by giving the court a road map of his argument. He would discuss the general nature of the act, the effect of the act on lawyers and on any person compelled to turn property over to the receiver, the legal contradiction between the sequestration aspect of the act and the writ of garnishment issued by the receiver, and, finally, the argument that the writ of garnishment process violated Confederate and international law.

Although he lacked some of the colorful analogies Petigru used, Whaley said he believed the act, passed in a spirit of retaliation against the U.S. Congress's First Confiscation Act, operated as an "inquisition of the most stringent character and the most lawless purpose." No human power had the authority to force its provisions on him or any other citizen of South Carolina. The law made it the legal obligation of every citizen to inform on one's neighbor. A law that purported to indemnify Confederate citizens placed a more onerous burden on them than the loss of property to the Union army.

The act compounded the evil by failing to make any allowance for special relationships. Whaley argued that those persons standing in a fiduciary relationship to others could not simply throw that obligation away. The status of a fiduciary had been acknowledged from time "immemorial." Notwithstanding the arguments appearing in the press and made by other state officials, such as Louisiana Attorney General Thomas Semmes, war did not destroy relationships of trust and obligations of fiduciaries, it merely suspended them. If belligerents did in fact exist in a state of "utter occlusion" as Semmes maintained, Whaley argued, that placed all confidential relationships in suspension until the hostilities could be resolved. It did not emasculate those relationships.

Whaley asserted his legal right to make "no answer" to the writ on the grounds that as an attorney, to do so violated his confidential relationships with his clients. When he accepted his commission as an attorney from the State of South Carolina, he took the attorney's oath—as a trustee. Citing *Greenleaf's Evidence* and the English Lord Chancellor Brougham, Whaley insisted the attorney-client privilege knew of no qualification by "proceedings pending or matters contemplated." Any communications, papers, letters, or other document sent or received by or from an attorney while acting in that capacity remained confidential, and no court could compel their disclosure. Whaley contended that no "ex post facto" law passed after he had sworn an oath to uphold the trust and confidences of his clients could change the nature of the privilege. In the war between Spain and France in 1684, not one Spanish factor betrayed his French correspondent, despite living under a monarchial government with all the trappings of absolute power. If these men could preserve the trust and confidences of those with whom they were in a fiduciary relationship, surely the Confederacy could expect its lawyers to do no less.

Whaley argued that the provisions of the act sequestering debt and discharging the debtor could not survive scrutiny under international law. Nineteenth-century financial transactions depended on the strength of the paper that evidenced debt. The paper guaranteeing payment for goods purchased in New York was usually then "sold on the street, to French, English or even Southern money houses." The promissory note became "currency," and to discharge a debt in the manner contemplated under the act undermined international commerce. More important for Confederate citizens, when a debtor paid off the debt the person received the note or other evidence of indebtedness marked "paid." The return of the paper protected the debtor from any subsequent claim of indebtedness. The sequestration receiver could not deliver the debtor's paper because he did not hold it, and merely declaring the debtor freed of any obligation did not make it so.

The holder of the note had every right under international law to demand payment. The Confederacy could not protect its citizens against such a demand, and no nation would allow the Confederacy to confiscate debts of an alien enemy. Whaley cited *Wolff v. Oxholm*, a case arising out of the 1807 war between Denmark and England, where Denmark attempted to sequester debts due to English subjects. Tried before the King's Bench, Lord Ellenborough held the act void under international law. Whaley argued that the court could not ignore this legal authority and the unwillingness of the international community to recognize the seizure of debt. He warned that "everywhere out of our Confederacy [a Confederate citizen] would be liable again."

A more immediate concern than the law's effect on outsiders involved the security provisions of the act, which threatened to crush an otherwise solvent Confederate businessman and in the process expose him to arrest and confinement. Under section 6 of the act, a debtor owing money to an alien enemy could be required to post security for that debt. Prior to the war the Southern debtor and Northern creditor may have had an arrangement whereby the Southerner always maintained some debt, paying for goods as he collected his own receivables. In effect, they had a nineteenth-century system of revolving credit. The debtor met his financial obligations as they came due, and his business ran smoothly. The war obviously interrupted the normal flow of commerce, but by confiscating the debt the Confederacy could immediately bankrupt a Southern business by forcing it to pay immediately and in full, an obligation never contemplated to be repaid in that manner. Under the Sequestration Act the failure to pay or post adequate security set into motion a chain of events that rapidly pushed a Southern citizen through the sequestration process and culminated in the seizure and sale of his property! Whaley argued that when it came to sequestering debts, the act retaliated against Southern businessmen, not Northerners.

Before concluding, Whaley addressed the receiver's power to compel people to appear and answer his writs of garnishment. Whaley argued that the garnishment power gave the receiver unbridled authority to act beyond the oversight of both the court and the grand jury. Under section 4 of the act the judge charged the grand jury, and it was the grand jury's obligation to identify, locate, and report on alien enemy property. The receiver could then sequester the property in question, gain possession, and liquidate it. However, section 8 allowed the receiver to gather information and compel discovery beyond the supervision of the judge or the grand jury. This aspect of the act made the entire process an inquisition. When the receiver served Whaley with a writ, he believed the process came from the grand jury, but quickly realized that was not the case. The writ lacked any form of judicial oversight from a grand jury or the court because the receiver issued it without an ongoing legal proceeding of any kind. The receiver's writ was "discovery" without the underlying lawsuit. It looked like an inquisition.

Whaley closed by calling on the court to do its job. The entire act ran contrary to the common law of the land and the law of nations. Even if the Confederacy had the power to pass such a law, the judiciary had an obligation to scrutinize every aspect of its application. Whaley reminded Magrath that the "judiciary stood as the watchmen to the outer portals of the temple of our liberties," standing between the legislature and the people, with the constitution as its guide. Whaley denied that the Confederacy had the power to pass such a law, but even if it did, without some amendment "our past prosperity will be entirely obliterated." To allow the Confederacy to confiscate debts risked bringing wholesale ruin on the land. If the act was to be retaliatory, so be it, but not even the U.S. Confiscation Act purported to seize debts, money, bank stock, or land. It seized contraband of war. The Confederate law exceeded retaliation and in so doing exceeded "the bounds of wise legislation."

Whaley made an impressive opening assault. Nelson Mitchell followed, and whereas Whaley had been almost apologetic as he began his attack on the Confederate law, Mitchell's argument had an edge to it that Whaley's did not as he began by pointing out an apparent paradox. "It may naturally be a subject not only of surprise but of censure, that one whose daily duty is to appeal to the law in behalf of others, should be found in an attitude of apparent resistance to its commands." But Mitchell cautioned the court to be wary of appearances. This act may have "assumed the authority of law, . . . that though the crown and scepter might be exhibited, the Royal authority was wanting."

Mitchell attacked the constitutional authority of the Confederate Congress to sequester. The Confederacy presented an alternative to the U.S. Constitution and had expressly placed the states in the position of supreme sovereignty. By doing so the drafters limited the powers granted the central government under the Confederate Constitution. Mitchell argued that the present Congress "not only does not claim, but would reject anything like the [this] attribution of sovereign power." In every exercise of authority the Confederate Congress had to trace its actions to some specific clause of the constitution, or its actions were void. Only the power to declare war could possibly support the Sequestration Act, and Mitchell insisted that the war-making power, even when combined with the necessary-and-proper clause of the Confederate Constitution, fell woefully short of the authority needed to validate the sequestration of property and debts.

In order to support sequestration, Mitchell argued, the power to "declare war, or make war" not only had to be what was necessary and usual to conduct war but also had to extend to every conceivable cause and effect that might enable Congress to wage war. The act of war had to extend the power of the central government beyond its specifically enumerated powers and at the same time, by implication, eliminate any obstacles placed in the constitution that acted as a limitation on the Confederacy's power. Such a power would by necessity extend over the public presses, the state legislatures, and every form of public and corporate authority. "War," Mitchell contended, was so terrific that it "is natural to shrink from any effort to limit the extent of power which it draws after it and to conclude that its power [to wage war] is to be measured only by its requisitions." But, Mitchell insisted, the Confederate Congress in Montgomery, Alabama, did not take this position when it drafted the provisional constitution only eight months earlier. Whether the power to sequester debts and property existed in theory did not matter; the Confederate Constitution denied that power to the central government.

The Confederate Congress had the power to declare and wage war, limited, however, by the specific methods that followed, to wit: "to grant letters of marque and reprisal—to make rules concerning captures on land and water—to raise and support armies—to provide and maintain a navy—to make all the rules for the government and regulation of the land and naval forces." The drafters did not give the Confederate Congress the power to confiscate property and debts, and Mitchell argued that this omission came from the knowledge that historically sequestration had never been a necessary or proper power connected to the power to declare and wage war. Putting the notion of property aside for a moment, he said, the confiscation of debt had only been "attempted two or three times within as many centuries," and other nations had always refused to recognize such an act of sovereignty. If the drafters enumerated such basic powers as raising armies and issuing letters of marque, why omit something as extraordinary as sequestration if they intended that the Confederate Congress should have that power?

Nor, Mitchell contended, could one find evidence that sequestering property and debts flowed from any of the enumerated war-making powers. This was not a "capture" on land or sea. One cannot capture something that already lies within one's power or jurisdiction as did the property the Confederacy sought to sequester. A power such as the one at issue simply could not be deemed necessary and proper to conducting war when it had been resorted to so seldom, with such opposition, and without which nations nevertheless effectively waged war.

Mitchell recognized that it would not be enough simply to say the constitution prohibited the practice. He had to address the other sources, specifically international law and the precedent, if any, established by the United States in previous wars, either by its own legislative branch or the opinions of the U.S. Supreme Court. Aside from *Wolff*, no judicial decision had ever addressed the precise points at issue in the case, although the U.S. Supreme Court had touched on the question in *Brown v. United States* (1814).

Brown involved the confiscation of a load of pine timber by the U.S. district attorney for Massachusetts. Although the case involved the law of capture, and the facts did not match those at issue in the sequestration cases, however, the Court discussed the sovereign's right to confiscate enemy property during war and whether that right extended to the confiscating of debt. Both sides knew about *Brown*, and by being the first to address the decision, Mitchell could emphasize the beneficial aspects and then distinguish those that were not, before his adversary had the opportunity to address the court.

Mitchell conceded that *Brown* supported the proposition that confiscating debts lay within the power of the sovereign, but, quoting English Chancellor Kent, the power to confiscate debts, "a naked and impolitic right, condemned by the enlightened conscience and judgment of modern times . . . while still within the outskirts of the sovereign power of nations . . . is clearly not regarded as necessary and proper to the power of declaring war." Although Mitchell did not quote Justice Marshall's majority opinion, Marshall supported Mitchell's position, stating, "The universal practice of forbearing to seize and confiscate debts and credits, the principle universally received, that the right to them revives on the restoration of peace, would seem to prove that war is not an absolute confiscation of this property, but simply confers the right of confiscation." It is interesting that both Whaley and Mitchell overlooked this dictum. The dictum provided strong authority that debts should not be confiscated and the broader notion that war did not destroy all commercial and legal relationships among citizens of belligerents. War merely suspended these relationships, and if they were only suspended and not destroyed, then Whaley's argument that privileges and fiduciary relationships remained intact had merit.

Mitchell pointed to the United States and South Carolina during the American Revolution, arguing that the Articles of Confederation and the Confederate Constitution offered a good comparison of governmental systems and the rights conferred on the central government, including virtually identical war-making powers. Not only did the Continental Congress stay within the strict limitations of the power conferred on it, but when the issue of confiscating enemy property arose, the central government deferred to the states. When South Carolina did act, its confiscation law limited itself to property. It asserted jurisdiction over debts due alien enemies, not to seize them but to protect them. Rather than confiscate debts, South Carolina allowed alien enemies under certain conditions to sue in South Carolina courts to recover the sums due them. Thus, historical precedent established that the unlimited power to confiscate property was not within the power to declare war, thus voiding the Confederate Sequestration Act.

In his final remarks Mitchell took aim at the language of the act, terms so vague and so general that one could easily interpret the act to mean that every citizen must become an informer. It is one thing, he argued, to be subpoenaed as a witness in an equity proceeding to testify as to a particular person. This act allowed the receiver to "summon the community by sound of trumpet to inform generally as to a class of persons." One need not resort to legal precedent to distinguish between a witness and an informer. If the Confederate legislature could resort to the methods of the Star Chamber without any grant of authority, why not also employ all of its methods, including "the boot or the thumbscrew"? Although society rightfully had a legitimate claim to the loyalty of its members, in Mitchell's opinion it was an act of supreme stupidity to pass a law that could not be enforced. Maybe some people could be informers, but if so, they did so voluntarily. "A general may order his men on a forlorn hope, however certain their destruction; for spies he must resort to voluntary service."

Whaley and Mitchell took a good portion of the day, but enough time remained for Charles Richardson Miles to make the government's first presentation. As he stood to make his argument, several things had become apparent to everyone. Although Magrath presided over a district court, the defendants asked much more from a trial judge than simply to interpret the law and apply it to the facts. The Confederate Constitution provided for a supreme court, but no such entity ever existed, nor did the Confederacy ever establish its own appellate court structure. In time state supreme courts, most notably North Carolina's, filled the void and interpreted the constitutionality of Confederate laws. Now the defendants asked Magrath to fill that role.

Whereas the constitutionality of the act, the sanctity of the attorney-client relationship, and the status of fiduciary relationships clearly fell into the realm of legal questions, the argument as to the propriety of the writ of garnishment and the notion of sequestering debts involved policy. Simply because the Confederacy might have the power, and the legal authority existed to support its use of that power, did not mean sequestration was the right thing to do. The desire to punish or retaliate had to be weighed against the harmful effects on Confederate commerce and the danger of turning the Confederacy into a police state, with neighbors compelled to inform on one another or face criminal sanctions. In effect, Whaley and Mitchell begged the question as to what kind of nation the Confederacy would become.

Although no one had raised the issue, either in court or during the public debate that preceded trial, the Sequestration Act represented the first sign of the conflict becoming a "rich man's war–poor man's fight." The stated purpose of the act was to confiscate alien enemy property, liquidate that property, and then apply the proceeds to Southerners who lost property to Union confiscation. Although in theory any Southerner could have property confiscated, the real property at risk of being confiscated by the Union was slave property. Although the burden to inform and the attendant criminal penalties did not threaten life and limb in the same way conscription did six months later, the Sequestration Act nevertheless placed a burden on all citizens that ultimately benefited only the wealthier slave-holding class. Thus, when Miles stepped to the podium on the afternoon of October 14, he had to do more than simply provide legal justification for the Sequestration Act; he had to explain why it was the right thing to do.

Miles conceded his own shortcomings and felt "oppressed with the responsibility of my position in being called upon to defend the action of our Government in so important a matter and against such power and influence as were arrayed against me." Miles characterized himself as a man fulfilling a sacred duty, no different from the Confederate soldier on the field of battle. If overwhelmed by "the odds against me," he took solace knowing he fell in "the path of duty, in the cause of my country, and the defense of my government." Miles obviously did not share Petigru's belief that Magrath's presence on the bench made the outcome a foregone conclusion.

Miles left rebuttal to Hayne. He had already formulated his presentation, and he addressed four specific points: (1) does the sovereign have the legal right to sequester or confiscate all property and debts of alien enemies; (2) if so, does the Confederate Congress have the right and power to exercise that attribute of sovereignty; (3) is the method of exercising the power to sequester proper; and finally (4) does sequestration reflect sound policy.

Miles tried to eliminate any discretion Magrath might have to overturn the act on grounds of international law. A nation had the right to seize all property of its enemy found within its territory on the outbreak of war as a right inherent in sovereignty. Although the law of nations might soften or qualify the right from time to time, such relaxation of the general rule, absent an expressed treaty between nations, did not inhibit a nation's right to assert its sovereignty to the fullest. Only the sovereign itself could scrutinize the exercise of its inherent right. In *Ware v. Hylton* (1796), Associate Justice Samuel Chase succinctly stated the proposition that in the realm of international law "the nation was to justify her own laws, and her courts were to obey her laws."

One by one Miles laid out an impressive list of international scholars and English court decisions that supported the Confederacy's right to confiscate all property, including debts. Grotius, Vattel, Bynkershoek, and Wheaton all supported the Confederacy's right to seize any property. Miles had done his homework, and had he wanted to be even more emphatic, he could have added to that list such scholars as Puffendorf, Burlamaqui, and Rutherford. Miles used English case law to support the legal scholarship, bolstering Chase's stance on the place courts occupy in the interpretation of international law with Lord Thurlow's declaration in *Wright v. Nutt*. Thurlow held that the 1782 Georgia state law for the confiscation of the real and personal property of one Sir James Wright, including his debts, "was the law of an independent country, and the law of every country must be regarded in Courts of Justice, whether the law was barbarous or civilized, wise or foolish."

Miles's second point proved more difficult to support. Given that a sovereign right existed, even *Brown v. United States* held that the exercise of that right could not take place absent a legislative enactment. The defendants argued that the Confederate Congress lacked the constitutional authority to take such a step. Miles contended that the clause "and make rules concerning captures on land and water" acted as an expressed grant to the Confederate Congress of a substantive independent power.

Citing Marshall's opinion in *Brown v. United States*, he then argued that if the Confederate legislature had no expressed power, the power to confiscate existed by implication in the war-making power. The Confederacy's power over alien enemy property was no different from that over their persons. War makes citizens of other nations "enemies," and therefore to argue that the power to wage war did not include the power to deal with both the persons and the property of one's enemy limited the war power and placed the Confederacy at a disadvantage in its ability to wage war effectively. It did not matter that other nations rarely resorted to sequestration; the Confederacy could do so as part of its power to wage war against its enemy's persons and property.

If the Confederacy had the power, Miles argued, then how it exercised that power could not be questioned by either its courts or its citizens. At this point Miles moved from a purely legal argument to addressing aspects of policy, and he directed his argument toward the effect on alien enemies rather than the burden on Confederate citizens. Enemy citizens had no rights, and in a state of war the Confederate government could legally seize all property, including debts, limited only by "her own sense of duty." Such a right there-fore allowed the government to discover and seize that property by any and all means known under the law, and the only limitation re-quired that such a power be exercised by a means already acknowl-edged under existing law. This, Miles contended, the Confederate Sequestration Act did.

If alien enemies had no rights as to their property in the Confed-eracy, what right did a Confederate citizen have to resist a law de-signed to seize that property? The writ of garnishment as provided for in section 8 of the act had a historical equivalent in English com-mon law. The English exchequer exercised the same power in suits involving citizen indebtedness to the crown. How, Miles asked, is this writ any different from a bill of discovery in a Southern equity court, accompanied by interrogatories that required a person to dis-close information? Miles contended it was not. South Carolina's law provided for just such a remedy. Alabama's law went even further, allowing any creditor to file suit, even against an absent debtor, and serve a writ of garnishment on any citizen, compelling that person to answer as to whether the person held property or was otherwise indebted to the person named in the suit. These states allowed such processes to act on "citizens"; how could such an action be more onerous when acting on the property of one who had no rights at all? Once the alien enemy lost any rights in one's property, the argu-ment that the act burdened the Confederate citizen fell apart. A cit-izen is asked to do exactly what citizens are required to do under state laws where the debtor is a citizen.

Miles finally addressed what had become the real focus of the proceeding: should the Confederacy be doing this in light of the burden on its own citizens? Miles argued that the issue did not be-long before the court. Such arguments should be addressed to the legislature to modify or repeal the law, not to the court to set it aside. But to the extent that Confederate citizens continued to suffer "inconveniences" in complying with the law, Miles believed, those problems could be overcome by a lenient and equitable application of the law by the courts. If people chose to bring their grievances before a judicial tribunal, so be it. At least, Miles argued, allow the court to ameliorate any hardship on a case-by-case basis.

Miles's long presentation ended the first day of the trial. Under the circumstances he had done well for himself and his client, but certain questions remained unanswered. No one doubted that a sovereign possessed the power and authority to seize virtually any kind of alien enemy property. Although no nation had formally recognized the Confederacy, and the United States denied it any attributes of nationhood, no one in the Charleston, South Carolina, court questioned the Confederacy's legal existence. But, although the power to confiscate existed, the defense questioned whether this sovereign, under its own organic law, could exercise that power. As Mitchell pointed out, the Confederacy presented a different type of democracy on the North American continent, and using U.S. Supreme Court opinions that construed the U.S. Constitution to support the actions of the Confederate government seemed inappropriate.

In the period leading up to the Civil War, Chief Justices John Marshall and Roger Taney worked diligently to expand the power of the federal government under the Constitution. Under a governmental structure that placed the federal government at the top of the pyramid, such a position made sense. However, for more than thirty years the South argued the states were the preeminent political subdivision. The Confederate Constitution purported to reserve any power not expressly granted to the federal government to the states. It was not a document, at least in spirit, that availed itself of an interpretive scheme that expanded the power of the very government it purported to limit. This problem confronted the Confederacy for the remainder of the war. Notwithstanding the provisions of its own organic law, the exigencies of war compelled the Confederate government to take certain steps that, whether legal or not, were nevertheless necessary. Try as he did, Miles never got past this hurdle. No one denied that a sovereign could confiscate; the defendants' question was whether *this* sovereign could do so. In areas where no expressed grant of power existed, the Confederate constitutional scheme seemed to gravitate away from implied grants of power.

Miles's defense of the garnishment process likewise suffered from certain shortcomings. His claim that English law and the laws of several Confederate states provided for a discovery vehicle that compelled citizens to testify under oath as to the existence of property was technically correct. However, just as Mitchell and Whaley contended, those proceedings arose within the context of a specific lawsuit against a clearly defined defendant. The receiver's garnishment power required no specific suit or legal proceeding. It directed anyone named in the writ to tell whatever was known about any property belonging to anyone who might be an alien enemy. For the attorneys attacking the law, the question had much the same ring as another inquiry almost a century later during the McCarthy era: "Are you or anyone you know a member of the Communist Party?"

Miles's argument depended on a recognition that war destroyed alien enemy rights. If enemies had no rights in either their persons or their property, then loyal citizens had no right, and in fact no reason, not to comply with a law designed to seize property, no matter how vague the process or how general the inquiry. However, Miles provided little authority for the proposition that war destroyed all commercial relationships. His mention of the Confederate law of May 21, 1861, that provided for payment of debt owed to U.S. citizens into the Confederate treasury almost expressly recognized that war suspended commercial relationships, it did not destroy them. If that was the case, the Sequestration Act and any process designed to locate, seize, and liquidate debt seemed improper. If debts could be paid into the treasury and redeemed at the end of the war prior to the Sequestration Act, then by what magic had the nature of commercial relationships been changed from suspension to a legal nullity?

The legal issues aside, the case had become focused on two policy issues: should the Confederacy make people inform on their neighbors, and even if it could confiscate debt, in light of the effect on other nations, should the Confederate government seize and liquidate debts owed to alien enemies? The first issue went to the heart of how the Confederacy treated its own citizens. A passport law already existed in 1861 that severely regulated the ability of Southerners to travel. In less than a year martial law became a reality throughout Arkansas, with individual military commanders invoking it on an ad hoc basis to maintain order in other parts of the Confederacy. Although the act purported to seize enemy property, the burden of doing so fell on Confederate citizens. Putting aside constitutional issues as to which sovereign had the authority to pass such a law, the duty to inform came from a law passed by the one entity most Southerners despised the most, the central government. Although no one disputed that war demanded sacrifices from a nation's citizens, was this burden a necessary sacrifice for a nation not only struggling for international recognition but also striving to create some sense of internal cohesion among its own people? Even if citizens had to inform on one another, what of privileges and other legal exceptions? Miles offered no answers to these questions.

The district attorney also failed to address the larger issue of international relations. Although international law allowed nations to confiscate debt, international etiquette frowned on the practice. The Confederacy had already resorted to an outdated and disfavored mode of naval warfare when it launched its privateer fleet. Even though most of Europe had banned the practice in the 1856 Treaty of Paris, Spain, France, and England had allowed the Confederacy the latitude to seize prizes with only a minimum of interference. A law seizing debt struck directly at international commerce and finance. The Confederacy battled almost daily in both Paris and London for diplomatic recognition. A law that all but destroyed the ability of a British or French merchant to collect a debt from a Confederate citizen because the debt had originally been due to a U.S. citizen discouraged commerce between those nations and the Confederacy.

Confederate sequestration also demonstrated a selfish ignorance of what it meant to be a member of the community of nations. No one denied a nation's right to wage war. But war in the nineteenth century had limits, and nations not involved in the conflict expected belligerents to respect those limits. On at least two occasions during the war, the *Trent* incident and French intervention in Mexico, Lincoln took the position that discretion was the better part of valor, or as he put it, "one war at a time." Although no one threatened to go to war over debt confiscation, a nation badly in need of international recognition did not engender the goodwill of the community of nations by unnecessarily trampling on their ability to conduct business. Miles had missed this important point. In his zeal to demonstrate that the Confederacy could seize debt, he and perhaps his client had lost sight of the larger picture. The goal was to win the war at home and on the field. To do so required the full support and concerted energies of the people. International recognition proved crucial to colonial success in the American Revolution. The Sequestration Act threatened to undermine public support for the war at home and discourage foreign recognition. Miles had missed several other key points, and the next day James Petigru made certain to address every one of them.

CHAPTER 6

"I Lay This Offering of Age
on the Altar of Justice"

With the start of the piracy trials still a week away, the first day of the sequestration proceeding began, defining the legal and policy boundaries of the case. On day two, the day of trial everyone anxiously awaited, the issues became much more focused. On Tuesday morning, October 15, 1861, James Petigru stood up to argue his case against the Sequestration Act. Petigru, the most accomplished orator in South Carolina and perhaps in the United States, opened with little of the flair that characterized his distinguished career. He stated plainly that his "demurrer would be sustained" on two grounds: (1) the writ of garnishment was illegal and unwarranted, and (2) the confiscation of enemy debts was not within the competency of the Confederate government. His understated, businesslike opening proved to be the calm before the storm.

His close friend Joseph Pope sat in the courtroom that morning and years later recalled watching Petigru summon his strength and talent one last time. "Old, feeble, and slowly sinking into the grave, quivering in every limb, his eyes flashing, his voice rising, I can hear him as he uttered these words, 'I oppose this act of arbitrary power because I was born a free man!'" With these words Petigru launched into his assault and pressed his first point: the garnishment writ was illegal.

Admitting the sovereign's power to seize enemy property, Petigru denied that such a power had any lawful connection to the general inquisitional nature of the writ process. Petigru stripped bare Miles's argument that legal precedent supported such a tool. Yes, laws existed that allowed citizens to question others as to the nature and whereabouts of property, but such laws specifically called for, and in fact demanded, an underlying legal proceeding, something that made the request for information and the legal duty to disclose narrow and defined. These cases had no plaintiff or defendant. It is no more a judicial proceeding, Petigru argued, "than if the governor or general should call upon every man in the community to purge his conscience as to alien enemies."

The writ was a general warrant, a tool and instrument of tyranny. Although Petigru did not specifically refer to the colonial American experience, he could have. The dreaded Writs of Assistance added fuel to the growing fires of dissent in the 1760s. More commonly referred to as the king's "general warrants," they allowed British soldiers to search for smuggled goods at any time of the day or night, in any suspected house, without notice or warning. James Otis denounced the writs as contrary to English common law, and the Fourth Amendment to the U.S. Constitution reflected the American contempt for such methods: "No Warrants shall issue, but upon probable cause, supported by Oath or affirmation, and particularly describing the place to be searched, and the person or things to be seized." Both the provisional Confederate Constitution and the permanent document incorporated verbatim the Fourth Amendment to the U.S. Constitution.

When Petigru denounced the writs of garnishment as illegal, he meant they violated the Confederacy's own organic law. Miles's argument that, the thing being legal, the means was likewise legitimate, seemed to fall apart in the face of the prohibition against general warrants and even failed to meet Justice Marshall's famous "ends-means test" of *McCulloch v. Maryland.* Assuming the end was legitimate (i.e., war making or confiscating enemy property), the means must be "consistent with and not prohibited by the constitution." The garnishment writs had all the attributes of a general warrant and thus violated both the Confederate and the U.S. constitutions.

The Confederacy constantly invoked images of the American Revolution in defense of its own actions and characterized the present war as the "Second American Revolution." Petigru's argument suggested that the Confederacy had forgotten all of the lessons of America's first struggle for independence. As he attacked the government's legal arguments, he insisted the case spoke to the character of the Confederate nation and its people. Petigru could not divest the members of Congress from their beliefs and opinions, but, he said, his unwillingness to comply came from a higher power, telling Magrath that he (Petigru) was "a free man, and has the same right to withstand an inquisitional examination that a poor man has to close the door of his humble shed against the foot of power."

Petigru insisted that the Confederate Constitution resolved the antebellum debate that surrounded the U.S. Constitution as to whether the states and the federal government were coordinate branches, both sovereign in their respective spheres. The Confederacy created a central government of "special and limited powers." Miles's sarcastic comments notwithstanding, Petigru had not become a states' rights advocate. Consistent with the legal position he had held for most of his life, he simply believed the clear language of the document controlled. The Confederate Constitution had "positively, plainly, and without equivocation" excluded any encroachment on the "full and entire sovereignty" of the several states. No ambiguity existed; the Confederate government acted as "mere agent," empowered to act within the confines of the expressed authority granted it by the true sovereigns, the states.

As he approached the end of his argument, Petigru focused on the problem with sequestering debt and explained why the Confederacy had no jurisdiction over debts. Debts could not be "captured," as Miles suggested, because they cannot be "possessed" by the sovereign. Unlike tangible personal property that "exists" in a physical sense, debts exist as between creditors and debtors, and the debt itself actually resides in the physical possession of the creditor, who in many cases assigns it to another, and that person in almost every instance since the outbreak of war lived outside the physical boundaries of the Confederacy. Returning to the example of the American Revolution, Petigru insisted that South Carolina took the only logical course when it acted to protect debts owed to enemies. Once again Petigru returned to the moral implications of sequestration. Debt represented both a moral duty and a legal obligation. War could not destroy the moral obligations that ran between businessmen, and the Confederacy made a grave mistake by ignoring the ethical implications of its actions.

As Petigru sat down he assured the court that nothing short of the important principles at stake in this case could have moved him "now that the visions of hope have fled and the fire of youth is extinct, to venture into this arena." James Petigru had less than two years to live, and as he concluded his final argument, he wished that another person, someone perhaps more capable than himself, younger and stronger, could have undertaken this duty, but because no one stepped forward, Petigru told Magrath, "I lay this offering of age on the altar of justice, and am done."

The venom in Petigru's argument lingered, and the burden of responding fell on South Carolina Attorney General Isaac W. Hayne. Although no member of the South Carolina bar could match Petigru's skill, Hayne at least had the family reputation and professional status to step out of the considerable shadow Petigru cast on the proceedings. But reputation alone could not overcome Petigru's assault on the act; Hayne needed a legal argument, and his response came down to one simple word: necessity.

Hayne insisted that the "gentlemen" in this case had ignored "the very peculiar condition of affairs prevailing at the time." The Confederacy found itself as a new government, unacknowledged by the powers of the world, with the old Union denouncing Confederates as rebels and traitors and waging war to deny the South's right of self-government. The Union had all the prestige of the "old government," it outnumbered the South, and it possessed the navy. Facing fearful odds, the South's only hope lay in the unquestioned loyalty of its population to the Confederate government. Instead of the sympathy "which the learned counsel thinks so eminently due the weak as against the strong," the challenge to the Sequestration Act had been fraught with such words as inquisition, "Torquemada," tyranny, oppression, injustice, "Star Chamber," and "the rack."

Invoking biblical images of the Israelites and Noah's son who covered his naked father, Hayne insisted that everyone should follow the language of the poet and "be to her faults a little blind; be to her virtues very kind." Hayne had raised an argument, perhaps for the first time, that has resonated in the United States when future national crises have arisen: the exigency of the moment changes the government's ability to stretch the protections afforded by the Constitution. World War I, the Depression, World War II, the cold war, and even the present struggle against terrorism provide vivid, and sometimes shameful, examples of government action surviving judicial scrutiny because the emergency overrode the law.

Hayne's necessity argument exposed a weakness in the Confederate government. Its constitution, perhaps adequate for the demands of peacetime, possessed severe limitations when it came to waging war. Thirty years of fighting for states' rights made it difficult to argue that the Confederate Constitution, even though copied in some places almost verbatim from the U.S. Constitution, should be interpreted to expand the powers of the central government. As Petigru argued, secession grew out of a desire to limit the power of the national government. However, Hayne argued that the Confederate Constitution had the same meaning unless specifically changed by the drafters.

Hayne missed the point, or perhaps he understood the point and made the best argument he could under the circumstances. The drafters of the Confederate Constitution did not give the Confederate government the power to sequester or confiscate. They also rejected John Marshall's notion of the U.S. Constitution as a document with expanded and implied powers, and when the state delegates met in Montgomery in 1861, they created a government of limited power. Although the U.S. Supreme Court recognized an implied power to confiscate during wartime, that case law interpreted a different document, the similar or identical language notwithstanding.

Emphasizing the argument in *Brown v. United States,* Hayne insisted that the war power grant in the Confederate Constitution included confiscation and repeated his argument that had the Confederate framers intended to change the meaning of that clause, they should have expressly done so. Because the drafters had not expressly changed the war power grant as it had come to be interpreted under the U.S. Constitution, Hayne claimed that the Confederacy's confiscation power "is absolute, as absolute on that subject as the power of the Czar of Russia." The law of nations notwithstanding, the Confederacy had the right to act as any other sovereign and confiscate the property of alien enemies.

Arguing that the Confederate Constitution expressly addressed wartime confiscation proved difficult, but Hayne had a valid point as to the effect of international law. If the Confederate government possessed the power, international law controlled only the question of whether such an act was wise, not whether it was legal. But Hayne's argument demonstrated yet another dilemma all free nations face in times of war or national emergency: to what extent is a nation willing to compromise or destroy its most cherished principles in order to meet the crisis? Barely six months old, the Confederacy took a legal position totally contrary to the argument of states' rights proponents of the past three decades. Southern writers, newspapers, statesmen, and jurists had condemned the power of the U.S. government as both tyrannical and absolutist. Now one of its most prominent officials argued that the Confederate government possessed the same power and could use that power indiscriminately.

Hayne insisted that because confiscation served the public good the Confederate legislature could implement the law in any manner it deemed proper. Was it unreasonable or "unheard of" he argued, "to require good citizens to give their aid in the execution of that law?" Hayne equated the duty to disclose under the act with the English common-law offense of "misprision of treason." A person committed a crime if he or she witnessed or had knowledge of a treasonous act against the king and failed to report the act. The analogy offered an intriguing comparison and some chilling implications. Hayne analogized the failure to report the existence or whereabouts of alien enemy property with the failure to report a treasonous act and, by extension, Hayne argued, any felony. If a citizen can be required by law to report a crime or act of treason, why should that person not also be required to disclose information under the Sequestration Act? Both laws required general disclosure of a particular fact, and each carried a penalty for failure to comply. The chilling aspect of Hayne's argument lay in the possibility that failure to disclose the whereabouts of property might rise to the level of aiding and abetting an enemy.

Continuing with his "necessity" argument, Hayne suggested that even if the present law lacked a legal precedent, novelty alone did not invalidate the law and that nothing prevented Congress from compelling all citizens, including attorneys, generally to disclose information as to the nature and whereabouts of alien enemy property. Such a disclosure requirement might be inconvenient, but it deprived no one of liberty. In light of the prohibition against general warrants in the Confederate Constitution, Hayne's willingness to make such an argument revealed something about the Confederacy and the South.

The antebellum South had become accustomed to control on the exercise of speech and the dissemination of information. The rise of abolition in the 1830s had brought a strong reaction in the South. In an effort to suppress abolitionist ideas, Southern states censored mail, monitored speech, and passed the "Gag Rule," precluding petitions regarding slavery on the floor of Congress. Southern citizens accepted all of these measures as necessary for the public good to control the slave population and preserve the institution. Although some people chafed under such restrictions, most Southerners simply acknowledged them as a way of life. Neighbors closely scrutinized one another's conduct, not hesitating to report impermissible actions to the community at large. In this context Hayne's necessity argument seemed rational. The Sequestration Act and its disclosure requirements fit neatly into a cultural acceptance of speech control, but rather than a prohibition against certain speech and ideas, this act required the passing along of information to protect the public welfare.

Although his argument had some validity, granting government such broad power to seize property had no historical equivalent. Try as he might, Hayne's efforts to provide the Confederate law with a legal precedent failed, and in the end the act had only one justification: necessity. The public interest overrode any other consideration, Hayne argued, and although the act was harsh, war destroyed friendships and with them any possibility that Confederate citizens could be informing on their "friends." Hayne pointed to the numerous instances of Union confiscation and reminded the court that the act retaliated in order to compensate Confederate citizens for property loss and perhaps to check the enemy's confiscation efforts. Such a law, Hayne argued, deserved a "charitable construction" even if defective in some way. In a statement directed right at Petigru, Hayne closed by saying: "I would challenge the Counsel to produce from the history of the world a single instance of a Government under the same circumstances, where there has been a violent disruption, followed by a fearful war, which has evidenced such forbearance, regularity, and perfect freedom from injustice, extortion and tyranny in every shape as has been exhibited by our young Confederacy. I for one am proud of it."

Petigru did not respond. Perhaps in answer to his plea for someone younger and more able, Nelson Mitchell responded to Hayne's attack on the defendants' patriotism and the suggestion that their challenge to the Sequestration Act injured the country. Mitchell could not see how the "right to retaliate" changed the distribution of political power under the Confederate Constitution, and although "distress is entitled to indulgence," civil duty demanded the present challenge. Far from harming the country, challenging a breach of the constitution showed true faith and support. Who, after all, supported the government more: one who thought the constitution "too weak to endure safely any attempt to arraign proceedings like the present—or those, who having faith in its substantial structure . . . believe an act of congress or an opinion of the Attorney-General, may be questioned without impairing its strength?"

Mitchell's rebuttal ended the first phase of the sequestration cases. Magrath intended to take his time preparing an opinion and promised to inform each side on the morning before he rendered his decision. Magrath treated Petigru's demurrer as a separate case from James Wilkinson's demurrer and Ed McGrady's objections. Before rendering judgment, Magrath still had to hear the other two cases, and on the morning of October 17, James Wilkinson presented his objections.

Wilkinson made it clear that he had none of the ideological or constitutional objections that characterized the first two days of argument. He supported the act and the writs of garnishment. For him the key question was "to what extent, and under what limitations, if any, does the act intend that the attorney shall be compelled to give the information inquired to? Is a lawyer to be stripped of his privilege and forced to discover without reservation, or is he still entitled to the same protection afforded by the common law?" Wilkinson objected to the burden placed on lawyers, not the larger issues articulated by Petigru, Mitchell, and Whaley.

Wilkinson restated the common-law rule that the privilege exists regardless of circumstances. Without the privilege no person dared consult a professional or go into court either to retain redress or to defend one's own interest. Wilkinson cited *Greenleaf's Evidence* to support the existence and extent of the privilege. Although the attorney-client privilege had its beginnings in sixteenth-century England in the landmark cases of *Berd v. Lovelace* (1577) and *Dennis v. Codrington* (1580), evidence as a distinct study had come into its own only between 1770 and 1830. Simon Greenleaf, a Maine attorney, wrote the first significant treatise on evidence in the United States in 1848, and by 1861 his work represented the standard in the field. Wilkinson needed no further support but added *Greenough v. Gaskell*, an 1833 English case that reinforced the nature of the privilege as one not qualified by the existence or nonexistence of an actual case. Good law in 1861, *Greenough* is still cited today in British Commonwealth jurisdictions.

Nothing in the act addressed the attorney-client privilege or allowed the examination of deponents to go beyond the areas protected by the privilege. Without a specific provision abrogating the privilege, how could the privilege be changed for sequestration? The framers of the Confederate Constitution "understood well the nature and extent of this privilege and the tenacity with which the profession adhered to it." Lawyers were among the delegates to the Montgomery convention, and Wilkinson believed that had they intended to remove the privilege as an impediment to discovery under the act, they would have done so with clear, expressed language. Attorneys understood that, unlike business relationships, the state of war did not alter the nature of the privilege. Civil rights might have to bend to the exigencies of war, but not legally established privileges.

Wilkinson argued that attorneys existed as a part of the magistracy. As officers of the court they maintained an official connection to the branch of the government responsible for administering justice. Lawyers thus owed both private and public duties and swore an oath to the government to perform those obligations faithfully. When a court recognized privileges, particularly the attorney-client privilege, it recognized something it had invested in its own officers. When the government in turn held out this class of persons to the public at large as persons exempted from the general obligation to disclose communications made in confidence, it "invited the world to repose confidence in itself, under a pledge that it shall forever be inviolate."

The act specifically exempted Confederate bonds and stocks held by an alien enemy from the class of property subject to seizure. That exemption recognized such debts as a promise or obligation of the government to pay a sum certain. If it sequestered government securities, the Confederacy in effect reneged on its own obligation. Wilkinson argued that the creation of privileged communications rose to the same level. How, he asked, "would the court proceed under this act, to examine a wife, whose husband was an alien enemy, or visa versa?" Could the court presume that Congress intended the act to destroy the sacred nature of that relationship?

In a direct assault on Hayne's necessity argument, Wilkinson asked the court how any level of necessity could justify the destruction of relationships by invading the sanctity of the communications made within them, without simultaneously creating a distrust "that must repel mankind from the society of each other, and drive him to solitude for safety." Communications both between husband and wife and between attorney and client came into play under the Sequestration Act, and Wilkinson did not see how, under any legal or equitable construction, the Confederate Congress intended to destroy those privileges.

Wilkinson concluded his short but effective argument by voicing the same concerns about the Sequestration Act that others had articulated both during and prior to the trial: "Some of its provisions . . . weaken and despoil the citizens of the Confederacy and protect the enemy eventually against all loss and injury." Sequestration needed popular support to succeed. At present the Confederate government acted only as a steward; it froze property but had not yet been able to seize property physically and liquidate it into the national treasury. The law classified enemy property and took it out of the path of war's potential waste and destruction by placing it in the hands of Confederate citizens who might otherwise turn it over except that certain provisions of the act now compelled them to resist. Fortunately, the "careless penning of the act" did not prevent the court from adopting a construction giving effect to the objects of the act without "inflicting disaster upon the citizens of the Confederate States."

With that Wilkinson sat down, and Miles rose to respond. The effectiveness of Wilkinson's argument on this narrow point became immediately apparent. Miles could offer no legal authority in rebuttal, conceding everything "that had been so forcibly said by the Counsel." But he did draw one important distinction: property held by an attorney did not belong in the same category as communications made to an attorney. If an attorney held property in his possession, the writ of garnishment required him to say so and, on demand by the receiver, to turn it over. Doing so required no breach of a privileged "communication."

Wilkinson seemed to strike the first clear victory for the defendants. Although Whaley had been the first to raise the privilege issue during the trial, and Petigru had done so ten days earlier at the first hearing, neither had presented the argument as cogently as Wilkinson. Wilkinson not only addressed the legal issues surrounding privilege but also, like his codefendants, raised the more important question of what kind of nation the Confederacy would become. Treatises, both then and now, stress how the South possessed a folk culture, one in which community relationships and honor had real meaning. Would this culture now witness its own destruction, not from the North, but at the hands of its own government? Would, as Wilkinson suggested, a nation that professed to stand for a simpler time, one that had not been corrupted by the artificial and impersonal relationships characteristic of industrialization and immigration, now force its citizens away from community and society in order to protect themselves from each other and their own government?

Wilkinson's limited attack based on privilege partly explains his apparent success. To sustain his plea undermined neither the law nor the government. However, his argument carried more force than he cared to admit, and his objections applied beyond the mere protection of common-law privilege. The Confederate Constitution represented the law of the land even if it fell short as a mandate of all its people. Wilkinson's readiness to concede so easily that war abrogated civil rights might reflect the modern trend in the twentieth century, but his nineteenth-century codefendants refused to accept that the government owed any less of a duty to its people to safeguard constitutional protections than to protect certain privileges deemed essential to the orderly administration of justice. They most certainly rejected any suggestion that the Confederate Constitution carried the same implied expansive power as the U.S. Constitution. The Confederacy presented the world with a new variation of self-government, developed for almost thirty years and based on states' rights and a Jeffersonian vision of political economy. The Confederate dream helped push the nation down the path to war, and Whaley, Mitchell, and Petigru refused to allow it (the government) to alter that vision out of a professed "need" to fight that war with a method that not only violated the constitution but also, on the basis of historical precedent, hardly seemed necessary.

The court recessed until October 22, but Magrath's docket remained busy with sequestration matters. Two cases against sequestered estates concluded on the morning of the twenty-second and went to the jury. Immediately thereafter, McGrady presented his argument to the court. Despite having heard two days of argument and with an additional six days to prepare, he offered nothing new to the debate and based his opposition to the act on three points: (1) Congress lacked the power to pass the act under the provisional constitution, (2) if the act was unconstitutional, the writs of garnishment were unauthorized, and (3) even if Congress possessed the power to sequester, the writs were still improper. Although his arguments repeated those of his colleagues, his opening words placed the matter in the context of the times in an effort to show the court that patriotism demanded that the act be challenged in order to preserve the very thing the Confederacy had gone to war to protect.

McGrady's motives echoed those expressed by Mitchell, that patriotism demanded dissent. The legal basis for his objections came from Petigru's argument that the issue of state versus federal sovereignty had been resolved by the Confederate Constitution. McGrady pointed the court to the ordinances of secession passed by all eleven states. Every Confederate state claimed as a basis for secession that "inherent, intrinsic sovereignty" belonged only to the states. When the states granted the Confederate government certain powers, they did not "concede sovereignty to the federal government." Therefore, all arguments to support the Sequestration Act on the basis of the "sovereign" power of the Confederate government failed in light of the clear language in the Confederate Constitution.

McGrady's argument came to the same conclusion reached by his colleagues: even if the Confederate Congress had the power to sequester, the vagueness and generality of the writ went beyond any grant of authority, particularly when one stripped away the veneer of necessity based on the protection of the public welfare. Seizing on the example of the American Revolution that Petigru had missed, McGrady asked, "Is not this generality and vagueness the very objection urged against writs of assistance which empowered the officers of the customs to search for uncustomed goods in any house without specifically describing the particular house?" This, McGrady insisted, "our revolutionary forefathers held to be one of the highest acts of tyranny." The act had nothing to do with "public safety." The act indemnified those who lost property to the Union, slave property, and to accomplish this goal the Confederacy armed its sequestration receivers with the unprecedented power to summon a whole community into a court of justice without the slightest allegation against or concerning any one of them. "We must resist [the writs] until resistance becomes utterly vain, and then will have to consider the only choice left us, between submission and the prison."

Miles responded briefly to McGrady with a shorter version of his lengthy presentation of the previous week. Acknowledging McGrady's status in the community, Miles lamented that regardless of McGrady's sense of duty compelling him to resist the law, "the weight of the influence of his personal and professional reputation which he has cast in the scale in which this important action of the government is now being weighed . . . would not only influence those who look up to him with respect, but would also influence those whose opposition . . . would spring from motives less pure." After a brief presentation Miles rested, and the court adjourned for the day. The next morning McGrady briefly responded to Miles's rebuttal, and on the twenty-third of October, the arguments in the sequestration cases concluded. Magrath retired to consider the evidence and make his ruling. It had taken nine days to try the case with the court in recess for several days during that period. In a case with such weighty issues that had taken months to develop and a week to try, one might rightfully expect the verdict to take some time. It did not. On the morning of October 24, 1861, Magrath delivered his verdict in *Confederate States of America v. James L. Petigru, et al.*

———

In criminal trials quick verdicts normally do not bode well for defendants. However, more than a simple criminal proceeding, the trial had all the trappings of a supreme court case. If nothing else, both sides agreed that Magrath's decision stood to dictate the future course and application of Confederate sequestration and the methods used to implement the law. The arguments from both sides contained more than just law; they spoke of policy and need. The debate moved beyond questions of what the Confederacy *could* do in this situation to what the Confederacy *should* do in this situation. Each advocate couched the issues as he saw them, and from these various arguments Magrath distilled the case into three main questions: (1) was the act adopted by the Confederate Congress consistent with international law, (2) did the Confederate Congress possess the power under the constitution to pass such an act, and (3) if so, was the method of proceeding, specifically the seizure of debts and the broad garnishment power, inconsistent with moral obligations that society enforces or violative of privileges that belong to Confederate citizens.

Magrath's lengthy opinion took more than two hours to read and reflected the efforts of a jurist expecting public scrutiny both at home and abroad, even if his decision never found its way to an appeals court. To find the Confederate Sequestration Act consistent with international law, Magrath went beyond court decisions and referenced the opinions of scholars and jurists in any form he could find. He cited Manning, Martena, Chancellor Kent, Wildman, Bynkershock, Vattel, Grotius, Puffendorf, Comyn, and Wheaton for the proposition that enemy property belongs to the sovereign and can be confiscated during wartime. He went as far back as the Magna Carta for the proposition that "merchants shall have free ingress and egress to enter, stay and depart by land or water, to sell or to buy, except in times of war." At the onset of war, England held goods of foreign merchants, keeping them safe until it determined the treatment afforded by the belligerent to English merchants and their goods. The proposition seemed ideally suited for the Confederacy because its Sequestration Act came after the Union's expressed intent to seize and confiscate Confederate property.

Magrath briefly cited English case law and then moved to the opinions of American jurists on the issue of enemy property and the authority of the sovereign to seize that property. Citing Justices Story and Iredell, Magrath concluded that enemy property found in the ports of a belligerent could be detained and confiscated and that legal claims could likewise be seized by the sovereign. But seizing property in general only partly addressed the dispute. Provided the Confederate government had the power to sequester, the defendants had not denied that international law allowed belligerents to seize and confiscate one another's property. The property issue centered on a specific kind of property: debt. To deal with this argument Magrath had to address the only case on record, *Wolff v. Oxholm*.

Magrath reasoned that Lord Ellenborough's opinion in *Oxholm* rested not on the legality of confiscating debt but on the grounds that international scholars either did not recognize the right or questioned its viability. Ellenborough found no instance in the last 100 years where such a right had been claimed and thus denied the debtor's defense of payment to the Danish government when the creditor sued in an English court. Magrath distinguished between the existence of the legal right to seize debt and the unwillingness of nations to exercise the right. A historical unwillingness to confiscate debt did not prohibit the Confederacy from doing so under international law. Magrath conceded that much had been said as to the distinction between debts and other types of tangible property, but such distinctions had been based on policy, not on right. As to issues of policy Magrath said, "It is not necessary here to consider how far the confiscation of debt is just or politic. In courts of justice and in questions like this, the proper inquiry is, what is the rule of law?"

Having committed himself to the rule of law, Magrath held that the Confederate Sequestration Act did not extinguish a creditor's rights. When a Confederate debtor paid money owed to an alien enemy into the Confederate treasury, he received a certificate absolving him of that debt. But Magrath insisted that at the end of the war a foreign creditor could return and sue to recover his money, not against the debtor, but the government that seized the debt.

Magrath's interpretation of the act, or rather the "possibilities" that existed, had no legal basis. More important, his legal manipulation of the act did not alter the effect of debt seizure on international commerce during the war. A foreign, nonenemy creditor who came into possession of a note or other evidence of indebtedness owed by a Confederate citizen that began as a debt to an alien enemy found himself without recourse.

Having held that the Confederate government could legally seize alien enemy property, including debts, Magrath addressed the seminal legal issue of the case: did the Confederate Congress have the power under the constitution to do so, or did such power lie exclusively with the states? If, as the defendants contended, the Confederate Congress did not have the expressed power to confiscate debt under the constitution, the Sequestration Act was void.

Magrath found the necessary expressed grant of power within the provisions of the Confederate Constitution that gave Congress the power to declare war and establish rules of capture on land and water. Whether it regarded persons or property, the Confederate Congress had authority to regulate capture. Who could argue, he asked, that the Confederate Congress had properly exercised its authority as to persons captured by the Confederate Army? It did not matter in which state a Union soldier became a prisoner of war; the laws laid down by the Confederate Congress governed his treatment. Why distinguish between a captured person or soldier and "a booty or a prize"? Each situation involved capture and became subject to the rules laid down by Congress, well within its expressed authority.

All of Magrath's "capture" examples involved the seizure of persons or property by Confederate military authority on land or sea. However, the Sequestration Act had nothing to do with "capture" by military authority. It authorized government confiscation of civilian alien enemy property outside the immediate operational area of battle. Although "capture" represented the only expressed grant of power that could possibly be analogous to "confiscation," the two were not the same. As Magrath stretched to find a legal justification for sequestration, the differences did not matter. Magrath had admitted that the Confederate Constitution made the sovereignty of the states "perfect" and that therefore any construction of the act that upheld its constitutionality had to do so without violating that basic principle. "Capture" was all he had to rely on.

Clinging to his ruling that Congress had the expressed power to regulate capture, and notwithstanding his earlier assertion that law, not policy, must govern the case, Magrath then contradicted himself with a long policy argument focusing on the need for uniformity. To give credence to the defendants' argument that the states, not the federal government, held the power to confiscate destroyed uniformity in a law that not only undermined the effectiveness of the stated goal, to confiscate, but also made it difficult to deal with "the other belligerent." A different confiscation act for each state risked having a rigid system in one state and a lenient practice in another. In the process the Confederacy lost uniformity not only as to how it seized enemy assets but also in how the Union treated Confederate citizens' property.

The need for uniformity extended not only to a situation where the Confederacy sought to deal unilaterally with alien enemy property but also to the treatment of belligerent citizens' property established by treaty. A treaty had to bind all the states. To argue that the Confederate government could not address the confiscation of enemy property so as to bind every state in the Confederacy violated the central government's treaty power. The Confederate government under its war-making power had the expressed authority to negotiate peace and could address an area that might otherwise lie outside its authority.

Magrath fashioned this legal argument entirely on his own. Neither side had ever suggested the treaty power had anything to do with sequestration. Magrath reached beyond the legal arguments of counsel to bolster his "necessity" argument for Confederate confiscation. By giving examples of expressed grants of authority such as treaty making and peace making, which by their operation encompassed areas that seemed reserved for the states, Magrath justified the need to encroach on state sovereignty in order for the Confederate Congress to carry out its responsibilities. He rejected the comparison between the Confederacy and the United States under the Articles of Confederation, insisting that the Confederate Constitution created a government that cured the ills of the Articles of Confederation by allowing the central government more latitude while preserving the sanctity of state sovereignty. However, he cited no specific portion of the Confederate Constitution that worked this delicate balancing of the need for uniformity and the absolute sovereignty of the states.

Necessity also underscored the portion of Magrath's opinion sustaining the discovery methods authorized by the Sequestration Act. The key to his reasoning lay in the nature of the property addressed by the writ of garnishment process. Under the act all alien enemy property, wherever it existed within the Confederacy, immediately became the property of the Confederate States of America. The Confederacy's title to the property became perfect, and all other proceedings merely sought to identify the property and its whereabouts. If, as Magrath insisted, the government had lawful title to all alien enemy property, then it also acquired all other rights incident to that title, including the absolute right to know what that property might be and its location. The public had no right to conceal the nature and whereabouts of government property.

Magrath had justified the government's right to alien enemy property; however, he had still not addressed the effect on the average Confederate citizen. He reserved the right to do so in his opinion on Ed McGrady's challenge. The next day, in a short two-page opinion, Magrath struck down McGrady's challenge, returning to his theme of necessity. In his estimation the act did not harm Confederate citizens. The general nature of the inquiry did not divest any Confederate citizen of property; it did not touch his person, effect a search of his house, or seize any of his effects. The writ did one thing: it required the citizen to deliver or reveal the existence of property belonging to the Confederacy's enemies, enemies who now became the enemies of every Confederate citizen. What right did a citizen have to refuse to answer or give information as to property that the person had no right in and which properly belonged to the government? The obligation became even greater when the property in question worked a benefit on the nation as a whole, rather than on one individual.

Only James Wilkinson's privilege issue remained, and his short presentation yielded the only concession from the court. In less than a page Magrath determined that the attorney-client privilege extended to every communication that the client made to his lawyer for purposes of professional advice. The act contained no exception, and Magrath held that any communications made by a client to an attorney prior to the war that revealed the existence or whereabouts of property now deemed alien enemy property remained protected by the attorney-client privilege. His limitation as to the time of the communication reflected a built-in limitation on the privilege. Communications that served to further an ongoing violation of the law had never been protected by the privilege.

———

Petigru had been right. Neither he nor any of his codefendants could expect any help from Magrath. One of the South's most ardent proponents of states' rights fashioned a legal opinion that supported the Confederate government's first controversial effort to impose a national will on its citizens. The trial had revealed a gap between the type of government the South wanted to create and the government it needed to survive the war. Magrath's opinion in the main case came the morning after McGrady's final argument, perhaps indicating that Magrath's mind was made up after Hayne and Mitchell finished almost a week before. Magrath used the hiatus to begin drafting his verdict, a verdict that in many ways went beyond anything argued by either Hayne or Miles. In the end Magrath cared little for the notion that the act as drafted and applied seemed to violate key principles of the constitution. In war, the Confederate citizenry, including its lawyers, had to tolerate what he deemed only a minor irritant. Magrath had upheld the right to sequester property; he refused to address whether it was proper, either in how it affected its citizens or the international community. In time the Confederate Congress tried to soften the law and address some of the arguments made by Petigru, Whaley, Mitchell, and McGrady. For now the argument was over.

The emotions that accompanied the trial did not easily subside. On October 28, 1861, Ed McGrady spent "the whole day after twelve [noon] in making arrangements to prevent difficulties between Miles and Messrs Mitchell and Whaley." As so often happens in trials, the verdict merely defined legal rights; it did not alter opinions or diminish the zeal of the advocates. The surviving records indicate that William Whaley went on with his life. Nelson Mitchell continued the fight for at least two more years. But although the Confederacy had established a national authority over its own citizens, it came with a price, both in the infringement on civil liberties and in the limitation of state sovereignty. Meanwhile, north of slavery, two U.S. juries heard evidence that in a different way came to bear on the same issues litigated in Charleston, issues that went toward answering the question of how the rest of the world, and the United States in particular, defined the Confederacy as a nation.

CHAPTER 7

"I Cannot Insult and Ridicule the Feelings of Millions"

On the morning of October 22, 1861, as the sequestration cases came to a close and Andrew Magrath prepared to render his verdict, William Smith and his prize crew went on trial for piracy. The same sense of importance that characterized the proceedings in Charleston embraced the courtroom in Philadelphia as Hubley Ashton stood to deliver the government's opening statement. Faced with a formidable defense team and thrust into the limelight because of the illness of his superior, George Coffey, Ashton told the jury that as much as he might like this case to be the burden of another, more qualified man, he "dare not shrink, especially in the hour of our country's history, from the task which has been set before me." But the burden would not be his alone, and he impressed on the jury that "the determination of the fate of the prisoner, however, involves the determination of questions infinitely more important than whether he shall die or live." Ashton insisted that "the issues of the present mission of this court are fraught with consequences which reach far into the future. The verdict which you shall render will leave this room and find its record in the imperishable history of the land." The trial of William Smith provided the platform for lawyers on both sides to argue the question of what the Confederacy was.

Ashton's opening statement briefly detailed the events that led to the capture of Smith and his prize crew. By the time of trial everyone in Philadelphia knew the story of the *Enchantress*'s capture by the *Jeff Davis* and subsequent recapture by USS *Albatross*. Like most large newspapers in the North, the *Philadelphia Inquirer* had chronicled the exploits of the Confederate privateers from the time the *Savannah* had gone to sea. To a great extent Ashton's opening statement repeated what the jury already knew, facts not only a matter of common knowledge but also undisputed, even by the defense. The case quickly became a debate over the legal effect of Smith's actions. Whether Smith and his crew were pirates or naval combatants all came down to the Confederacy possessing sufficient attributes of nationhood and sovereignty, and the way the United States indicted these men made that question all the more vital.

Ashton distinguished between common-law piracy and the statutory crime. Common law defined piracy as the act of a person on the high seas who purported to be at war with all nations. That person plundered with the spirit and intention of "universal hostility" and committed offenses against every nation. He was deemed an enemy of the human race, and any nation could capture and punish him. By 1819 this definition had become so accepted within the international community that the U.S. Congress made common-law piracy a federal crime. However, Smith did not stand accused of common-law piracy.

Whether the Confederate letter of marque issued to the *Jeff Davis* protected Smith as a combatant, everyone, including the U.S. government, knew Confederate vessels preyed on the shipping of only one nation. Jefferson Davis's instructions accompanying the letters of marque impressed this point on Southern sea captains, and the subsequent conduct of the Confederate privateers did nothing to undermine the fact that the Confederacy made war only on the United States. Although Great Britain, France, and Spain refused to allow Confederate privateers to take prizes into their ports, they did not treat these men or their ships as pirates. Foreign countries, unwilling to recognize the Confederacy formally, nevertheless treated the conflict as something more than a rebellion. A "not guilty" verdict in a U.S. court might reinforce that amorphous existence, convey nation status on the rebellious South, and invite foreign recognition.

Ashton explained to the jury that Smith stood charged under two U.S. laws, the first passed in 1790 and the second in 1820, which created a statutory definition of piracy. Section 8 of the 1790 act made it a crime for any person to commit a robbery or murder on the high seas or any river out of the jurisdiction of any particular state, which if committed within the land body of the country would be punishable by death as robbery or murder under the laws of the United States. If convicted, such a person faced the death penalty.

Section 9 of the 1790 act took this statutory crime one step further by stating that if any citizen committed an offense as defined in section 8 or "any act of hostility against the United States or any citizen thereof upon the high seas under the color of any commission from a foreign prince or state, or on pretense of authority from any person, shall, notwithstanding the pretense of such authority, be deemed, adjudged, and taken to be a pirate, felon, and robber." Conviction of the crime also carried the death penalty.

The 1790 statute came under scrutiny in *United States v. Palmer* (1818) where Chief Justice Marshall interpreted the law to mean that the robbery or murder had to be committed "on board" an American ship. Acts committed against an American ship or citizen from a "foreign ship" did not fall under the statute. In several subsequent decisions, lower courts followed Marshall's holding, and two years later Marshall reaffirmed his interpretation of the 1790 act in *United States v. Klintock* (1820). The sole question in a prosecution filed under the 1790 act became the identity of the nation under whose flag the ship sailed, and the crime had to be committed on board an American ship for the statute to apply.

In light of these decisions the U.S. Congress attempted to clarify its statutory definition of piracy in May 1820. Section 3 of the 1820 act made it a crime for any person to commit the crime of robbery in or on any ship or vessel or on any ship's company of any ship or vessel, or the lading thereof, and any such person doing so would be adjudged a pirate. Ashton explained that once the vessel against which the crime was committed was shown to be American, the nationality or identity of the offender was irrelevant. Contrary to the common-law definition of piracy, such a person need not be the enemy of all, and he need not have committed any other piratical acts. One act of robbery involving an item of virtually no value, if committed against an American ship, constituted piracy.

As pled, the government's case gave the defendant only one real defense: the act was not robbery because it occurred in the context of a war between belligerents. The defense argued in the alternative that "duress" removed the "intentional" *mens re*, or mental state necessary for robbery, but ultimately Smith's fate depended on his status as a combatant. Ashton and his co-counsel knew this. A "not guilty" verdict meant that Smith had committed an act of war. An act of war required at least two warring nations or belligerents, and if he was not a pirate, the flag under which Smith sailed had some international status.

In October 1861 the war had just begun, already punctuated by three Union defeats on land, engagements Ashton referred to as his opening statement came to its conclusion. This case could therefore decide some of the very issues being played out on the battlefield. Ashton reminded the jury that "independently of the consideration which affects merely the personal fate of the prisoner, the case which we present will probably involve the practical determination by you of the great question which is now shaking the continent of America to its center, and finding its everlasting solution on the battlefields of Virginia and Missouri." He insisted that only on the battlefield could the Confederacy establish its identity, and he implored the jury to agree that the "pretended authority under which it may be claimed the crimes of the prisoner were committed, cannot avail him, before this tribunal, either to justify or excuse them."

Ashton's reference to Bull Run and the battlefields of Virginia and Missouri reminded the jury that the trial was taking place within a larger context. The Union defeat at Manassas shocked the Northern public. Newspapers proclaimed "Black Monday," and Horace Greeley, whose *New York Tribune* had pushed for Union military action, wrote to Lincoln, encouraging him to sue for peace. A second defeat at Wilson's Creek in August 1861 further dampened spirits. But while newspapers spread a message of defeat, the Northern public refused to despair. Enlistments went up as Northern communities recommitted themselves to the task. Rather than dampen the fires of patriotism, battlefield defeat stoked the embers. On October 21, 1861, the day before trial, a Union disaster outside Leesburg, Virginia, resulted in 1,700 casualties. The debacle at Ball's Bluff only added fuel to the fire. Smith's defense team faced a jury already tainted by adverse publicity, and Ashton encouraged them to submit to their bias and use the trial to strike a blow for the Union.

While the armies fought during the summer and fall of 1861, both the Union and Confederate legislatures waged war. The Confederacy implemented both the Alien Enemies Act and the Sequestration Act in August, a clear message of Southern intentions to make war on Union citizens and property. In July the U.S. Congress convened a special session to address the rebellion. After declaring a "state of insurrection," Congress passed a series of bills confirming Northern intentions to do whatever necessary to crush the rebellion. Such revenue measures as the first federal income tax and allowing the secretary of the treasury to borrow $22,000,000 through the sale of treasury notes affirmed the government's commitment to finance the war. The First Confiscation Act escalated the conflict by adding an attack on slavery to the goal of preserving the Union. A juror sitting on a piracy case in either Philadelphia or New York in October 1861 knew that both sides had mobilized all their resources for war and that the trials had become another battleground in the larger context of war.

The defense reserved its opening statement for its own case in chief and asked the court to invoke what in modern jargon is "the rule." It requested that while one prosecution witness was being examined, all other prosecution witnesses wait outside the courtroom until after they had testified. The purpose is to prevent witnesses from hearing prior testimony and making their own consistent with what they have heard. The court granted the request, and the prosecution went to work.

In rapid succession the prosecution called the owner of the *Enchantress*, one of its charterers, and its first officer. The first two witnesses established that the ship was American owned and operated, sailing from an American port, and therefore that the robbery occurred against an American vessel. Valued at between $5,000 and $6,000, the ship carried a cargo of 75 sacks of corn; 20,000 feet of lumber; sundry barrels of mackerel; boxes of candles; and barrels of hams, pork, soap, and glassware. Although Ashton had insisted that robbery under the statute applied to the taking of an object of "almost inappreciable value," he demonstrated that this robbery involved goods of substantial value. The third witness, Charles Page, corroborated the nature and size of the cargo and testified to the seizure of the *Enchantress*.

Ashton's inexperience as a trial lawyer evidenced itself during the prosecution's case. He went to painstaking measures to establish that the crime occurred on the high seas, until both judges finally told him to move on; everyone had conceded that the ship had not run aground when it encountered the *Jeff Davis*. At times his examination of his own witnesses lost its flow as he skipped forward or turned back in time. Finally, the defense objected, and Judge Grier told Ashton to let his witnesses tell their story as it unfolded.

Page recounted sighting the *Jeff Davis* and how the privateer flew a French flag until it pulled alongside the *Enchantress*, when the Confederate colors finally appeared. He testified about the *Jeff Davis*'s armaments and that it forcibly took the Union ship under the threat of its five guns. Page confirmed William Smith's presence on board the *Jeff Davis* and his transfer to the *Enchantress* with four of his shipmates. Consistent with his inexperience, Ashton seemed not to know when to stop. Judge Grier finally stopped Page's direct examination by telling Ashton he had established all he needed to with this witness. Perhaps realizing he had pushed the court's patience to its limits, Ashton passed the witness.

George Wharton and Nathaniel Harrison took turns cross-examining Page. Wharton inquired about the *Jeff Davis*'s use of a French flag to approach the *Enchantress* and then established that Page had never seen a Confederate flag prior to this incident. He tried to determine when Page saw Smith for the first time. On direct examination Page testified that he had the opportunity to observe and hear the interaction among the Confederate crew and officers. Wharton pressed Page about a "commission" held by the *Jeff Davis*. Page testified that he did not see a commission but that when the Confederate boarding officer set foot on the *Enchantress* he stated, "You are a prize to the Confederate brig *Jeff Davis*." Wharton tried to establish the existence of the letters of marque carried by the Confederate privateer because the defense never obtained original documents from the Confederate government. Page admitted that he and his fellow prisoners received good treatment from the time of their capture until their release, undermining the government's position that Smith participated in a violent seizure of the ship. Page's testimony made the incident look more like a ministerial act of war, accomplished without harm or bloodshed, with the crew treated as prisoners of war.

Harrison established that Page had never seen Smith before the day of the incident but that he visited Smith and the other prisoners twice since their capture. Harrison suggested that Page had gone to see Smith in order to prepare his own testimony and that he could not identify Smith as the prize master of the *Enchantress*. After all, Page had seen him only briefly as the *Enchantress* crew moved over to the *Jeff Davis*. He might have wrongfully identified Smith as the person in charge. A juror picked up on Harrison's suggestion and asked whether Smith took charge or acted in a subordinate role. Page replied that Smith assumed command of the Union ship. William Kelley then briefly took Page on redirect for the prosecution, inquiring about the dress of the crew. Did they have uniforms? Did the crew dress alike? Page said "no," suggesting the absence of a formal military organization.

Then the prosecution called Jacob Garrick to the stand. Garrick provided the only testimony of what happened after Smith and his prize crew boarded the *Enchantress* and headed for Charleston. Now a twenty-five-year-old cook, Garrick had gone to sea in 1852 as a seventeen-year-old and served as a steward on board the *Enchantress*. He testified that Smith came on board and told Garrick and the rest of the crew to gather up their possessions and move to the *Jeff Davis*. When asked why he remained on board, Garrick explained that just as he prepared to board the *Jeff Davis*, he heard someone say to "take that colored individual back." Garrick returned and remained on board the *Enchantress* for sixteen days until its recapture by the *Albatross*.

On that fateful day the *Enchantress* prize crew sighted the Union warship coming toward them. One of the crew members instructed Garrick to go forward, and if the *Albatross* crew called his name, he should respond and put the Union ship at ease. Garrick insisted on remaining in the galley from where he watched the approach of the *Albatross* through the galley door. He heard Smith instruct each member of his crew to take the identity of a member of the real *Enchantress* crew in the event the *Albatross* passed close enough to converse. The prize crew lacked one man of the full crew's complement, and Garrick heard Smith tell his men to say that their missing shipmate had washed overboard while at sea.

When the Union ship drew near, it raised the American flag, and Smith ordered the crew of the *Enchantress* to do likewise. Garrick testified that the captured vessel flew the American flag from the time the *Jeff Davis* seized her until her recapture. When the Union ship came within speaking distance, Garrick moved up on deck, jumped overboard, and began yelling that the Confederate ship *Jeff Davis* had control of the ship. Within minutes William Smith's brief career as a prize captain came to an end.

The defense briefly cross-examined Garrick, but neither Wharton nor Harrison accomplished much. In response to questions from both, Garrick testified he did not know the name of the *Jeff Davis* captain and did not see William Smith again after he disappeared below the deck of the *Albatross*. At the time the cross-examination seemed irrelevant to the proceedings. But the defense questioned the Philadelphia court's jurisdiction, and attempts to trace Smith's route north after his capture served to establish that he could not properly be tried in Philadelphia because the act in question had not been committed there, nor had Smith been initially held in Philadelphia. Wharton and Harrison wanted the defendants tried in Virginia or with the crew of the *Savannah* in New York. The *Enchantress* lay at Hampton Roads, Virginia, for almost a week before being towed to Philadelphia. Although the prize might be properly adjudicated in Philadelphia, the defense argued, Smith and his crew could not.

After Garrick testified, the court adjourned for the day. Garrick's testimony should have been irrelevant. The previous three witnesses established the character of the ship, the nature and value of its cargo, and the circumstances surrounding its seizure by the *Jeff Davis*. But Garrick's story depicted a Confederate crew acting not like sailors, but like pirates. Efforts to conceal the true identity of the prize crew and flying the American flag did not comport with men acting as Confederate sailors. Garrick's testimony painted Smith and his cohorts as something other than combatants. Garrick journeyed to Charleston not as a free man of color and a ship's cook, but as property, destined for sale. Already tainted as "rebels," Smith and his men looked more like simple thieves out for money, rather than acting in the service of a nation, and willing to profit from the evil institution that many people believed lay at the heart of the rebellion.

On the morning of the twenty-third, the prosecution resumed its case. John C. Fifield, the captain of the *John Welsh*, an earlier victim of the *Jeff Davis*, took the stand. On board the *Jeff Davis* as a prisoner when it took the *Enchantress*, Fifield identified Smith as a *Jeff Davis* crewman and the *Enchantress*'s prize master. Fifield supported Page's testimony as to the weapons on board the Confederate privateer and its use of the French flag to draw near its prey. He also testified that the *Jeff Davis* used hemp sails. American vessels used cotton; hemp made the Confederate ship appear "foreign," adding to the deception of flying a foreign flag. The guns remained covered until the merchant ship came within close range. The crew wore no distinctive uniforms, suggesting the Confederates had no military affiliation, and masqueraded as a civilian vessel solely to plunder. Fifield recounted the *Jeff Davis*'s seizure of his ship, going into detail about how the privateer fired a live round at the *John Welsh*. Finally Judge Grier questioned whether Ashton had gone beyond the scope of the trial, and Harrison objected, asking the court whether Smith stood accused of seizing the *John Welsh*. Ashton stopped and passed the witness.

Wharton questioned Fifield about the officers on board the *Jeff Davis*, including Captain Coxetter. Fifield admitted the *Jeff Davis* had a clear command structure, including a surgeon, just like any other warship. Fifield clearly remembered a captain of marines and testified to the exchange of papers between Coxetter and Smith. Wharton suggested that Fifield saw the *Jeff Davis* letters of marque. Fifield admitted that during his captivity he ate well and moved with almost complete liberty around the ship. Harrison cross-examined Fifield for less than a minute, establishing that the *Jeff Davis* never fired at the *Enchantress*.

The prosecution called U.S. Deputy Marshal Thomas B. Patterson, who confirmed Smith's arrest warrant and described how Smith and his crew came to Philadelphia. On cross-examination Wharton asked to see Smith's "papers," still trying to get the original letters of marque, but Patterson knew nothing of any documents. Wharton also asked for the affidavit that supported Smith's arrest, but again Patterson had neither a copy of the warrant nor the supporting affidavit. Although the effort was a long shot, the warrant, if defective, could be thrown out, but Patterson could not help.

Although far from spectacular, the prosecution established all the elements necessary to convict Smith and his crew of statutory piracy: a robbery on the high seas against a U.S. registered vessel, with the requisite intent both as to the seizure of the *Enchantress* and Smith's actions as her prize master. Although both sides debated whether the seizure was violent or humane and whether the perpetrators seemed to be military men, legally Ashton's case satisfied the statutory requirements.

The defense struggled to establish the existence of letters of marque and, without them, used circumstantial evidence to prove that the seizure of the *Enchantress* was an act of war. But Jacob Garrick's testimony depicted the *Jeff Davis*, Smith, and his prize crew as men trying to deceive the Union rather than openly fighting the Confederacy's war on the high seas. Even worse, Smith willfully took a free man back to Charleston for sale as a slave. Somehow that fact alone undermined the argument that this had been an act of war rather than one of piracy and profit. This distinction became particularly important as the defense put on its case, a case premised on Smith's status as a citizen in a place where the U.S. laws and courts did not operate, as a man who owed an allegiance to the only government that existed, making his actions those of war and not piracy.

———

John O'Neill had remained silent for the entire trial thus far. On the afternoon of October 23, 1861, his silence ended as he stood up and gave the defense's opening statement. Mindful that the statutes made no exception for acting under the authority of another nation, O'Neill and his co-counsel nevertheless relied on the Confederate letters of marque as the foundation of their case. Smith stood accused of committing robbery on the high seas. O'Neill argued that robbery required a "guilty intent, that disposition for theft which is the very heart of this indictment, and in the absence of which he must be acquitted." Smith had no intention of "stealing" anything, but rather was obeying the orders of the only duly constituted government existing in Georgia, South Carolina, and the other nine Confederate states. O'Neill argued that the present state of political affairs in the South, although "unfortunate and . . . deeply wrong," must be Smith's "shield and protection" no matter how much the members of the jury deplored the rebellion. Although O'Neill shared the jury's contempt for the "Southern Confederacy," it nevertheless existed. The Confederacy had a government, and that government issued letters of marque. Smith acted in compliance with those letters, and for that reason alone he found himself on trial for his life.

Smith's defense rested firmly on the question of "what was the Confederacy." O'Neill's opening statement claimed that in addition to any legal status under international law, the Confederacy had a practical existence that could not be ignored. Contrary to what the U.S. Supreme Court said years after the war with the rebellion crushed, the laws and courts of the United States did not operate in the South in 1861. William Smith lived under a government that passed its own laws, and as the sequestration cases had demonstrated just a week before, it had the power to interpret and enforce those laws. Confederate citizens could not look to the U.S. government for protection, and for a people whose homes, families, businesses, and livelihoods had been and continued to be in the South, noncompliance with Confederate law carried severe consequences. The defense offered Smith's entire life as evidence to repudiate any notion that he acted as a pirate when he helped seize the *Enchantress*.

O'Neill did not discuss the sequestration cases, in part because given the state of news reporting, the outcome did not reach Northern newspapers for several days. However, his colleagues made reference to sequestration laws as proof of the Confederacy's power over persons within its borders. But, before offering proof of its laws, the defense had to establish the Confederacy's "factual" existence. This seemingly obvious fact proved the first obstacle to Smith's successful defense, an impediment that for very practical reasons the defense never completely overcame.

Legal trials present an interesting contradiction. It is often irrelevant what everyone knows; it only matters what is proved in court. Every person in the courtroom on that October afternoon knew that eleven Southern states seceded, that they formed a government and adopted a constitution, and that the government created under that constitution raised an army that for the time being successfully waged war against the U.S. Army. However, try as he might, Nathaniel Harrison could not secure original copies of the Southern secession ordinances, the Confederate Constitution, or the letters of marque issued to Coxetter and the *Jeff Davis*. Harrison explained to the court that without postal communication, the defense had no way to obtain certified copies of any Confederate documents.

As a result, the evidence it offered came from Moore's *Rebellion Record*, a three-volume collection published in New York City that contained copies of the secession ordinances, the Confederate Constitution, and other documents. Harrison offered the books not as proof of the "authority of the Southern Confederacy" but to show the conditions that existed when the defendant committed the acts for which he was now on trial. In other words, he offered the books to show that a government in fact existed and was administering justice and regulating those persons within its jurisdiction. Grier considered the request and then asked the government if it objected. Ashton replied, "Yes sir, we object." When Grier asked why, Ashton said there was no evidence that the copies in the book were correct copies, and, furthermore, whether the copies were correct or not, admitting them did not change the outcome of the case because their existence did not excuse Smith's crime.

In modern jargon Ashton questioned the authenticity of the documents and raised the "best evidence rule." The best evidence to prove the content of a writing is the original document. Modern codified rules of evidence soften the requirement of an original by allowing a duplicate unless some question exists as to the authenticity of the original document, in which case the duplicate is of no use. Judge Grier moved past the originality requirement and addressed Ashton's claim that the documents, even if authentic, did not provide a legal justification for piracy.

Grier worried that Ashton wanted the court to "decide what may be the grave question of the cause on a mere point of the admission of testimony." Grier moved to admit the documents in the book, but Ashton pressed him, citing the *Hutchings* case (1817), a U.S. Circuit Court decision out of the Richmond, Virginia, circuit, where Chief Justice John Marshall held that in a trial for piracy, a commission as a privateer from a government unrecognized by the United States could not be evidence of a valid commission and therefore could not justify piratical acts. Grier ignored *Hutchings*, telling Ashton he never excluded evidence of a defense even if later the evidence did not support the defense. Although Ashton may have been correct, Grier refused to decide a case of such importance by striking Smith's only defense.

The court admitted into evidence the documents in Moore's *Rebellion Record*, but excluded any comment or opinion by the author as to the legal effect of the documents either in the United States or in the opinions held by foreign governments. In addition to the secession ordinances and various proclamations of Jefferson Davis concerning letters of marque, Mr. Harrison offered proof of the Confederacy's legal authority within the eleven states it controlled. Part of that proof came in the form of Confederate militia laws calling for men to enlist and the Sequestration Act and Confiscation Act that seized alien enemy property.

With their documents in evidence, the defense began its case by calling Edward Rochford, an Englishman and a member of Smith's prize crew. Rochford testified about Smith's life in Georgia prior to the war. The prosecution objected to the testimony as irrelevant background, but Grier disagreed. The defense then asked Rochford about Georgia's militia laws that required young men to serve in the army or navy. The militia law proved that once war broke out, men such as Smith had to serve or face the consequences. Thus, even if no one forced Smith on board the *Jeff Davis* at gunpoint, the war compelled Confederate citizens to render military service. To avoid service Smith either had to leave his home and property and abandon his wife and child or move his entire family. This dilemma created a type of duress or compulsion that made Smith's military enlistment involuntary. The prosecution vehemently objected to the entire theory.

Having allowed the defense's unusual offer of documentary evidence, the court drew the line. Rochford had no legal expertise and could not testify on the legal effect of a Georgia militia law. Second, the court balked at the duress argument. The "compulsion" Smith acted under came from public opinion and the fervor of the times, in effect a sort of community pressure. Judge Grier hesitated and asked Wharton directly, "If there is a great insurrection, on this theory may not every fellow say, 'I had to go with them; there was so much violence and excitement, that I was forced to act with them,' and thus may not the whole hundred or hundred thousand escape?" Wharton argued this was the only way to deal with communities and the concerted action they compel on the part of their members. But neither Grier nor Cadwalader accepted this notion of compulsion as rising to the level of a legal duress defense.

Wharton briefly addressed jurisdiction, claiming Smith and his companions came to Philadelphia from another jurisdiction and should be tried there. The court listened but did not seem impressed, and Wharton quickly returned to the heart of his defense. He questioned Rochford as to whether the U.S. courts operated in Georgia. Again the prosecution objected, but Grier overruled the objection because everyone knew the U.S. courts no longer operated in the South. Rochford then testified as to Smith's reputation as a peaceful man and respected member of his community, and Wharton passed him to Ashton.

Sensing the court's resistance to the defense's community compulsion argument, Ashton focused his cross-examination of Rochford on the existence of any real duress. No one "confined" Smith on board the *Jeff Davis* before it sailed, although he needed the captain's permission to go ashore. Rochford conceded that the *Jeff Davis* crew expected to receive a share of any prizes it seized and that Smith, as an officer, would receive a larger share. Then Ashton tried to show that Smith had acted out of his own free will, but his inexperience surfaced yet again. He pressed Rochford to admit that Smith voluntarily traveled from Savannah, where he enlisted, to Charleston, where he joined the *Jeff Davis*. "No sir," answered Rochford. "I will not say that. He did not go voluntarily. The laws of the Southern states—" Ashton cut him off. "Never mind about the laws," he said. But Ashton had opened the door, and despite attempts to withdraw the question, Judge Cadwalader allowed Rochford to answer, and Grier agreed, instructing Rochford to give the complete answer as to why he believed Smith was compelled to go. "I say every man was compelled to join the army or navy; and he [Smith] being acquainted with the sea life, like every seafaring man, thought it better to go into the navy than the army."

Despite Ashton's error, no one forced Smith into the Confederate military. The Confederacy did not draft until the spring of 1862, and any "duress" Smith experienced would have come from either a state militia law or a sense of community pressure. Neither source compelled him to join the *Jeff Davis*. Confederate enlistment records show that not everyone immediately responded to the call. In fact, James Chestnut of South Carolina claimed that by early 1862, about half of South Carolina's eligible male population refused to volunteer. Judge Grier kept looking for some form of real duress, and finally, exasperated by Rochford's continued reliance on the "laws of the Southern States," he gave up, saying, "Oh! Never mind!" The defense called one more member of Smith's crew, Daniel Mulliner, to testify as to Smith's competence as a pilot and his reputation in the community as being peaceful. The prosecution did not cross-examine him, and with that the defense rested. With no rebuttal testimony offered, the court adjourned for the day to allow both sides to prepare closing arguments.

The presentation of the evidence took but two days, with the defense witnesses requiring barely half a day. The case came down to the legal arguments. The prosecution established the essential elements of piracy; the defense's entire case depended on the documentary evidence and historical facts that showed the Confederacy possessed a legal substance sufficient to protect those who committed acts of violence against the United States while serving in the Confederate military.

The trial demonstrated the difficulty of constructing a legal defense dependent on the testimony of persons who could not attend because they were part of the rebellion. However, the defense missed some key opportunities to put on available testimony to support its case. Union military officials could have testified, albeit unwillingly, about the Union prisoner exchange policy. Although privateers at sea fell into an admittedly gray area, the exchange of land prisoners supported an argument that seafaring prisoners deserved the same treatment.

Union naval officers and officials could have also testified about the blockade, as could Smith, Rochford, or any of the other prisoners captured by a Union ship performing blockade duty. Under international law, nations could only blockade other nations, or entities with some status under international law. Using live testimony, or even Northern newspaper accounts, the defense could have established that the Union had blockaded "something" and could not simultaneously blockade the Confederacy's ports and coastline and deny its legal existence. The defense raised this contradiction during closing arguments, but Union officials forced to admit the contradiction in front of the jury could have made a stronger impression.

George Earle had been sitting quietly for the entire trial. His moment finally came as he rose and presented the government's closing argument on the morning of the twenty-fourth. Earle reminded the jury that Smith's trial occurred within the context of a rebellion in which Smith took an active part. Despite the rebellion, Smith received a fair trial and presented the best defense possible. Having done so, Smith could not escape the simple and undisputed facts. Earle suggested that the court could render an opinion just on the basis of facts as presented and bypass the jury. In effect, that is what happened.

Earle argued that although born in South Carolina and a resident of Georgia, Smith remained a citizen of the United States and could never divest himself of his allegiance to that nation. He traveled voluntarily from Savannah, Georgia, to Charleston, South Carolina, and became a crew member of the *Jeff Davis*. He accepted the risks of capture and its attendant consequences in exchange for monetary profit. He had no one to blame but himself for his predicament, and his actions knew but one definition: piracy. Most civilized nations denounced privateering, and even the United States recently consented to its abolition. Earle neglected to tell the jury that the United States refused to join other nations in 1856 in abolishing the practice and that its recent willingness to do so stemmed from the Confederacy's intent to invoke the practice.

Legality aside, Smith's privateering defense depended on a commission from a government in rebellion purporting to authorize him to plunder the ships of his own nation, the United States. Although U.S. citizenship did not have a legal definition until 1868, and it remained unclear in 1861 whether one could voluntarily relinquish it during peacetime, international law did not allow a person to take up arms against his country as part of an internal rebellion and claim to no longer be a citizen. Earle made certain the jury understood that Smith made war on his own country.

Earle then took the jury through the voyage of the *Jeff Davis* and its capture of the *Enchantress*. He cited the U.S. Supreme Court cases of *United States v. The Brig Malek Adhel* (1844) and *United States v. Tully* (C.C. Mass 1812) for the proposition that the statutes

Smith stood accused of violating defined robbing and stealing as "piratical aggressions" and that the intent to plunder is inferred from the acts themselves and did not require "personal violence." Earle all but eliminated any notion that the bloodless seizure of the *Enchantress* made it any less a piratical act. The crew of the *Enchantress* made the seizure bloodless because once the members realized their plight they did not resist.

The most damning portion of Earle's closing argument came with his presentation of Smith's role in taking Jacob Garrick to Charleston. Earle insisted Smith acted free of any duress when he told his crew that "we will take him to Charleston, where he will bring $1500." Everyone knew Garrick was a free man of color, and unlike the 1850 Fugitive Slave Act that required the return of runaway slaves, Smith took a free man to Charleston intending to enslave him. Garrick could have stayed on board the *Jeff Davis* and returned with the other prisoners. But Smith willfully took him to Charleston, violating the laws of South Carolina, Georgia, and the United States by enslaving a free man. In doing so Smith committed "an offense without feeling, because to tear a man from his home and enslave him forever, against the usages of warfare, stamps this transaction just in the light I wish you to look at it . . . a piratical, outrageous aggression, without any of the colors or forms of law." Earle argued that Smith acted as a slave trader and deserved no protection.

Earle offered other examples of men acting under the color of authority. He discussed *United States v. Klintock*, where the defendant, accused of piracy, claimed to have acted under a commission from a General Aury. Aury claimed to be a brigadier of the Republic of Mexico and a generalissimo of Florida and granted the defendant a commission to seize ships after the United States took possession of Florida from Spain. Justice Marshall held that Aury had no power to issue a commission, and the defendant's good-faith reliance on that commission did not excuse him of piracy. Earle argued that if the "good faith" argument failed in that case, how could the United States possibly cloak Smith's actions with any legal protection when he claimed to act in "good faith" on a commission from an entity "which aimed a blow at the very existence of our government, and which aims a blow at the very existence of this court?"

Only the U.S. government could issue a valid letter of marque, and Earle argued the Southern rebellion changed nothing. In *Rose v. Himley* (1808), the Supreme Court held that until other nations recognized the rebel government of Santa Domingo or France relinquished her colony, the sovereign power of France over Santa Domingo subsisted. Earle insisted the real issue in the case did not involve Smith's fate, but rather how a rebellion is to be defined. "In the case now before you the point [formal recognition] rises to the dignity of the national existence, and the question involves the recognition of the right of a portion of the country to revolt and destroy the government." Earle asked the jury to do its duty and said that "while you mete out justice to the prisoner under the charge of the court, you will also reflect that the interests of the community are in your hands, that the interests of the government are in your hands."

Nathaniel Harrison began the defense's closing argument, and George Wharton concluded. Together they gave an exhaustive summation, arguing points to the court and jury that they had been unable to present during the evidentiary portion of the trial. Before beginning his oral argument, Harrison handed the court a written list of the five points he intended to cover:

1. The Confederate States of America was a government, either in fact or in law, with authority to issue letters of marque. The defendant acted under those letters and was a privateer, not a pirate.

2. At the time of the alleged offense the Confederacy physically controlled and occupied the territory where the defendant lived, and he did not commit treason against the United States by rendering allegiance to that government.

3. At the time of the alleged offense the U.S. courts were suspended or closed in the Southern Confederacy, unable to administer justice or enforce U.S. law. Unable to protect him, the defendant became absolved from his allegiance to the United States.

4. At the time of the alleged offense the defendant was unable to obtain either civil or military protection from the United States, and at the same time he was compelled by the circum-

stances to take up arms for the Confederacy or to leave the country. Had he chosen to leave, his property would have been subject to sequestration and confiscation. As such, the situation amounted to legal duress sufficient to justify an acquittal in this proceeding.

5. The court had no jurisdiction because the defendant was apprehended on the high seas and first brought to another district where jurisdiction attached.

Harrison told the jury that he faced more than just the skill and ability of the prosecution counsel. In addition, he said, he contended with "the excited condition of the public mind, and in the popular prejudice and prejudgment, which, in surrounding the questions now before you, may be said to surround even the prisoners themselves." He added that he had no right to complain; given the times no man could divest himself completely of prejudice. However, he only hoped the jury felt an "honest prejudice" and not one that "usurp[ed] the place of reason, and turn[ed] a deaf ear to fact as well as argument, [so] that the trial becomes a farce, and that the jurors simply meet . . . to render a foregone conclusion." He meant no offense to any member of the jury, but asked that if he offended them, they allow him the same latitude of uninterrupted discussion as they afforded Mr. Earle.

Harrison laid before the jury all of the documentary evidence chronicling secession and the creation of the Confederate government. Once formed, the Confederate government acted. The Confederate Congress convened and adjourned twice, raising an army and putting a navy on the seas. It financed and supplied its military, and that military successfully conducted war consistent with the rules of civilized nations. The Confederacy's president issued letters of marque, and the defendant, Smith, acted under those letters notwithstanding the claim by the United States that those letters afford him no protection from the charge of piracy.

Harrison repeated the definition of a pirate at common law, one at war with all nations. Although Smith had not been charged with common-law piracy, Harrison argued that the same intent necessary for piracy under common law attached to piracy under the statute and that Smith had no intention of robbing anyone. More important, the piracy statute did not abolish privateering. The United States had the opportunity to do so in 1856 and declined. Could the United States refuse to recognize English or French letters of marque? No, Harrison said, and argued it had to honor the Confederacy's commission. Harrison reemphasized the Confederacy's de facto existence and argued that no matter how wrongful the government might be, an established government had the right to commission privateers.

Harrison continued, saying that even if the United States refused to acknowledge the right of secession, not even Daniel Webster during the nullification debates denied the "right of revolution." Did not the United States begin in this very way? During the American Revolution American privateers preyed at will on British shipping. One of America's greatest naval heroes, John Paul Jones, was a privateer. "Was his commission any less valid than the one Smith sailed under because we admit the right of our own revolution, yet deny the right of the South to do likewise?"

Pointing to something not in evidence, Harrison remarked on a recent prisoner exchange. How could the United States treat Southern soldiers as prisoners and yet ask the jury to condemn these men as pirates? Other nations recognized the Confederacy as a belligerent and dealt with its government. Great Britain's Lord Russell declared the Confederacy a belligerent on the floor of Parliament. The British admiralty refused to distinguish between Confederate privateers and sailors on board U.S. men-of-war. The French government allowed Confederate privateers to remain unmolested in its ports for up to twenty-four hours. From an evidentiary standpoint this argument had no support, even though it was commonly known and acknowledged by both sides. Harrison's next point also lacked an evidentiary foundation, but he took advantage of one of Judge Cadwalader's own opinions to highlight the inherent contradiction in the Union position of on the one hand blockading the South and on the other trying Smith as a pirate.

Whereas Justice Grier's duties involved him almost exclusively in appellate matters, Cadwalader sat as a federal district judge in Philadelphia. Although he had been on the bench only three years when the *Jeff Davis* came to trial, the nature of his experience rather than the duration of his tenure on the bench made Cadwalader an important part of the case. Under the Judiciary Act of 1789 Congress gave exclusive jurisdiction of admiralty cases to the federal district courts and excluded them from jury trial. The act also gave each federal court the power to establish its own rules for disposing of prize cases. Therefore, from the time the Union blockade went into effect, Cadwalader presided over prize cases, cases in which the district attorney, George Coffey, represented the interests of the United States. These cases not only gave Cadwalader a familiarity with the district attorney's office but also exposed him to the very legal issues that became such a prominent part of the piracy cases.

Legitimizing a captured ship as a prize required affirming the legality of the blockade. That question in turn forced the judge to address the legal status of the Confederacy. Although Cadwalader tried to avoid the issue in the prize court, the Confederacy's belligerent status became almost a prerequisite to condemning its ships as prizes of war and validating the blockade. Cadwalader's court records showed that in most cases he condemned ships as being "enemy property" without defining the "enemy." However, presiding over the trial of Smith and his crew, Cadwalader now had to address the "enemy." But affording the Confederacy belligerent status might legitimize Smith's conduct as an act of war under international law and provide the Confederacy with a status somewhere between rebellion and official recognition. Such a status went beyond what the federal government wished to convey early in the war and ran against the current of public opinion that wanted these men convicted as pirates and traitors.

Harrison now offered a decision rendered by Judge Cadwalader in the *General Parkhill* case. On May 18, 1861, USS *Niagara* seized the *General Parkhill* as it attempted to run the Union blockade. The Charleston firm of Peterson and Stock contested the prize proceeding. Cadwalader upheld the Union captain's claim to the prize. He ruled that as residents of the Southern Confederacy, the firm and its members, whether personally loyal or disloyal, were an entity in a state of hostility against the government and thus forfeited all claim to national citizenship and with it the right to any proprietary status in a U.S. prize court. Harrison argued that Cadwalader's *General Parkhill* decision had conveyed belligerent status on the Confederacy.

The defense raised a strong point. The language in Cadwalader's *General Parkhill* opinion flew directly in the face of George Earle's contention that William Smith remained a U.S. citizen. Harrison contended that although ignorance of the law was seldom an excuse, in cases of a clear difference of opinion, a diversity of opinions on the law, or, as in this case, an absence of any law governing this situation, ignorance, or at least confusion, provided a legal justification. At a minimum, Cadwalader's *Parkhill* opinion created legitimate confusion as to the Confederacy's status.

Harrison took the jury through a detailed discussion of secession and revolution. Drawing on the writings of Puffendorf and Thomas Paine, Harrison argued that "government was more the result of accident than of art." William Rawle, a Pennsylvanian and a federal district attorney under Washington, wrote a treatise on the Constitution, stating that if the people hold the power and choose to secede, then they sever the ligament of the Union. Beginning with the American Revolution, New Hampshire's initial resistance to the Constitution, and the efforts of Virginia, Kentucky, and later South Carolina to nullify federal law, Harrison contended that the entire history of the United States up to that point provided "a practical exhibit of secession, nullification, or revolution at some time and in some shape or the other."

Whether right or wrong, Harrison argued that the legal status of a seceding group or entity had never been resolved. He referenced a letter from a Judge Sharswood, a Philadelphia judge and legal scholar, to a Mr. E. Spencer Miller dated October 4, 1860, wherein Sharswood conceded that the doctrine of secession remained an open question. Even Abraham Lincoln's 1848 speech on the floor of Congress conceded secession as a right: "Any people, anywhere, being inclined and having the power, have the right to rise up and shake off the existing government, and form a new one that suits them better. This is a most valuable and sacred right—a right which we hope and believe, is to liberate the world."

By this point both the court and the jury questioned Harrison's loyalties. He must have sensed the rising level of discomfort because he reiterated his disapproval of secession, saying his exhaustive list of authority simply demonstrated that learned men could and did disagree. That being the case, how could the government convict a man of treason and piracy under circumstances where the legal status of the government he acted under remained so unclear?

Harrison then offered both legal and historical authority suggesting that the nature of the hostilities, as being organized revolution rather than unorganized insurrection, gave the Confederacy a legal status. That legal status in turn justified Smith's conduct and precluded convicting him as a pirate. Reaching back to the America Revolution, Harrison cited Sir Edmund Burke's speech in Parliament on March 22, 1775. On the eve of the American Revolution Burke stated that there was "a wide difference in reason and policy, between the mode of proceeding on the irregular conduct of scattered individuals, or even bands of men who disturb order in the state, and the civil dissensions which may from time to time, on great questions, agitate the several communities which compose a great empire." Burke conceded that as to the American colonists, "I do not know the method of drawing up an indictment against a whole people." Furthermore, "I cannot insult and ridicule the feelings of millions of my fellow creatures." Harrison then argued that if all of America was not indictable for its revolution and attempt to sever its bonds with Britain, how could the Confederacy be indicted, and, more important, how could one man acting in the military of that revolutionary government be indicted?

Returning to Cadwalader's opinion in the *General Parkhill* case, Harrison offered the judge's own words that if a conflict became a civil war, as distinguished from merely an unorganized insurrection, "such other governments may lawfully treat the revolted insurgents, not as mere pirates, but as entitled, in the war to the same immunities as ordinary belligerents in a foreign war." Harrison argued that Cadwalader took the same position as Burke. During an ongoing revolution, the only difference between rebel and patriot could not be the success of the rebellion. Harrison was forced to add Cadwalader's limitation that "the right to revolutionize could not be considered here [in *Parkhill*] until the power to revolutionize had been established." But Harrison argued that Cadwalader's distinction had nothing to do with the "effect" of a revolution, and even if it did, the Southern Confederacy had more than demonstrated the power to revolutionize. To his argument he added the weight of several scholars on international law, including Emmerich de Vattel, who distinguished between unorganized insurrection and organized revolution as the guide for determining the treatment of combatants.

Harrison gathered momentum, making direct reference to the surrender of Fort Hatteras and the newspaper accounts of the surrender terms, which included treating the defenders as prisoners of war. If prisoners on land, why not at sea? he asked. Why had no Southern land prisoner been punished as a traitor? He admitted that beyond the newspaper accounts he had no evidence. He had tried to get official U.S. documents concerning Confederate prisoners of war, but the government refused.

But even without official documents Harrison had a compelling argument. Everyone, North and South, followed the war in the newspapers and knew that a prisoner-of-war exchange policy existed. If all rebels committed treason, how could the Union exchange men who actively killed U.S. soldiers and yet threaten to hang men who at least in this case had never fired on a Union warship? Ideally, Harrison would have liked to point to the exchange of Confederate sailors as part of the program, but in 1861 the privateers were the Confederate Navy. CSS *Alabama* and CSS *Florida* had yet to embark on their infamous careers that devastated the Union merchant marine, and the ironclad naval wars on Southern rivers did not begin in earnest until 1862. But treating men on land differently from those at sea made no sense, and Harrison hammered away at the contradiction.

According to Harrison, Smith acted under duress. In the absence of any U.S. authority in the South, and the ability the Confederate government demonstrated to enforce its own laws, Smith had little choice but to show his allegiance and render support when the government called on him. Harrison cited Hugo Grotius, the renowned international law scholar, for the proposition that all consent requires three things: a physical power, a moral power, and a serious and free use of both. Harrison contended that events in the Southern Confederacy inhibited both Smith's physical and moral power to consent.

The summation came to a close as Harrison argued that the case properly belonged in the Eastern District of Virginia where the Union took Smith prior to his removal to Philadelphia. Finally, turning to Mr. Earle, he chastised him for trying to blame the conflict on the South and to use that blame to prejudice the jury against Smith. Ultraists and extremists on both sides brought the war, and the jury did not have to assign blame to resolve the issues in this case. If they had any doubt as to Smith's guilt, they must acquit. "The law requires no sacrifice, it demands no victim at your hands. It would rather that ninety-nine guilty persons should escape from punishment than that one innocent man should be made to suffer."

George Wharton then stood to give his summation. Harrison's "full and exhaustive" closing almost made it unnecessary that he consume any more of the jury's time. But, Wharton added, he owed a duty to Smith, who until three days ago was a total stranger, and he had to discharge that duty to the fullest.

Wharton covered little in the way of new ground. He spent considerable time arguing that the federal piracy statutes did nothing more than make common-law piracy a federal offense. Therefore, if not a pirate at common law, Smith could not be deemed a pirate under the statutes. Wharton insisted, as Harrison had, that Smith did not fit within the definition. He did not make war on all nations, and he lacked any of the intent necessary to make him a pirate. Wharton reiterated the uniqueness of the case and the inadequacy of prior judicial decisions to construe a situation involving a civil war.

In an effort to personalize Smith, Wharton retraced his life up to the time he went on board the *Jeff Davis*. He painted the picture of a simple, honest man caught up in events far beyond his control. His civilian skills as a pilot placed him in the venue where he was best able to serve, and he went aboard the Confederate privateer as a sailor in service of the only government in existence in the South. Wharton asked the jury to put themselves in Smith's position and to ask themselves whether any of them could simply have abandoned home and state as the prosecution suggested Smith should have done.

Turning to the subject of the *Jeff Davis*, Wharton described the vessel as a military one, complete with a crew, each holding specific military rank. Referring to the proclamations issued by Jefferson Davis, Wharton argued that Confederate privateers sailed under specific instructions that required them to at all times comport themselves in a manner consistent with international law. As a member of the *Jeff Davis*, Smith had done so. In 1856 the United States refused to join other nations in condemning privateering, and in the war so far, the major European powers had not condemned the South's use of the practice, even if they did not allow prizes to be taken in their ports.

Wharton suggested that Earle's use of certain authorities on international law had the taint of personal bias. Earle's suggestion that privateers deserved "any invective you might choose to hurl at them" grew out of his personal opinion as a peace advocate. His source for that statement was Jonathan Dymond, a Quaker whose treatise, *An Enquiry into the Accordancy of War with the Principles of Christianity*, condemned privateering because he found war itself inconsistent with Christian beliefs. Although that point of view might reflect the religious sentiments of one group, Wharton said, it did not represent the state of international law. Wharton cautioned the jury not to confuse the two positions, and to reinforce his point he briefly traced the history of American privateering through 1813.

Wharton concluded with perhaps the defense's strongest point: how could a Confederate soldier be one thing on land and another at sea? "Ask yourself a plain question," he said. "What is the difference between fighting the United States on the ocean and fighting the United States on the land?" If we take the course suggested by the government, "then erect a line of gallows from Philadelphia to the Potomac." But, Wharton cautioned, "be prepared to see ten men executed in the South for every one we hang here." As much as the government denied the fact, the Confederacy established a de facto government, and the laws of the United States no longer operated there. Quoting from Vattel, Wharton explained that a sovereign never fails to label as rebels those persons openly resisting its authority. But, Wharton said, when the resistance involves so many, as it does in this case, compelling the sovereign to make war to enforce its authority, it must content itself with the title of "civil war," and accord combatants all the rights and privileges commonly associated with war between civilized nations. Although it might be politically inexpedient to admit belligerent status on Smith and his crew, justice demanded the United States do so.

The defense's closing argument took twice as long as its evidentiary case and contained much of the force and appeal lacking from its presentation of proof. The contradictions in Union policy could not be ignored, particularly in light of the language in some of the prizes cases. The big question remained as to how much of this legal argument the jury either heard or understood. Public prejudice ran high, and Smith's defense team conceded he committed the acts in question. The defense had the unenviable task of arguing in support of the legal effect of a rebellion that struck Northerners as wrong at a gut level.

Four months of editorial commentary in the North had only strengthened the sentiment against Smith, which in turn drew strength from the string of Union defeats that, although low in comparison to later years, had cost the lives of Northern soldiers. Could the jury separate its contempt for the rebellion from Smith's personal situation when the prosecution insisted Smith's acquittal might sanction the Confederacy's existence? Both Wharton and Harrison steered clear of as many emotional issues as possible, Jacob Garrick's seizure in particular. But the defense did not have the last word. William Kelley and the prosecution went last, and Kelley not only reminded the jury of Garrick's seizure but also reaffirmed what was at stake in the case.

Kelley denied that Smith acted under duress. He argued that Smith could have sent his wife and children north and then once in command of the *Enchantress* simply steered it north to safety. Citing British authority in *Foster's Crown Case* (1792), Kelley admitted that one was not a rebel if he acted under duress but that he had to take the first opportunity available to escape. He reminded the jury that Smith willingly tried to return Garrick to Charleston and sell an otherwise free man into slavery. Using the defense's evidence problems to his advantage, Kelley argued that there was no documentary proof of any letter of marque, only the testimony of men on trial for piracy and the argument of their counsel. Jefferson Davis's proclamation calling for privateers did not prove the *Jeff Davis* sailed under such a commission. Even if one assumed that the letter of marque did exist, Kelley argued, acknowledgment of its validity by the court and jury would put an end to the U.S. Constitution by legitimizing secession and in the process "render that which was to be perpetual, finite." If Harrison thought Earle's argument had been unduly emotional, it soon seemed tame in comparison to Kelley's.

Kelley painstakingly went through most of article 1, section 8 of the Constitution and then read from the portion of section 10 that sets forth the prohibitions against the states. States could not grant letters of marque, make treaties, or do anything else reserved to the U.S. government. To validate the letters of marque validated states' rights. Kelley was "amazed by the effrontery of the defense." They claimed to not be guilty of piracy because they were guilty of a higher crime, treason. It would be like "an apology for inflicting a blow on the king which consists of an earnest assurance that it was intended for the queen." Smith's defense was that he did not steal from Englishmen, Frenchmen, or Spaniards, only from Americans!

At this point Kelley abandoned any effort to address the case. He attacked Smith's claim to have injured no foreigner. Referring to the defendant and his "cruel and wicked rebellion," Kelley argued that "free, republican America is the promised land of oppressed millions toward which they journey when hope gilds their dreams" and that the U.S. Constitution was "the pillar of fire by night, and the cloud by day, to weary, oppressed, and longing multitudes." Smith's actions hurt these poor people by destroying the only real hope they had for fulfillment. Smith was not a pirate, Kelley stated facetiously, because he was at work "tearing apart the Constitution." Smith acted in support of a "mad ambition" to carve away a portion of the United States and tried to "obliterate the glorious memories and forever dispel the blessed hopes of the American people."

Kelley dismissed the defense argument that secession remained an open question. His summation degenerated into an emotional appeal to convict Smith in order to save the United States. He conceded that the recent prisoner-of-war exchanges seemed to admit of the Confederacy's existence, but denied that the U.S. government had sanctioned any exchange of prisoners. Although Kelley's argument had become an emotional appeal, it had not been ignored, at least not by the court. When Kelley touched on the issue as to whether the rebellion had reached a sufficient level that it demanded some form of legal recognition, Cadwalader interrupted in an apparent effort to guide Kelley to a particular point. Was there any legal or historical authority, Cadwalader asked, "to support the establishment of a revolutionary government which is organized under a contest, while the contest continues?" Grier then asked whether it ceased to be a rebellion in that case. Kelley understood the importance of the questions and in response made perhaps his most important legal point, that "neither the power nor the right of revolt against a government can be asserted in its own courts."

Kelley offered no authority, and Mr. Wharton finally asked where the argument was going. Perhaps smarting from Harrison's use of his *Parkhill* opinion, Cadwalader explained that he believed that a revolutionary government could be recognized only after it had been "established" for at least some period of peacetime and not while it "was engaged in the very contest that purported to determine its survival." Redirected by the court to the salient issue, Kelley drew on historical examples, claiming for instance that even though the United States recognized Texas's independence, a Texas letter of marque carried no weight in a Mexican court before Mexico gave up its military efforts to subdue the region. As he sat down, Kelley admonished the jury that its verdict might well inspire the enemies of the United States and to bear that in mind as they deliberated. Kelley had resorted to the same tactic Magrath used in South Carolina when he charged the grand jury. In this instance a "not guilty" verdict could be construed as giving comfort to the enemy and might encourage others to follow in Smith's footsteps. In 1861 patriotism in both the North and the South exacted a heavy price in the forfeiture of constitutional rights and the subordination of fundamental justice to national interest.

Kelley's closing brought the day to an end. What it lacked in legal substance it compensated for in its emotional appeal to the larger issues at stake. The trial went beyond Smith's guilt or innocence; it became a legal debate over the status of the Confederacy. The next day Judge Grier charged the jury. It did not take long, and Grier's instructions made the outcome almost a foregone conclusion. The elements of piracy required the following: First, there had to have been a robbery, defined as a felonious and violent taking of any money or goods from another with intent to do so. Second, there did not have to be actual violence, and the goods needed only to be in the legal possession of the owner, and not on his person. Finally, the acts had to be committed on the high seas. Having defined the elements of the crime, Grier then destroyed the defense's legal argument.

Grier instructed the jury that no rebellion designed to overthrow the government can be recognized as a legitimate government regardless of its size or power. Every government by the law of self-preservation has the right to suppress insurrection. The existence of a civil war is proof that the United States does not recognize the Confederacy. As such, this court, sitting under the authority of the United States and charged with executing its laws, can view those in rebellion only as traitors and anyone acting under any authority who seizes property on the high seas as pirates and robbers. Grier denied the right of secession and proclaimed the Constitution to be perpetual. "Judge the tree by its fruits," he said, "and we see the results of this miserable political heresy in the present situation of our country."

Grier refused to entertain the legal and academic debate as to when a civil war is entitled to some recognition. He also declined to give any instruction on the lack-of-jurisdiction argument. In Grier's opinion, "Of the main question of the guilt of the prisoner there is no dispute." Privateers had no legal right in a civil war to be treated in the same fashion as land prisoners in accord with the principles of war between nations. Exchanging prisoners as opposed to executing them remained a matter of government policy. Although privateering might be legal, commissions from a government in rebellion were not. Finally, any argument that the defendant acted under duress lost its validity when, as the prize master of the *Enchantress*, Smith chose to remain in the service of the Confederacy even after he ceased to be a subordinate and assumed control over his own fate.

The jury retired and within forty-five minutes returned a "guilty" verdict. On October 28, 1861, Harrison moved for a new trial and an arrest of judgment. On the same day three members of Smith's prize crew stood trial, including the two who testified on Smith's behalf, Edward Rochford and Daniel Mulliner. The trial lasted until five o'clock on the afternoon of the twenty-ninth, whereupon the jury found the men guilty. The one remaining member of the crew was acquitted after testimony that he steered the *Enchantress* south by day, but at night steered north, thus keeping the vessel at sea longer and bringing about its capture.

Smith and three members of his crew stood convicted of piracy. Grier's jury charge made that a certainty. No one disputed the facts.

However, over the course of four days the nation had been forced to evaluate the Confederacy, and although the court refused to accept many of the arguments, the presentation of those arguments articulated the legal contradictions in how the Union fought a civil war. Cadwalader found himself confronted with the language of his own prize case opinion that seemed to convey the very status the government did not want to give William Smith.

This case had been a jury trial in name only. The resolution of the legal issues made the jury's verdict a mere formality, much as Harrison had feared. Grier's acceptance of Kelley's statement that a government could not admit of a rebellion in its own courts ignored the fact that in determining the status of prizes and legitimizing the blockade, the U.S. courts had already done so. Although clearly not a pirate, Smith stood convicted as one because to do otherwise added weight to the growing fear in the North that the Confederacy might be something other than a rebellion. It just might be a nation.

The verdict in the trial of William Smith did not bode well for Baker, Harleston, and the rest of the *Savannah* crew on trial in New York. Their ordeal began on October 23, 1861, and continued for almost a week after the Philadelphia jury decided Smith's fate. But as so often happens, what seems to be a legal certainty becomes muddled with a different jury, in a different place, and in the hands of different attorneys and different judges. The United States was about to be reminded of this fact as the question of "what was the Confederacy" moved north to a federal courtroom in New York.

CHAPTER 8

"For God's Sake, Leave This to the Clash of Arms"

At the moment a jury in Philadelphia was deciding the fate of William Smith, the trial of Baker, Harleston, and the crew of the *Savannah* had barely reached its midpoint. The New York proceeding began on October 23, 1861, only a day after Smith's trial in Philadelphia had gotten under way. On the first two days the prosecution presented its case, and the court held an evidentiary hearing on the same issue Harrison had raised in Philadelphia: the court lacked jurisdiction because the defendants first came under arrest in the Eastern District of Virginia. Whereas the court in the *Jeff Davis* case all but ignored the jurisdiction issue, Justice Nelson and Judge Shipman allowed almost a half day of testimony and argument regarding how the defendants came to New York. Ultimately, the defense team for the *Savannah* proved no more successful than William Smith's lawyers.

When the government arrested Algernon Sullivan, the defense obtained the assistance of additional counsel, unsure if and when Sullivan would be released. By the time of trial, the twelve defendants had four other lawyers in addition to the three-man team that began the case at the arraignment stage. Jeremiah Larocque, Joseph Dukes, Isaac Davega, and Maurice Mayer joined the defense just prior to trial. However, if one believed the newspapers, the size and quality of the defense team made no difference. On the day of trial the *New York Times* reported, "It is difficult to see how the parties can escape conviction under this indictment. Their act, whatever it was, [was] done on the high seas. . . . That the taking of the *Joseph* and her cargo . . . was forcible and by violence, there can be no doubt, and this would seem all there is required for a conviction." As the case unfolded it seemed the prosecution believed its own press. The government proceeded as if the outcome was a foregone conclusion. The defense had other ideas.

The *Savannah* case took an interesting twist almost immediately. Before the case arose, Daniel Lord had formulated the *Savannah's* defense, and Brady and Larocque implemented Lord's theories by using the government's indictment to confine the issues in the case. The indictment serves as the guide or blueprint for what the prosecution seeks to prove. It also apprises the defense of the government's allegations. It must be detailed and clear, and the prosecution is bound by the allegations of its indictment. A comparison of the indictment in the *Savannah* case and that in the *Jeff Davis* case shows similar factual allegations; both alleged a violation against the "form of the statute of said United States." But in Philadelphia, in addition to the actions of the *Jeff Davis* in seizing the prize, the indictment detailed the seizure of the *Enchantress* by the *Albatross*, and as a result, during the course of the trial, the prosecution argued and presented evidence that the Confederates "resisted" the efforts of the U.S. government vessel and thus committed both treason and piracy.

In New York, the prosecution pled facts that brought the offenses under sections 8 and 9 of the 1790 act, and section 3 of the 1820 act, charging the defendants with piracy, but they did not allege treason. The defense argued that because the prosecution alleged only piracy, the only relevant facts went to the outfitting of the *Savannah* and its actions up to the time it seized its first and only prize, the *Joseph*. Any acts of aggression or violence thereafter, specifically regarding the battle with USS *Perry*, should be excluded. The indictment mentioned nothing after the seizure of the *Joseph*, and the defense team insisted all evidence had to stop at that point. The court agreed, and having established the limits of the prosecution's evidentiary case, the defense then stipulated that the *Savannah* sailed as a privateer under authority of the Confederate government and that it had seized the *Joseph* and its crew and cargo while acting in that capacity. Despite Mr. Evarts's best effort to show that the *Savannah* fired on and resisted capture by a U.S. vessel, the court refused to allow the evidence. In effect Brady and Larocque limited the prosecution's case and then took the emotion out of the proof by stipulating to the offense. By the second day of trial the prosecution rested, with most of its case consumed in an argument over jurisdiction.

The record does not address why the prosecution did not seek leave to file an amended indictment. Delafield Smith pressed for the earliest possible trial date and insisted that the outcome of the case was a foregone conclusion. Perhaps the prosecution feared that an amended indictment might provide grounds for a delay of the trial with a Northern public hungry for a conviction. It might also have demonstrated weakness and an admission that the defense had out-maneuvered the prosecution. For whatever reason, the prosecution chose to stand on its original indictment, and on the afternoon of the second day, the defense opened its case.

Jeremiah Larocque began by personalizing his clients. He portrayed them as men on trial for their lives, far from home, and confined without contact with loved ones for more than four months. They were twelve individuals caught up in a rebellion that the New York newspapers that very morning had described as "two great armies arrayed against one another across the country . . . numbering no less than seven hundred thousand." These men were certainly not pirates, and for the government to ask for convictions under either the 1790 or the 1820 statutes represented a "monstrous stretch."

Larocque told the jury that as this trial proceeded, Confederate sailors stood trial in Philadelphia on the same charges. Both proceedings became necessary because almost immediately after the war began, President Lincoln issued a proclamation threatening to treat privateers as pirates. Larocque characterized Lincoln's proclamation as one made in haste and argued that the U.S. government secretly wanted a verdict of acquittal, thereby disembarrassing it from the hasty pronouncement made at the beginning of the war that almost every day saw armies battling from Maryland to Missouri. Larocque believed that not even Union soldiers wanted these men tried as pirates.

District Attorney Smith's opening took a few minutes and consumed but five pages of the court record. The defense's opening ran for hours and consumed the remainder of the day. Larocque explained that lawyers became the alter egos of their clients, and in this case he and his colleagues had a duty to point to the history, laws, judicial precedents, and Constitution of the United States to show that the trial of these men did not comport with "our own" history and laws. Contrary to Smith's opening, which portrayed these proceedings as a matter of form, Larocque insisted that much was at stake and that a guilty verdict at a minimum meant the forfeiture of these men's lives. With that disclaimer, the defense argument proceeded through a painstaking process to address virtually every legal and factual allegation made by the prosecution.

Larocque argued that everyone knew the definition of piracy and that pirates do not create "prize crews," bringing ships back to the port of their own nation. The use of the American flag by the *Savannah* to trap the *Joseph* was nothing more than a naval trick. Reading from James Fenimore Cooper's *History of the Navy of the United States of America*, Larocque told how the British raised the American colors to lure USS *Constitution* into a trap during the War of 1812. Larocque's opening statement became an oral brief of both the law and the facts, citing case law and legal treatises for everything from the definition of piracy to common-law robbery. He pointed out that under one section of the statute, the guilty parties had to be U.S. citizens and that only four men were citizens. The remaining eight were from Europe and Asia and had never been naturalized. Insisting that, under the government's indictment, if a majority of the defendants could not be convicted, then none could, Larocque stated that two-thirds of the defendants did not even come under the statute.

Reading from the legislative history of the piracy statutes, Larocque argued that the entire purpose of the law was to prevent a person like King James II, who abdicated his crown, from going to some other physical location and authorizing men to seize the ships of a particular nation, in that case England. In such a situation the would-be sovereign issued commissions as a ruler without territory and without the power to protect the innocent or punish the guilty or in any way administer justice, and any commission he issued could not be considered as coming from an established government; but rather from one that, regardless of prior status, now acted outside the realm of civil society. That was simply not the case here. Just as the defense had done in Philadelphia, Larocque argued that one could not dismiss the Confederate government as a nullity. It had substance and controlled vast areas of the country where U.S. law did not operate and where the United States provided no protection.

Unlike in the *Jeff Davis* case, the defense in the *Savannah* case obtained copies of the letters of marque. When the prosecution framed its indictment, it had alleged, consistent with section 9 of the 1790 piracy act, that the defendants had acted under the pretense of authority from one Jefferson Davis, attempting to set up the charge that the defendants had acted under the authority of some foreign "prince" or individual. Using the de facto existence of the Confederate government as its basis, the defense attacked the charge, arguing that a government issued the commission, not a foreign prince or individual. Jefferson Davis signed the commission by virtue of the power invested in him under the Confederate Constitution, and the commission therefore fell outside of the conduct covered by the statute.

Larocque cited a wide range of international legal authority and U.S. Supreme Court decisions as to the allegiance owed to a de facto government by the citizens within its physical boundaries. Reading from Judge Cadwalader's opinion in the *Parkhill* case, he pointed out that in order to claim Confederate ships as prizes, the U.S. courts had been forced to recognize the Confederacy as a de facto government and a belligerent. At one point Mr. Evarts objected to Larocque arguing from documents and treatises not in evidence. Nelson overruled the objection, allowing Larocque to refer to the defense's anticipated evidence as part of his opening.

Larocque then addressed secession. In a sense he had no choice. The case before the court had come out of the secession of eleven states. Larocque couched the conflict in terms of a dispute between two sovereigns, both recognized by the U.S. Constitution. The federal government and the state governments in the South had reached a point of impasse. That impasse compelled the state sovereigns to form a compact to contest the dispute. Legally, this dispute placed citizens in the seceding states in a position of conflict between two sovereigns, both demanding their allegiance and loyalty under circumstances where only one, the state, and its creation, the Confederacy, had physical and legal possession of the territory in which they lived. Although the dispute might be unresolved, one could not deny the existence of the government in the South or that it controlled the allegiance and conduct of its citizens. The U.S. Constitution made no provision for such a dispute, and to punish individuals caught up in the controversy because they harkened to the call of the only government that existed where they lived was wrong.

Larocque insisted that the acts of the Confederacy passed after secession and the initiation of hostilities had the same validity as the acts of the colonial governments and Continental Congress in 1776. Regardless of Lincoln's statement in April 1861 calling the conflict a rebellion by Southern citizens, by July 1861 the United States recognized that a state of war existed. So, whether one termed it a civil war or a war between two competing sovereigns, both of which the U.S. Constitution recognized, the actions of the twelve men on trial could not be piracy. As he prepared to sit down, Larocque implored the jury, "For God's sake leave this to the clash of arms, and to regular and legitimate warfare, and do not expose us to the double hazard of meeting death on the field, and meeting an ignominious death if we are captured."

Before resting for the day the defense put into evidence some of its documentary proof, including Lincoln's proclamation raising troops and extending the blockade, as well as South Carolina's ordinance of secession. Delafield Smith told the court the prosecution intended to object on relevancy grounds but offered to wait until the defense tendered all of its evidence. As the court adjourned for the day, several things had become clear. First, Smith and Evarts's belief that the defense team posed a formidable opponent proved correct. The defense in the *Savannah* case came to trial much better prepared than its counterpart in Philadelphia. Second, because the defense came better prepared, the jury in New York saw a different case than that put on in Philadelphia.

The New York case had none of the appeal of the *Jeff Davis* case. Without Jacob Garrick and his testimony portraying William Smith as enslaving a free man, the New York case became a legal debate. By stipulating to the facts, the defense cut off any emotional appeal the prosecution might have made to the jury. Finally, the court in the New York case seemed more willing than its Philadelphia counterpart to allow the defense to argue the legitimacy of the Confederate letters of marque. This became even more apparent the next morning when the defense offered the bulk of its documentary evidence.

Brick by brick the defense built a documentary case to show that the Confederacy existed. When the prosecution objected, the court overruled its objections. The New York court allowed the admission of twenty-three documents from Putnam's *Rebellion Record*, a contemporary counterpart to Moore's *Rebellion Record* used by the defense in Philadelphia. The documents covered the period from South Carolina's secession through the May 6, 1861, proclamation of the Confederate Congress recognizing the state of war and encompassed the creation of the Confederacy, the Fort Sumter crisis, Davis's call for privateers, and Lincoln's call for 75,000 volunteers and his institution of the blockade. Defense counsel also read from another contemporary source, *Diary of the Rebellion Record*, to give the dates of Davis's inauguration as Confederate president, his nomination of his cabinet, the Confederate Congress's declaration of free navigation on the Mississippi, and South Carolina's ratification of the Confederate Constitution.

Then the defense admitted into evidence the papers found on board the *Savannah*, including its privateering commission. The record is unclear as to the source, but the defense also admitted Davis's instructions to private armed vessels; the May 21, 1861, act relative to prisoners of war; extracts from Lincoln's July 4, 1861, message to Congress in its special session; and portions of James Buchanan's December 4, 1860, address to Congress. From the *Rebellion Record* the defense offered the proclamations of both the queen of England and the emperor of France as to the existence of hostilities and the recognition of the Confederacy as a belligerent. To this they added the articles of capitulation of the Confederate forts at Hatteras Inlet and the advertisement in the *Charleston Daily Courier* describing the filing of a libel suit in the Admiralty Court of the Confederate States of America, South Carolina District, announcing the sale of the *Joseph*. Finally, the defense offered a Confederate judicial law relating to the administration of an estate in due course of law to demonstrate that the Confederacy had a judicial system established under its own government.

The court admitted everything offered by the defense. More important, it did not qualify the use of the evidence. In Philadelphia the court had admitted similar documents for historical purposes only, to show that certain events had happened as a matter of historical fact. However, it refused to allow the documents to serve as evidence of legal significance. The secession ordinance could show that

South Carolina purported to leave the Union, but it could not be persuasive evidence of a separate government. In New York the court imposed no such limitation. The court in Philadelphia refused to admit documents showing how European powers viewed the conflict; the New York court allowed documentary evidence from both Great Britain and France. The court allowed the *Savannah* defendants to present the best possible picture of what the Confederacy was in 1861. Using documents from the United States, the Confederacy, and European nations, the defense team could put before the jury a case that, right or wrong, the Confederacy had a legal substance that could not be ignored.

Why did the New York court admit so much evidence and allow it to be used for such a broad purpose, whereas the Philadelphia court severely restricted the defense's evidentiary case? Again, the judges did not explain themselves, nor did they have to. Perhaps in Philadelphia, Grier and Cadwalader feared the jury might acquit if faced with the mountain of evidence in support of the Confederacy's existence. New York, as the financial capital of the nation, had always had strong ties to the South and its cotton empire, a relationship that generated fortunes for men in both sections. However, such a bias hardly explains the different approaches taken by the judiciary. The Confederacy's legal existence involved political considerations in that only if the coordinate branches of the federal government recognized its existence could it truly claim to exist.

However, simply saying the Confederacy did not exist proved nothing. Nelson and Shipman may have believed that recognition, even as a belligerent, required looking to the totality of the evidence, that is, not just the government's words but also its actions. The prisoner-of-war situation provided a good example. More important, what the government said had changed over time. Lincoln's bold pronouncements in April as the war began gave way to more sanguine observations by July, observations that a jury might conclude pointed to some form of recognition even if short of full nationhood. If most of Europe treated the Confederacy as a belligerent, could not twelve American jurors reach the same conclusion? In New York, Nelson and Shipman made the case a test of the American jury system as much as anything else.

The legal significance of what transpired in New York as the defense put on its case seemed lost on the general public. The *New York Times* reported the events of the trial in detail, but offered little commentary. However, even if the public did not understand every legal nuance, the trial captured the city's imagination. Every day saw hundreds turned away for lack of seating as people crowded in to hear the testimony and judge for themselves. On October 25 the crowd heard the admission of the documentary evidence and then saw the defense put on its case: one witness who responded to nine questions and faced no cross-examination.

The defense recalled prosecution witness Second Lieutenant Daniel D. Tompkins of the *Harriet Lane*, the ship that received the *Savannah* crew from USS *Minnesota* and transported the men to New York. First, it asked Tompkins if he had ever seen flags of truce going back and forth between Union and Confederate naval forces near Fort Monroe. Tompkins had seen flags, but had never personally received one. The defense hoped to show that both sides observed rules of civilized warfare on the sea as well as on land, thus strengthening its argument that the defendants should be treated in the same manner as land prisoners.

The second point went to the issue of the official military bearing of the prisoners at the time of their transfer. Tompkins testified that although none of the other defendants wore uniforms, Captain Baker had a "regular uniform" with metal buttons, although he could not describe the buttons. When asked if he had any knowledge of the prisoner exchange policy between the United States and the Confederacy, Tompkins replied he did not. With that short exchange the defense case came to a close. The prosecution offered no rebuttal testimony, and the two sides prepared to give their summations to the jury. Before doing so, Justice Nelson told both sides to present their legal propositions to the court.

Evarts quickly moved through the prosecution's authorities. Referring to the English common law he provided the definitions of treason and robbery, and in response to the defense's contention that the prosecution had limited its own case by failing to indict for treason, he argued that piracy was a species of treason, where one committed the piratical acts against one's own government.

Forced to address Larocque's argument of dual sovereignty and its effect on Southern citizens, Evarts provided legal precedent for the proposition that even where two sovereigns seem to exert a conflicting claim to a citizen's fidelity, a lawful prince (or government in this case) who had the prior allegiance of his subject could not lose that allegiance without that subject willfully resigning himself to another government. In other words, one had to choose, and that choice did not exonerate a citizen from the claim of treason by the government to whom he relinquished his fidelity.

Perhaps the most important legal point Evarts made came from the case of the *Santissima Trinidad*, that "although a parent government may find the magnitude and power of the rebellion such as to induce or compel it to resort to warlike means of suppression, so that toward neutral nations there will grow up such a state of authority as will compel the recognition by neutral nations of the rights of war and belligerents," the parent government still maintains sovereignty and can enforce its laws by all those sanctions against its rebellious subjects. Civil war does not destroy the duty of allegiance or the ability of the sovereign to punish its subjects for treason.

Evarts's legal authorities addressed some of the more salient points of the *Savannah*'s defense, particularly the assertions of dual loyalty and the effect of civil war on the obligations of the citizenry in the rebelling territory. However, as important as the law may be, jury trials often turn on how the jury feels about certain issues. How people feel about a particular issue or dispute often turns on how persuasive the competing arguments are for each side. If people hear only one side, even if they are initially prejudiced against that position, they tend to lose sight of arguments to the contrary.

The court had already undermined the prosecution's case by limiting the evidence under the indictment. The defense's willingness to stipulate to the operative facts further diminished the prosecution's ability to have the jury actually hear its side of the case. Aside from Evarts's brief presentation of the law, the defense took the entire third day of trial presenting its legal position. After adjourning on Friday afternoon, the trial resumed on Saturday morning, October 26, with the defense continuing its legal presentation for most of the day. Only after it finished did Evarts reply by adding to his earlier brief presentation of authorities. The summation by counsel to the jury consumed all of the following Monday, Tuesday, and a portion of Wednesday. During that period the defense held the floor for more than a day and a half, its argument broken up only by Evarts's closing summation, which came after the defense had concluded.

Six defense attorneys argued for the defense, whereas for the prosecution the case had become William Evarts's to win or lose. Delafield Smith completely deferred to Evarts, and despite his strong reputation and the prejudice of the Northern mind in October 1861 against anything Confederate, the jury spent most of the last four and one-half days of trial listening to the defense tell it why these twelve men deserved to go free: the Confederacy existed, and that existence cloaked these defendants with an authority that precluded convicting them of piracy.

Daniel Lord began the defense's presentation of legal authorities. Although the argument ultimately failed, he spent most of his time addressing the court's lack of jurisdiction. Lord then attacked the indictment and explained to the court the legal distinction between the two provisions charging the defendants with piracy. Section 8 of the 1790 act held that "if any person shall upon the high seas commit the crime of robbery, in or upon any ship or vessel, or upon any of the ship's company of any ship or vessel, or the lading thereof, such person shall be adjudged to be a pirate; and being convicted before the Circuit Court of the United States for the District into which he shall be brought, or in which he shall be found, shall suffer death."

Lord argued that the statute did nothing more than restate the definition of common-law piracy and required proving that the accused was the enemy of all nations and attacked ships with that specific intent. As Larocque pointed out earlier in the trial, the section spoke to "persons," not "citizens." Section 9 of the 1790 act stated that "if any citizen shall commit any robbery or piracy, or any act of hostility against the United States, or any citizen thereof, upon the high seas, under color of any commission from any foreign prince or state, or any pretense of authority from any person, such offender shall, notwithstanding the pretense of any such authority, be deemed and adjudged and taken to be a pirate, felon and robber, and on being thereof convicted, shall suffer death."

This, Lord argued, was "statutory piracy" and required first and foremost that the perpetrators be citizens, not just persons. He pointed out this distinction to Justice Nelson, and Nelson acknowledged the difference. In neither case did the prosecution claim the defendants acted treasonously. More important, because of the legal and/or de facto status of the Confederacy, the eight non–U.S. citizens could not be convicted under section 9, and the four U.S. citizens could not be convicted under section 8. Under section 8 none of the twelve men engaged in piracy, because they simply lacked the intent to prey on the shipping of all nations. Whether or not one conceded the legitimacy of the Confederate letters of marque, those letters clearly showed an intent to attack the ships of only one nation, the United States. Thus, common-law piracy could not be shown.

As to section 9, the charge depended on proving first that the defendants were U.S. citizens, a fact that immediately removed eight of them. Then the government had to nullify the letters of marque by showing they were issued under the pretense of authority from a foreign prince. Using his documentary evidence, Lord argued that the Confederacy, whether right or wrong, was a government, and that even Abraham Lincoln had acknowledged its existence in his proclamation of July 4, 1861. Four months after characterizing the hostilities as an "obstruction of the laws of the United States" in the seven states that had seceded by February 1, 1861, Lincoln characterized the same insurrection as "an ordinance [which] has been adopted in each of these states, declaring the states respectively to be separated from the National Union. A formula for instituting a combined government of those states has been promulgated, and this illegal organization, in the character of the 'Confederate States' is already invoking recognition, aid and intervention from foreign powers."

Even before his address in July, Lincoln recognized the state of war between the two powers and authorized Union ships to seize Confederate ships and take them as "prizes of war." As much as the Union wished to deny the distinction, what began as an insurrection, even treason, had escalated into a civil war. Citizens under both governments had but to look at the Confederacy to conclude it had substance and power within its own territory, including the power to compel the obedience of its citizens. To claim the *Savannah*'s commission created only the pretense of authority ignored reality. Again, referring to the proclamation issued by the British government, Lord told the court that foreign nations, as yet unwilling to recognize Confederate independence, nevertheless treated its sailors as combatants and not pirates.

Larocque immediately picked up where Lord left off. Although the argument had become somewhat repetitious, by narrowing the case, the defense also narrowed the issues, and even with less ground to cover, the defense had the right to argue those issues fully. The prosecution had claimed the outcome was already decided; the defense did not agree. With the time that remained on Friday afternoon, Larocque concentrated his legal argument on the obvious contradiction between the government's position and the weight of U.S. case law that recognized belligerents even where national independence had yet to be realized.

Citing the opinion of Judge Livingston in the *Joseph Segunda* case (1825), Larocque pointed out that in the dispute between Spain and her South American colony of Venezuela, the United States recognized the Venezuelan privateer as a belligerent, refusing to deem it or its crew pirates even though Venezuela's independence remained uncertain. Larocque forced the court and the government to address the clear contradiction between blockading the Confederacy while simultaneously denying its legal existence. Even if the Union refused to recognize the Confederacy as a nation for fear of others doing likewise, it could not deny the Confederacy a belligerent status. A Confederate citizen could justifiably rely on its authority over them and commit an act of aggression protected by the laws of war.

Larocque returned to his theme of dual sovereignty and the notion that states retained rights under the U.S. Constitution, including the right to protect themselves. In that capacity, states had the right to extract the obedience of their citizens, whether acting alone or in concert. As the day concluded, Delafield Smith informed everyone that the jury in Philadelphia had reached a verdict in the case of *United States v. William Smith*. Prosecutor Smith telegraphed Justice Grier and asked for a copy of his jury charge and told the court that the prosecution intended to refer to it as a legal authority, given the similarity between the two cases. The court agreed and adjourned for the day. By Monday everyone knew that the defendants in Philadelphia had been convicted. On Saturday the court saw the first evidence of that verdict. Larocque continued his argument that states could defend themselves even against the federal government.

Citing everything from the *Federalist Papers* to the Dorn rebellion, Larocque came dangerously close to legitimizing secession. He wanted to demonstrate the novelty of the conflict and the right of the states to demand obedience from its citizens when the U.S. government could no longer provide protection. However, Evarts grew weary and demanded that Larocque explain how a state could constitutionally justify allowing its citizens, under any pretext, to commit acts of aggression against the United States. Larocque said that he thought he had done so, but before the debate got out of control, Delafield Smith told everyone that he had both Judge Grier's jury charge and Judge Cadwalader's opinion in the *Jeff Davis* case.

Brady demanded to know who reported the charge and the opinion. Smith replied that he received it by telegraph from a Philadelphia attorney and a copy of newsprint from a Philadelphia newspaper. Brady questioned its accuracy but conceded that they all might recognize Grier's writing style. Smith read the charge, and Brady recognized immediately what had happened in Philadelphia. "Tell me what question of fact that was left to the jury?" Brady asked. He told the court that Grier had decided the case and had left nothing for the jury. As the defense continued its presentation of the law, that thought weighed on everyone's mind. The key lay in the court's charge to the jury, and if it resembled Grier's in any way, there would be nothing for the jury to decide, and the defendants would all hang. The defense had to convince the court that a fact issue existed as to whether these men had actually committed piracy. They had to convince the court that sufficient difference of opinion prevailed as to the Confederacy's legal existence to allow the question to go to the jury.

———

Maurice Mayer followed Larocque and focused almost entirely on the foreign defendants. The substance of his legal argument addressed the treatment by the United States of privateers of other nations under similar circumstances. Mayer insisted that "it is known by all Europeans" that although England did not initially recognize America as a belligerent during its own revolution, before the revolution ended, England had done so. The notion of belligerent rights in a revolution "has entered into the flesh and blood of every European." With this understanding of events and the law, the eight foreigners on trial became Confederate privateers. They saw Charleston blockaded and understood legally that a blockade implicitly conveyed belligerent rights. As outsiders, they looked at the Confederacy and saw an established constitutional government and never dreamed that if they embarked on a privateering enterprise they would be treated as pirates.

Mayer understood the legal maxim that "ignorance of the law is no excuse." However, his clients knew the law, and under everything they understood as European sailors, they did not engage in piracy. The U.S. piracy law did not address foreigners, but even if it had, how could these men be aware of the "fact" of its existence? Knowledge of the facts, Mayer argued, goes to the heart of the intent necessary to convict men of piracy. These men knew the law of belligerency, and they could judge for themselves the character of the hostilities between the United States and the Confederacy. Having done so, they concluded that although they placed themselves in harm's way by sailing aboard a privateer, they risked death in combat, not execution as criminals. One of Mayer's own clients, a German named William Clarke, best summed up his plight and his defense when he told his lawyer, *"Mitgegangen, mitgefangen, mitgehangen!"* ["Gone along, caught along, hanged along!"]

The foreign defendants added an important element to the case in New York, one absent from the Philadelphia trial. The defense emphasized how other nations, governments, and rulers viewed the conflict and in turn conceptualized the Confederacy. The eight sailors offered insight into how ordinary people in other countries saw the Confederate nation and its struggle with the Union. To outsiders looking objectively at the war, the Confederacy had substance, and despite the unique nature of the struggle, they conceptualized the Confederacy in terms roughly equivalent to their own historical understanding. Regardless of the Union's position on the rebellion, and its understandable need to avoid foreign recognition of that rebellion, certain legal and factual realities could not be ignored. The eight foreign sailors brought that home.

As William Evarts concluded the presentation of the legal arguments and authorities, the *Jeff Davis* verdict loomed large. The prosecution in Philadelphia succeeded in making the Confederacy a legal nullity, notwithstanding its de facto existence. Grier had decided the case by refusing to allow the jury to consider the legal existence of the Confederacy. The same opportunity existed in the *Savannah* case. All of the defense's legal maneuvering and carefully orchestrated strategy meant nothing if Evarts convinced Nelson and Shipman that no nation had to recognize or legitimize a rebellion in its own courts. For almost a day and a half the court and jury had listened to only one side. Evarts now had the opportunity to undo some of the damage by going last.

The jurisdiction issue threatened to end the trial without addressing the merits, and it consumed a large part of Evarts's presentation. He argued that the defendants were not formally "arrested" until brought to New York. Judge Nelson sensed that Evarts stood on shaky ground and questioned whether the piracy statutes allowed a sea captain actually to "arrest" a pirate. Evarts emphatically said no. No sooner had Nelson stopped questioning Evarts than Larocque objected to Evarts's legal authorities. An argument ensued over whether the defense had properly raised the jurisdiction issue, a debate that consumed valuable time in the prosecution's argument and detracted from the real issues.

Finally, Evarts reached the seminal legal issue in the case: were these men privateers, or were they pirates? Once again, the defense spoke up as Brady objected to Evarts's characterization of the defense theory. Evarts presented legal arguments showing privateering on the decline in the international community. Brady insisted that it did not matter, that it remained a legal mode of warfare, and that the defense cared only that the *Savannah* crew acted in good faith. Evarts conceded Brady's point; if the acts took place "under conditions which, by the law of nations, relieved it from punishment," as a matter of law it could not be piracy.

The defense kept pushing the prosecution into conceding key elements of its case, and Evarts made a huge concession in admitting that a good-faith reliance on the factual circumstances relieved the defendants of liability, something the prosecution and the court in Philadelphia had refused to do. Having made the concession, Evarts identified the two conditions necessary to turn piracy into privateering: a state of war and a commission from a public, national, sovereign power. Did a state of war exist, and if so, did the Confederacy possess a public, national sovereignty?

Evarts argued that France and England had every right to concede the Confederacy "belligerent" status. But if either had chosen to treat Confederate privateers as pirates, would the defense be in English or French courts arguing they could not lawfully do so? Evarts did not think so, and if those nations had the right to make their own determination as to the legal status of the Confederacy, so did the United States. Lincoln's proclamation of April 19, 1861, stood as a clear statement of the right of the United States to choose how and when it recognized other nations, and Lincoln deemed the Confederacy rebellious and its sailors traitors and pirates.

Again, the defense objected, claiming that the legislative branch of the United States had made no such pronouncement. Evarts responded that the whole course of legislative activity demonstrated an outright refusal to recognize the current hostilities as anything but a rebellion that could not "rightfully go on." Evarts insisted that as part of the U.S. government, the court had no choice but to follow the lead of the executive and legislative branches. As far as executing men for treason, whether on land or sea, that decision lay in the hands of the government. Although good faith might relieve men of liability, Evarts argued that these defendants could not claim they acted in good faith: "Make the number of them what you will, if in the eye of the law they assume an authority which is on its face criminal and illegal, and even though it is part of a general scheme and organization for violent military resistance to the authority of the country, no Court can dispense from the punishment, but must inflict it through the general and ordinary criminal authority in respect to the crime in question, leaving the question of dispensation to the clemency, humanity and the policy of the government." In short, the defense's legal authorities stood only as evidence for what other governments chose to do with regard to recognizing South American governments as nations or belligerents; they did not bind the United States. With that, Evarts rested his legal case, and the court adjourned until Monday morning.

Monday belonged exclusively to the defense. In succession, Dukes, Sullivan, Davega, and Brady summed up the defense case for the jury, with Brady's argument running into the next day. The eloquence of the arguments increased because both sides now argued directly to the jury, but the substance remained the same: the United States could not ignore its own history. Although the U.S. government insisted on denying the Confederacy's legal existence, it had the same legal status America enjoyed in 1776, and the United States could not treat this conflict any different from the one some eighty years before.

But as Joseph Dukes said at the outset of his opening, civil war changes everything. "Civil wars strike deepest into the manners of the people—they vitiate their politics; they corrupt their morals; they pervert their natural tastes and relish of equity and justice." The defense feared that the jury might not be able to rise above the conflict. But despite any fears, Dukes expressed confidence that if justice prevailed anywhere, it would be before a jury of New York City citizens—"a city which if any city in the world possesses large, liberal and enlightened views, we may hope to find them."

Each of the four defense attorneys took a slightly different approach in his summation. Dukes provided numerous historical examples, including the American Revolution, to demonstrate that historical precedent simply did not support the U.S. government's position. The suggestion that plunder alone motivated the defendants missed the point. Plunder or not, taking prizes injured one's enemy, and the decisions rendered by such judges as Cadwalader in Philadelphia showed that U.S. vessels seized Confederate prizes on a regular basis. In fact, argued Dukes, those very prize cases admitted the Confederacy's status as a belligerent, thus placing the prosecution at odds with the legal opinions of its own judiciary. Men seized on land became prisoners of war, and no one challenged General Benjamin Butler or Commodore Silas Stringham when they negotiated the capitulation of the Confederate forces at Hatteras Inlet.

Why, then, Dukes said, were these men on trial for their lives—because in the heat of the moment in April 1861, Abraham Lincoln scrambled to counter the efforts of Jefferson Davis to raise a navy and declared his intent to execute any man captured while sailing under a Confederate commission. Now cooler heads prevailed, and the jury should not be bound by a proclamation made in such haste that it hardly measured up to the country's own sense of justice. Dukes implored the jury to "meet this issue like men. . . . Stand firm, do justice and discharge these prisoners." If the members of the jury chose not to, however, if they turned "deaf to the promptings of reason, of justice, and of humanity . . . impelled by political rancor and passion" and condemned these men to die, Dukes assured them that the final appeal of the case would be lifted to "a far more august tribunal than this, before whose unerring decrees, courts and nations alike must bow with awful reverence."

Algernon Sullivan went next. Perhaps more than any member of the defense bar, Sullivan had paid a high price for his willingness to defend the crew of the *Savannah*. As noted earlier, he had been imprisoned until almost the day of trial. He now stood before the members of the jury and reflected on what they must be feeling. He knew they heard the "voices in their ears" telling them to deal most severely with the enemies of their government now helplessly before the bar. But Sullivan implored the jury to resist the impulses of popular opinion and remember that this very country existed because of the "imperishable doctrine of revolutionary right." To find these men guilty meant "strike[ing] a parricidal blow, conspicuous in the eyes of the world, against the ever sacred doctrine which our ancestors transmitted to us as their best legacy and part of their own good name."

Sullivan described the *Savannah*'s preparation, voyage, and capture and then asked the seminal question: under the circumstances that prevailed, could the men on that vessel not justifiably rely on the Confederate commission? Of course, answered Sullivan. The *Joseph* fell victim to the *Savannah* not as a private seizure or plunder but as a prize of the Confederate States of America. With the original letters of marque in evidence, Sullivan pointed out that in every way the men complied with the code of war as recognized by all civilized nations. Equally important, the captain and crew of the *Savannah* followed Davis's instruction to the letter and not even the prosecution had suggested otherwise.

On reaching Charleston, the ship, together with all of its crew, papers, and documents, remained intact for all to see. The *Joseph* was sold as a prize of war not at a private auction but libeled in a Confederate prize court "on precisely the same basis, and enforcing the identical rules of law as the United States Prize and Admiralty Court, which convenes in the room adjoining to that which we now are." Nothing about the seizure and sale of the *Joseph* suggested anything remotely connected to piracy. Convicting these men of piracy required denying that the Confederate States of America possessed the right to issue letters of marque. That position, Sullivan maintained, "involves them [the U.S. attorneys] in inextricable embarrassments, and must expose the fallacies which lie at the bottom of the erroneous reasonings of the prosecution."

Sullivan explained that to take the position that only a successful revolution entitled the Confederacy to recognition, even as a belligerent, meant that "once a sovereign, always a sovereign." In effect, so long as the United States refused to recognize the Confederacy, even fifty years later, it had no right to any status. Such a proposition ignored reality. Citing numerous international law sources and examples ranging from Italy to the Republic of Texas, Sullivan stated, "A de facto government, merely, must be allowed by every sound jurist to possess in itself, for the time being, all the attributes of a government de jure. It may properly claim for itself and the citizen may rightly render to it, allegiance and obedience, as if the government rested on an undisputed basis." After comparing the Confederacy to the American Revolution, Sullivan concluded by telling the jury to "listen therefore to the better voices whispering to each heart. Remember the honor and consistency of the United States are involved in this case. . . . Tell your Government to wage manly, open, chivalric war on the field and ocean, and thus not at all; that dishonor is worse even than disunion."

The defense asked the jury to reach a verdict that, although contrary to the government's initial position in April 1861, comported with America's own history and legal precedent and the evolution of the Union's treatment of the Confederacy as the war progressed. In effect, they argued to "let Mr. Lincoln off the hook" by refusing to ignore the obvious facts and the great weight of legal authority amassed over the last 300 years. They said the Confederacy existed, it had real substance, and had any of the participants been in Magrath's courtroom only two weeks before, they would have seen just how strong a hold the Confederacy had on its citizens and the deep concern many of them expressed for the unprecedented nature and breadth of that hold.

Both Dukes and Sullivan pointed to the internal inconsistencies in the present conflict: men captured on land treated as prisoners and the Confederacy acknowledged as a belligerent in Union prize courts. Isaac Davega continued this theme in his brief closing statement, describing how the public flocked to see the "Pirates of the *Savannah*," the "monsters of the deep," expecting images of Captain Kidd and Jackalow, both legendary pirates. Instead they saw, led through the streets in chains, "gentlemen of character, intelligence, refinement and education." Davega argued that these men should be subject to military authority, not civilian. A war existed under every recognized definition of the term, and the defendants served the Confederacy as naval combatants. They acted in good faith on the commission of the only government in existence in the South and strictly adhered to the mandates of their commission and the law of nations. Davega insisted the jury had to do its duty. The suggestion from the prosecution that, even if convicted, the president would pardon the prisoners, was, in his estimation, "a delusion." He advised them to follow the golden rule, that is, "Do unto others as you would that they would do unto you."

The defense's summation concluded with James Brady. The finest defense lawyer in New York, and perhaps in the United States, Brady took the remainder of Monday and part of the next day. Brady offered nothing new, but his closing made it clear why the defense had taken so long in its presentment of legal authorities and why the admission of its voluminous documentary evidence had been so critical. Brady's passionate argument built on Larocque's presentation of the law as he read excerpts from it and the documentary evidence throughout his closing. Brady combined all of the arguments into one final presentation to convince the jury that the government had no case.

Nineteenth-century trials were events. People crowded into the courtroom to watch real-life drama and tragedy unfold. Attorneys made up a central part of the spectacle, and on October 28 and 29, everyone had come to watch one of the best. Brady did not disappoint his audience, and a curious thing occurred as both sides struggled to define the Confederacy and thus the fate of its twelve sailors; everyone learned something about the United States.

Brady lamented that the trial occurred while emotions were running so high and found it absurd for anyone to argue that no war existed. He found it equally troubling that no one could really explain why the nation went to war. Was it about recovering property, subjugating a rebellious province, or holding a people in the Union against their will, or was it about abolition? Whatever the reason, Brady said, he felt assured that "if it be for the purposes of mere subjugation . . . of establishing a dictatorship, or designedly waged for the emancipation of all slaves, our people will never sustain it at the North!" The crowded courtroom erupted in applause, which the court quickly silenced. If the audience reflected the sentiments of the jury in any way, the twelve men judging the case were not "mere automata" blindly ready to follow the dictates of their government.

The *Jeff Davis* verdict had become a matter of public record. Already battling a strong public predisposition against the Confederate sailors, Brady had to address the Philadelphia verdict. His plea to the jury actually addressed the court. He knew and respected both Judge Cadwalader and Justice Grier, but they left nothing for the jury to decide. To base any part of the decision in this case on the verdict in the *Jeff Davis* case would, he argued, deprive the defendants of a fair trial before their peers. Brady knew that if Nelson and Shipman rejected the defense's legal arguments, if they chose to believe that no nation could admit of rebellion in its own courts, the *Savannah* crew could expect the same fate as the men on the *Jeff Davis*.

Brady covered everything in his effort to destroy the government's case: the definition of piracy, the legal requirements of privateering, the status of the Southern states, the de facto existence of the Confederate government, the many parallels between the present struggle and the American Revolution, and how even Britain acknowledged America's status as a belligerent power. Citing Vattel, Wheaton (an international law authority), and even Daniel Webster, Brady repeated the proposition that a civil war demanded all of the general usages of nations accorded in a war involving two distinct nations. As Brady's lengthy summation came to a close, he spoke to his own role in almost a tacit recognition of the danger that the jury might reject the message because it condemned the messenger. Advocates, Brady said, are of very little use "in the days of peace and prosperity." It is only "when public opinion, or the strong power of government, the formidable array of influence, the force of a nation, or the fury of a multitude, is directed against you, that an advocate is of any use."

Brady reminded the jury of an insurrection of black persons in New York during America's colonial period and how public ire prevented the New York bar from stepping forward to defend the accused. On the basis of groundless charges, the colonial authorities hung most of the innocent defendants, including a poor priest. Following the Boston Massacre several British soldiers stood trial for murder, and that time, two men, Mr. Adams and Mr. Quincey, stepped forward to defend the soldiers. Mr. Quincey's father implored him not to take this unpopular defense, yet the son, ever loyal to his father, could not forsake his duty as an advocate and the obligation of his official oath. Brady and his colleagues faced the same dilemma and came to the same conclusion as young Mr. Quincey.

In the last minutes before yielding the floor to the prosecution, Brady called on the spirits of Hamilton, Adams, Jefferson, Washington, Moultrie, Marion, Greene, and Putnam. Not one of these founding fathers who fought for America's independence "would not say to you that you should remember, in regard to each of these prisoners, as if you were his father, the history of Abraham when he went to sacrifice his son Isaac on the mount—the spirit of American liberty, the principles of American jurisprudence and the dictates of humanity, constituting themselves another angel of the Lord, saying to you . . . 'Lay not your hands upon him'" With that Brady sat down, the applause of the audience once again ringing in his ears.

After what must have seemed like an endless onslaught by the defense, William Evarts rose to give the government's summation. Evarts had not attained the professional status and reputation he had within the legal community without just cause. An accomplished trial lawyer, he set out over the course of October 29 and 30 to unravel the defense that Brady, Lord, Larocque, and their colleagues so meticulously constructed over the preceding five days. Brady had dictated Evarts's course, and the prosecution's lead attorney painstakingly took the jury over the same ground the defense covered.

Faced with the analogy between the present rebellion and the American Revolution, Evarts traced the development of the United States from colonial times to the start of the Civil War. The Confederacy had no claim to being like the American colonies. America rebelled against the tyranny of the British Parliament; the Confederacy simply did not want to live with the election of 1860. It was a hollow argument in that it compared the American colonies' perception of tyranny with that of the Confederate states and found the latter's pleas of oppression wanting. But, in front of a Northern jury it might prove effective.

The defense tried to give the Confederacy legal substance in order to cloak the defendants with the protection afforded a nation and its combatants during time of war. Evarts countered the only way he could, by arguing that regardless of the Confederacy's de facto trappings of government, no sovereign had to recognize a rebellion as legitimate or to treat the citizens of a rebellious section as anything other than traitors. Then he painted the Confederacy and its component states as undeserving of any recognition or sympathy by addressing the conflict between federal and state sovereignty.

When it seceded, South Carolina took the position that "when any interest ceases to be the majority in a government, it had a right to secede." Ten other Southern states followed South Carolina's lead. But what, Evarts asked, was the injustice done to these states? Evarts traced the history of the federal government's protection of slavery, pointing to the numerous points along the path to secession where the government defied the majority in order to protect the South's sacred institution. The Confederate states were not oppressed, they were ungrateful.

When Evarts stripped away the hyperbole from the defense's case, it came down to a distinction between the right to rebel and the power to do so. The Confederacy had no right, and the fact that it seized on the power did not dictate how the U.S. government treated the rebellion. Isolated instances where military or civilian authority chose to give the Confederacy and its soldiers some of the protections afforded prisoners of war under international law did not bind the government to treat these men as anything other than pirates, just as Lincoln warned.

As Evarts brought his lengthy summation to its conclusion, the issues at stake for the prosecution became very clear. By virtue of the defense's arguments, the case had moved beyond "the simple issue of the guilt or innocence of these men under the statute." "It is not our fault," Evarts argued, "that you have been invoked to give, on the undisputed facts of this case, a verdict which shall be a recognition of the power, authority, and right of the rebel government to infringe our laws, or partake in the infringement of them to some form and extent." Evarts did not mince words. The jury's duty went beyond the guilt or innocence of men accused of piracy and became a sacred obligation to sustain the U.S. Constitution against the alleged power, right, and authority of the rebel government as manifested in the letter of marque issued by Jefferson Davis. An acquittal meant an admission that the power of the U.S. government had been overthrown by that of the rebel government, replacing "Liberty and Union now and forever" with the mournful confession, "Unworthy of freedom, our baseness has surrendered the liberties which we had neither the courage nor the virtue to love or defend."

Now the case rested in the hands of the court and jury, and Justice Nelson wasted no time in charging the jury. Like the court in Philadelphia, Nelson immediately crushed the defense's jurisdiction argument. Under section 14 of the 1825 Act of Congress, prisoners accused under the 1790 or 1820 piracy statutes could be tried either in the district where they were first brought or that in which they were apprehended under lawful authority for the trial of the offense. Thus, the court had jurisdiction. Turning to the merits, the court instructed the jury that it could find the prisoners guilty of a statutory violation of piracy even if they were not guilty of piracy as defined by common law. They need not be shown to be the enemies of all nations to fall under section 3 of the 1820 act or section 9 of the 1790 act.

Nelson laid out the elements of piracy and told the jury that it, not the court, had to decide the issue. Nelson conceded that only four prisoners claimed U.S. citizenship and that the other eight men could not be found guilty under the statute that made it an offense for "any citizen" to commit robbery or piracy on the high seas. Thus, as to five of the ten counts, the eight foreign defendants could not be convicted. The remaining five counts that applied to "any person" who committed robbery on the high seas did apply to the eight foreign defendants, but, under international law, a valid commission or letter of marque issued by a nation in a state of war with another nation afforded protection from the charge of piracy. The court seemed to have embraced the defense argument. However, although the court acknowledged certain international law defenses as to some of the counts, it went only so far. The defense had to hope that the jury saw the opening and would take advantage of the court's latitude.

In Philadelphia, Grier and Cadwalader had instructed the jury that it could not use the de facto existence of the Confederacy as the basis of any legal defense legitimizing the letters of marque. Although Justices Nelson and Shipman did not go that far, they refused to afford the Confederacy any recognition on their own. They stated that recognition "involves the determination of great public political questions, that belong to the department of our government that have charge of our foreign relations." Until the executive and legislative branches made a determination as to the Confederacy's status, the courts had no choice but to recognize that the "ancient state of things remains unchanged." The court could recognize the Confederacy's existence only after the other political departments "of the mother country" had done so. For that, they said, "we must look to the acts of these departments as evidence of the fact . . . these gentlemen, are all the observations we deem necessary to submit to you." The jury retired at 3:20 P.M. on October 30. The fate of twelve men and two nations rested in its hands.

In the William Smith trial, the court had told the jury it could not recognize the Confederacy. In New York the court told the jury that to recognize the Confederacy one had to look at the actions of the executive and legislative branches. The difference in the two charges allowed the *Savannah* jury to decide for itself whether the blockade, the military's treatment of land prisoners, or Lincoln's address to Congress on July 4, 1861, amounted to a recognition of the Confederacy as a de facto government. If it thought so, it had the latitude to take the next step and find that the prisoners had properly acted under that authority and acquit them of piracy. Nelson and Shipman gave the jury the authority to judge the actions of the U.S. government and in the process to try to define the Confederacy. With the door wide open, time would tell whether the jury would be willing to walk through it.

The Philadelphia jury had decided William Smith's fate in forty-five minutes. By six o'clock in the evening the *Savannah* jury had not reached a verdict. One juror, a Mr. Powell, seized on the issue of whether a state of war existed, and the jury requested additional instructions. The court repeated that it could offer nothing further. The jury went back and deliberated all night. At 8:20 A.M. on October 31 the foreman announced to the court that the jury had not reached a verdict and that there "was no prospect at all that we can come to an agreement." Mr. Powell and a Mr. Cassidy rose and confirmed the deadlock. The jury had hung. Nelson had no choice but to dismiss them, and Delafield Smith immediately asked for a date to impanel a new jury. Nelson's schedule made it impossible to retry the case during the court's present term.

————

The count stood at eight to four to convict when the jury gave up. The November 1, 1861, edition of the *New York Times* told a sad tale. "We regret to see that our anticipations as to the result of the trial of the privateers of the *Savannah* proved correct." Why had this happened? The press could not believe anyone could disagree. The charge seemed clear and the conduct admitted. Were there secessionists on the jury? The editors could not say, but some voiced the concern that Philadelphia acted with more loyalty than New York because that jury convicted its pirates. The *Times* laid some of the blame at the feet of the able lawyers who stepped forward to defend the Confederates. Daniel Lord did not comment, but expressed surprise that the government contemplated retrying the *Savannah* crew.

For the next week the newspapers pondered the outcome. People feared the verdict might embolden the South to increase its privateering efforts. How could the government prevent the same result?

Perhaps, some argued, the jury should have been "separated," or sequestered, thus preventing jurors from being subjected to "improper influences." Others believed the verdict, or lack thereof, showed disloyalty and that like government officials, clerks, and employers, jurors should be required to take an oath of allegiance. In the end no one knew why the jury hung because no records of the deliberations or posttrial comments survived. However, Nelson's charge clearly lay at the heart of the result in the *Savannah* case.

Nelson refused to ignore reality and the federal government's contradictory treatment of the Confederacy. The prosecution took the position that because the government tried these men as pirates, it had not given the Confederacy any status other than that of "a rebellion." As a judicial officer, Nelson could not "recognize" the Confederacy, but he could and did allow the jury to weigh the government's actions since the war began and determine for itself whether the United States had recognized the Confederacy as anything other than a rebellion. From the resulting deadlock, one can assume that at the very least, men disagreed as to the effect of the treatment of prisoners of war, the blockade, and Lincoln's own redefinition of the conflict in July 1861.

Nelson believed that the physical and legal control the Confederacy exerted over persons residing in its states altered their status under the law. A week after the *Savannah* trial concluded, Nelson charged a New York City grand jury in a treason case, saying that "citizens or subjects residing within the insurrectionary district, not implicated in the rebellion, but adhering to their allegiance, are not enemies, nor to be regarded as such." Despite the pressure to do otherwise, Nelson and Shipman recognized that the Confederacy's de facto existence made the government's charge of piracy uncertain. The jury could not resolve the ambiguity. For the time being, the crew of the *Savannah* remained safe, while their compatriots from the *Jeff Davis* stood to hang for the identical conduct. Yet one more contradiction existed in the Confederate enigma.

"Other Unlawful Combinations"

The conclusion of the *Savannah* trial brought an end to a remarkable three-week period. In eighteen days, three trials in three different courthouses forced both the North and the South to address the question of what the Confederacy was. Although buried in obscurity today, the sequestration cases and piracy trials captured the attention and the imagination of the American public in both sections of the country. Tried before packed courtrooms and followed in detail by the newspapers, the legal issues in all three cases went to the heart of the Confederacy's existence, both as a nation in the eyes of the international community and the United States and as the source and protector of basic civil liberties for the millions of citizens under the control and authority of the new Southern nation. So, what was decided? What was the Confederacy?

The South seceded from the Union based on notions of states' rights and condemning the oppressiveness of the U.S. government, yet it found itself as a nation unable to wage war effectively without a strong central government. Confronting a struggle for its very survival, the Confederacy resorted to extreme measures. Its populace applauded the revival of privateering and hailed the success of the South's makeshift navy. However, sequestration, even though aimed at the North, not only created severe problems for the South's merchant class but also gave Confederate receivers virtually unbridled discretion to exact information from Confederate citizens. Notwithstanding the potential harm to its international relations caused by a law that in effect undermined the currency system of the nineteenth century, the Confederate judiciary placed national interest over pleas of personal civil liberties. In so doing, the Confederacy became more like its adversary, the United States. Although legally Andrew

Magrath's decision did not bind other Confederate district courts, no state or Confederate court ever overturned his verdict. Sequestration continued throughout the war and proved to be an important source of income. But little of this money ever reached the Confederate citizens who lost property as a result of Union confiscation. Each individual compensation claim required a separate act of Congress, and only a few such bills ever passed.

The division and criticism engendered by sequestration never ended. Conscription and taxation proved just as contentious, and other men continued the sequestration battle the five Charleston lawyers had begun in 1861. In fact, one of the "Charleston Five" refused to give up the fight. Unable to defeat the Sequestration Act on constitutional grounds, Nelson Mitchell actively defended people accused of violating the act. He took cases in South Carolina, Georgia, and Tennessee and successfully defended both businesses and individuals from claims that they were "alien enemies" or that the debts they held were due to an alien enemy. Mitchell's most active sequestration client was Mordecai Solomon. Originally from New York, Solomon relocated to South Carolina after the war began. Before moving south, Solomon bought up debts originally due to several New York companies and began trying to collect. The Confederate government initially treated him as an alien enemy, and Mitchell filed or defended lawsuits throughout the South to perfect Solomon's claims until at least May 1863.

William Whaley and James Wilkinson returned to their legal practices. Edward McGrady did likewise, and after the war, he and his son became actively involved in building the "New South" and restoring its prewar social order in the absence of slavery. Andrew Magrath became governor of South Carolina in December 1864 and joined the chorus of other state governors condemning the Davis administration. Captured and imprisoned after the war, he returned to Charleston, South Carolina, after his release and enjoyed a lucrative law practice until his death in 1893. For James Petigru the sequestration battle ended an illustrious career, and he died in March 1863. All of South Carolina mourned his passing.

Although Mitchell continued the fight, he did not do so alone. In the fall of 1862, John Harmer Gilmer, an attorney and state representative from Albemarle, Virginia, objected to the interrogatories served on him by a receiver under the 1862 amendment to the Sequestration Act. Gilmer refused to answer the discovery or turn over any property in his possession. His objections mirrored those made in Charleston the year before, and his challenge suffered a similar fate. Confederate District Judge James Halyburton, sitting in Richmond, Virginia, struck down all of Gilmer's objections. Unlike Magrath, Halyburton made no exception for attorney-client communications, finding the privilege contrary to the act.

Having lost his battle with sequestration, John Gilmer continued fighting the Confederate government, becoming a vocal opponent of conscription in 1863. In November 1864 he published a letter originally sent to William Rives concerning the suspension of the writ of habeas corpus, claiming the action by the Confederate Congress "has no parallel, save in the Lincoln Dynasty from which we are seeking to escape." The destruction of state sovereignty by the Confederate government lay at the heart of all of Gilmer's objections.

The Confederate judiciary's willingness to support sequestration did not diminish the hostility toward the act. In an effort to shore up some of the defects and to address more clearly the issue of promissory notes as property subject to seizure, the Confederate Congress amended the Sequestration Act in 1862 and 1863. An 1862 case in New Orleans involving a promissory note threatened to undermine the act by excepting promissory notes as property subject to seizure. The Confederate Congress expressly defined promissory notes as debt.

As the Confederate government amended and enforced the Sequestration Act, state governments joined private individuals in resisting the law. On March 20, 1863, the Virginia State Committee on Confederate Relations issued a report and passed a resolution on the Sequestration Act. The report denied the Confederate Congress's power to confiscate or sequester property, and the resolution demanded that Virginia's senators to the Confederate Congress "use their best endeavors" to call for a repeal of the August 30, 1861, Sequestration Act.

On the basis of the surviving court records, one can see that neither Virginia nor any other Confederate state succeeded in slowing down sequestration. In 1864 the Confederate Congress tried to expand the reach of its confiscation act. Desertion from the Confederate army grew so prevalent that an amendment to the act sought to declare Confederate deserters "alien enemies" and to sequester their property. Nathaniel Harrison had argued that this would have happened to William Smith had he tried to leave the Confederacy in 1861. The amendment did not pass, but just the effort shows the Confederacy's continuing attempt to assert its national sovereignty.

In 1861 sequestration helped define the Confederacy. The week-long fight in Charleston, South Carolina, revealed a nation torn between its aspirations of a government where states held the highest level of sovereignty and the reality that, to win the war for its survival, states had to defer to central authority and control. That deference not only undermined the notion of state power but also required an encroachment on civil rights greater than that which popular Southern rhetoric accused the Union and the Lincoln government of perpetrating before and during the war.

Not only did the sequestration cases help define a nation; they helped define its people as well. Although many Southerners seemed willing to accept certain limitations on personal rights, the best example perhaps being the passport system that operated throughout the war, others resisted Confederate authority. Although Confederate courts deferred to the government, state courts showed a willingness to defy Confederate authority. North Carolina Supreme Court Justice Richmond Pearson provided the most glaring example in 1863 when he denied the Confederacy's right to use North Carolina's state militia to enforce Confederate conscription and desertion laws.

The fight over sequestration did more than simply define the Confederate nation at home; it placed the Southern experiment into an international context. Despite claims of Southern "uniqueness," the trial in Charleston demonstrated that what the Confederacy wanted to do had been tried before. The unique aspect of sequestration came with the Confederacy's willingness to fly in the face of historical and legal precedent. True, the vast weight of authority concluded that a nation could sequester debt, but that same body of law denounced the practice because of its adverse effect on international law and the unwillingness of other nations to recognize the right.

Despite convincing arguments from respected Southern lawyers that the disclosure provisions and discovery tools in the Sequestration Act ran contrary to fundamental search-and-seizure rights in both the Confederate and U.S. constitutions, Magrath upheld sequestration and its procedures as both legal and necessary. To the extent that legal cases become a mirror into which a people or a nation can look and see itself, the reflection cast by the sequestration cases in 1861 showed a government ready and willing to use all those powers that most Southerners found contemptible in the U.S. government and revealed a people troubled over the difference between the Confederate dream and the reality of what it had already become just six months into the war.

———

As autumn turned to winter in 1861, the prize crew of the *Jeff Davis* contemplated death from the gallows. The crew of the *Savannah* basked in the victory of a stalemate, but could only wonder what might happen the next time around. The crew of the ill-fated *Petrel*, cut down by USS *St. Lawrence* before ever taking a prize, awaited trial in New York on charges of piracy and treason. Like the *Savannah* crew, the men of the *Petrel* rotted away in the dingy confines of the Tombs. However, none of the Confederate privateers ever stood trial again, in great part because the Confederacy refused to stand by and allow the Union to execute its sailors.

Almost immediately after William Smith's conviction, Jefferson Davis made good on his earlier threats to retaliate. On August 30, 1861, the Confederate Congress authorized Davis to do "as may seem to him just and proper" to protect Confederate prisoners. On November 9, 1861, the Confederate War Department ordered General Samuel Winder to select hostages from Union prisoners of war, matching the numbers and ranks of the convicted crew of the *Jeff Davis* and the as yet unconvicted members of the *Savannah*, and hold the men in cells commensurate with those that housed the Confederate privateers in the North. Davis announced that for every Confederate executed, he would hang a Union hostage. His threats proved effective.

Faced with the prospect of executing men based on charges that at least one jury had been unable to convict on, and knowing that such an action assured the deaths of Union prisoners, the Lincoln administration relented and moved the privateers from the jails they occupied since their capture and placed them in military prisons. In due course the Union exchanged all the privateers as prisoners of war. For some the exchange came too late. At least two members of the *Savannah* died in prison or during the journey home. Most of the privateers returned home so destitute that the *Charleston Mercury* ran an advertisement seeking public donations for the men.

The Sequestration Act provided a glimpse into the future of the United States, given how its disclosure requirements resembled the "witch hunts" of the McCarthy era. The piracy cases provided a window into another aspect of the United States in modern times. The Union held the Confederate privateers in much the same way as the U.S. government currently holds "detainees" at Guantanamo. Both groups represent men purposely denied any legal status in order to circumvent constitutional protections or rights of international law normally afforded to accused persons or belligerents in war. The Union recognized a state of war in order to blockade the South and seize its ships as prizes. Yet, it denied men who took up arms on the high seas for the Confederacy any status as "warriors." The same situation prevails today, as the government tells the American people that we wage a "war" against terrorism, yet denies accused terrorists status as either combatants or regular civilians.

The privateers who survived their imprisonment, and the lawyers who represented them, returned to their prior lives, although history does not record what happened to most of them. Following the *Jeff Davis* trial Nathaniel Harrison left Pennsylvania and resurfaced in Richmond, Virginia. After the war he returned to Mercer County, West Virginia, serving as a local judge until 1870, when the West Virginia legislature instituted proceedings to remove him from office. Harrison's distinguished co-counsel, George Wharton, died in 1870, and the local papers mourned the loss of "one of [its] ablest lawyers and most distinguished citizens." Hubley Ashton, the young prosecutor thrown into the fray on the illness of his superior, moved on to become the assistant attorney general of the United States. William Kelley, nicknamed "Judge," served thirty-six years in the U.S. Congress, where he championed high tariffs and where his tireless efforts to protect the iron and steel industry earned him the title "Pig Iron" Kelley. William Smith, the man at the center of attention in 1861, drifted back into obscurity.

The two men responsible for commissioning the *Savannah* both survived the war. John Harleston enlisted in the Confederate army, saw extensive combat, and was wounded three times. Thomas Harrison Baker could not resist the allure of the sea and secured a post as the captain of yet another privateer, one both bigger and better armed. James Brady returned to his practice and died in 1869. His able co-counsel, Jeremiah Larocque, died the year before. On his death his law firm reorganized, and in 1870, Judge Shipman, who presided with Nelson over the trial, became a partner in that firm. William Evarts, the lead prosecutor, served a distinguished career as a U.S. senator, and in 1891 his bill, the Evarts Act, created U.S. circuit courts, thereby ending the practice of Supreme Court justices riding the circuit.

The 1861 cases continued to affect both Justice Robert Grier, who presided over the *Jeff Davis* trial, and Justice Samuel Nelson, who tried the *Savannah* case. The issues both men had grappled with in those two cases returned when a group of four prize cases found their way to the U.S. Supreme Court. As described earlier, Grier had refused to allow the jury in the *Jeff Davis* case to consider the possibility that the United States had afforded the Confederacy any recognition, and William Smith's conviction reflected the rigidity of that jury charge. Nelson had declared that as a member of the judiciary he could not afford the Confederacy any status, but he did allow the jury to make its own determination as to whether the Lincoln administration or the U.S. Congress had accorded the Confederacy a legal status. The hung jury seemed to result in part because of that factual question.

The piracy cases probed into many of the issues that came before the Supreme Court in 1863, including whether a state of war existed and the status of the Confederacy with regard to instituting a blockade. However, neither case ever went up on appeal. The resolution of those unresolved issues by the Supreme Court came in the *Prize Cases*. Almost every federal prize court upheld the taking of Confederate prizes, but the various judges arrived at their decisions by different routes. In 1863 the Supreme Court tried to bring uniformity to the problem by deciding the *Prize Cases*.

In a 5–4 vote Grier delivered the majority opinion, and Nelson dissented. None other than William Evarts argued for the government. In sustaining lower-court decisions holding captured Confederate vessels as war prizes, the majority upheld the legality of the Union blockade. Although the conflict was deemed a civil war, a state of war clearly existed, allowing Lincoln the power to recognize a state of war and institute a blockade to fight that war. However, in order to sustain Lincoln's actions and validate the blockade, Grier conceded that the president created belligerent rights and obligations as recognized by international law and that even in a civil war:

> The people of the two countries become immediately the enemies of each other (i.e., enemies by virtue of their residence in enemy territory, not because of personal allegiance. Hence neutral residents in one belligerent were enemies of the other belligerent) . . . [as a result] all treaties between belligerent parties are annulled. The ports of the respective countries may be blockaded, and letters of marque and reprisal granted as rights of war, and the law of prizes as defined by the law of nations comes into complete and full operation, resulting from maritime captures *jure belli*.

Grier affirmed what the defense in both the *Jeff Davis* case and the *Savannah* case insisted: whether or not the United States recognized the Confederacy as a nation, it had to acknowledge belligerent rights, and by doing so, its captured sailors operating under letters of marque became prisoners of war and not pirates. In his dissent Nelson argued that a state of war never existed under the Constitution and that therefore actions grounded in executive war powers were unconstitutional. He insisted that when these particular prize cases arose the federal legislature had not declared war and that a subsequent ratification of war could not legitimize the prizes.

It is hard to determine what effect Grier's experience in the *Jeff Davis* case had on his opinion in the *Prize Cases*. However, given the intensity of the arguments in both cases and the blatant contradictions in Union policy in 1861, the piracy trials must have weighed on the minds of both Grier and Nelson. Although the Union public and press continued to call Confederate ships "pirates," a title used with particular zeal when it came to CSS *Alabama*, the public and political pressure so prevalent in 1861 to deny the Confederacy any existence save that of a traitorous government did not exist in 1863. Faced with the factual realities of the Confederacy's existence and the international law that assigned status to such an existence, the United States finally did, as Larocque had insisted, leave "the conflict to the clash of arms." A victorious Union thereafter denied the Confederacy ever existed.

Grier's opinion in the *Prize Cases* validated other aspects of the defense arguments in the piracy trials. The defense insisted that certain "facts" simply could not be ignored. Grier finally agreed. The war was a fact, and the court could not ignore its existence. Moreover, Grier contended, the Supreme Court could not ignore the importance of how other nations viewed the conflict. Citing the *Santissima Trinidad* case, Grier argued that the U.S. government's recognition of hostilities and claim of neutrality in a civil war between Spain and its colony made each party a belligerent nation and entitled them to the "sovereign rights of war." When Queen Victoria issued a proclamation on May 13, 1861, declaring Britain a neutral power, other nations followed. It became impossible to deny the Confederacy's belligerent status.

Following the defense argument in both piracy trials, Grier described the magnitude of the war and how the court could not ignore a conflict that "all the world acknowledges to be the greatest civil war known in the history of the human race." To meet such a threat the president could take the steps he did, including blockading the South and treating captured vessels as prizes. However, whereas in 1861 Grier denied the jury in the *Jeff Davis* case the latitude to determine whether the U.S. government's actions afforded the Confederacy any status under international law, in 1863 he had to concede that Lincoln's actions, followed by the legislature's subsequent ratification of those actions, made the Confederacy a belligerent.

The *Prize Cases* did not expressly overturn any of the actions taken with regard to the Confederate privateers, even if the language in the opinion nevertheless destroyed much of the prosecution's argument in those cases. In January 1864, ten months after

Grier's decision, a Canadian court in the case of *In Re David Collins* reaffirmed what the rest of the world already knew and that the United States had finally conceded: the Confederacy existed in the community of nations at least as a belligerent, with rights of war that shielded its citizens from prosecution as pirates.

In December 1863, a small group of men purporting to act under the authority of a letter of marque from Jefferson Davis boarded a Union merchant ship, the *Chesapeake*, in New York harbor, pretending to be passengers. Once the vessel put to sea, the men seized control of the ship, killing one man and wounding another in the process. After several days the Confederates abandoned the ship, unable to bring it to a safe port, and they were subsequently captured by the Canadian authorities. The United States tried to extradite the Confederates on charges of piracy. The Confederates raised the defense of acting under a duly authorized commission from Jefferson Davis. The case took the form of an extradition and habeas corpus proceeding. Although some question arose as to the authenticity of the letters of marque, the Canadian magistrate acknowledged without question the Confederacy's status as a belligerent. Ultimately, the Confederates went free because the court found defects in the arrest warrant. But in the process of making that determination, the Canadian government acknowledged not only the fact of the Confederacy's existence but also its rights under international law.

———

The Sequestration Act as a symbol of the Confederacy's de facto existence got lost in the debates in Charleston, Philadelphia, and New York City. With the lives of Confederate sailors at stake in two Northern courthouses, and their hopes pinned to a defense that the Confederacy had substance and controlled the actions and loyalties of those who lived within its borders, sequestration offered convincing evidence of that power. Grier did not have to address the issue of the Confederacy's de facto existence in the *Prize Cases*, even though his opinion implied that the Confederacy's size and power attributed to the magnitude of the war. However, when the war ended, with the South in shambles, the Sequestration Act offered the United States the first opportunity to speak directly to the very issues raised in the piracy cases, not in the context of privateering but in the Confederacy's seizure of debts due to Northern citizens.

The defense in both the *Jeff Davis* case and the *Savannah* case had focused on the Southern Confederacy's de facto existence. Between June 1867 and June 1869, the chief justice of the U.S. Supreme Court, Salmon P. Chase, addressed the question of a de facto rebellion government. In three circuit court cases, one each in North Carolina, South Carolina, and Virginia, Northern plaintiffs owed money by Southerners prior to the war filed suit to recover on debts that had been sequestered under the August 30, 1861, Sequestration Act. Operating in the shadow of the *Prize Cases*, Chase pronounced judgment on what the Confederacy "had been" in a way consistent with Grier's opinion.

In *Shortridge Co. v. Macon* in 1867, Chase found for the Northern plaintiff in a promissory note debt case. He stated that the rebellion had been treason and that "it is the practice of modern governments, when attacked by formidable rebellion, to exercise and concede belligerent rights. These are concessions made by the legislative and executive departments in the exercise of political discretion. They establish no rights except during the war." The following year in *Keppel's Adm'rs v. Petersburg R. R. Co.*, Chase held a Virginia defendant liable on debts sequestered during the war. Following the lead established in the piracy cases, counsel for the Petersburg Railroad Company raised the Confederacy's de facto existence and the monumental proportions of the Southern rebellion as factors that exonerated the railroad from any claim of debt.

Chase took the opportunity to confront both concepts head on. De facto government, Chase admitted, had no fixed and definite meaning, but he defined the term as "signifying any organized government established for the time over a considerable territory, in exclusion of the regular government." However, nothing distinguished a de facto government from "other unlawful combinations." Such a government could not define itself solely by its power and territorial control, but depended on the policy of the national government from which it tried to separate. The Confederacy, regardless of its size and control, had been an ongoing act of treason and, in his estimation, never became a de facto government. Therefore, its legislative and judicial actions had no validity.

In June 1869 Chase returned to the scene of the sequestration cases and from his circuit seat in South Carolina did expressly what his two previous decisions had implicitly done: declared the Confederate sequestration acts null and void. In *Perdicaris v. The Charleston Gas Light Company*, Chase declared all actions of the Confederate government, or any state hostile to the United States and prejudicial to the rights of its citizens, void and incapable of conveying any title. The Sequestration Act clearly prejudiced the rights of U.S. citizens and was therefore void.

Chase's decision in *Perdicaris* came several months after his April 1869 opinion in *Texas v. White*. That opinion reflected the certainty of what the Confederacy "had been." Reading Chase's earlier circuit decisions on the Sequestration Act, one could see his opinion in *White* crystallizing. By the time Noah Swayne wrote that the Confederacy "was if it was not," the issue had been decided. As significant as these Supreme Court cases were, and are today as to the question of what the Confederacy was and how future generations could legally conceptualize rebellion, they would not have been possible were it not for the fact that the Confederacy had real substance, both factually and legally, within its own borders and in the eyes of the international community during the four years of the war. In the wake of Union victory it became a simple matter to say what the then dead Confederacy had been. But to understand what it was while it lived and the complexity of the question of national existence while a rebellion is inchoate, one must look to that obscure body of law created in October 1861 that put the issue of defining the Confederacy on trial.

CHRONOLOGY

February 1861	The seven Confederate states that seceded between December 20, 1860, and February 1, 1861, form the Confederate States of America in Montgomery, Alabama.
April 12, 1861	Confederate forces fire on Fort Sumter, and the Civil War begins.
April 17, 1861	Jefferson Davis announces his intention to issue letters of marque and calls for Confederate privateers.
April 19, 1861	Abraham Lincoln issues a proclamation announcing that anyone acting under a commission from the Confederate States of America will be treated as a pirate.
May 6, 1861	Confederate Congress passes an act recognizing the existence of war and authorizing the issuance of letters of marque and reprisal.
May 18, 1861	The *Savannah* is commissioned as a Confederate privateer.
June 3, 1861	The *Savannah* is captured by USS *Perry*.
June 18, 1861	The *Jefferson Davis* is commissioned as a privateer. It sails from June 28, 1861, until August 16, 1861, when it runs aground off the coast of Florida and is destroyed. During the time it sails it takes ten prizes.
July 22, 1861	William Smith and his prize crew are captured off the coast of North Carolina.
August 6, 1861	United States Congress passes the First Confiscation Act.
August 8, 1861	Confederate Congress passes the Alien Enemies Act.
August 30, 1861	Confederate Congress passes the Sequestration Act.
October 14, 1861	Trial in the sequestration cases begins in Charleston, South Carolina.
October 22, 1861	The trial of William Smith of the *Jeff Davis* begins in Philadelphia.
October 23, 1861	Trial of the *Savannah* begins in New York City.
October 24, 1861	Judge Andrew Magrath hands down his decision in the sequestration cases, upholding the constitutionality of the act.

October 25, 1861	William Smith is found guilty of piracy. On October 29, 1861, all but one of the remainder of his crew are found guilty of piracy.
October 31, 1861	The jury in the trial of the *Savannah* announces it cannot render a verdict and is dismissed.
February 2, 1862	The Confederate privateers are transferred from civilian prisons to military prisons and subsequently released.
March 1863	The U.S. Supreme Court decides the *Prize Cases*.
April 1869	The U.S. Supreme Court decides the case of *Texas v. White*, invalidating all actions of the Confederate government that aided in the rebellion.

Berd v. Lovelace, Cary 61, 21 ER 33 (1577)

Brown v. United States, 12 U.S. (8 Cr.) 110 (1814)

Confederate States of America v. Petigru, McGrady, Mitchell, Whaley, Wilkinson, Confederate District Court, South Carolina, private reporter (1861)

Dennis v. Codrington, Cary 100, 21 ER 53 (1580)

Folliet v. Ogden, 1 H. Bl. 123 (1789)

Foster's Crown Case, chap. 2, sec. 8, 216, London ed. (1792)

General Parkhill, U.S. District Court, Eastern District of Pennsylvania, Prize Court (1861)

Greenbough v. Gaskell, 1 My & K, 39 ER 618 (1833)

Hickman v. Jones, 76 U.S. (9 Wall.) 197 (1869)

Horn v. Lockhart, 84 U.S. (17 Wall.) 570 (1873)

In Re David Collins, privately reported (1864)

Joseph Segunda, 23 U.S. (10 Wheaton) 312 (1825)

Madzimbamuto v. Lardner-Burke, 1 A.C. 645 (1969)

Prize Cases, 67 U.S. 635 (1863)

Rose v. Himley, 8 U.S. (4 Cr.) 241 (1808)

Santissima Trinidad, 7 Wheaton 283 (1822)

Texas v. White, 74 U.S. (Wall. 7) 700 (1869)

United States v. Baker, U.S. District Court, Eastern District of Pennsylvania, private reporter (1861)

United States v. The Brig Malek Adhel, 43 U.S. (2 How.) 210 (1844)

United States v. Klintock, 5 Wheaton 144 (1820)

United States v. Palmer, 3 Wheaton 610 (1818)

United States v. Smith, U.S. District Court, Southern District of New York, private reporter (1861)

United States v. Tully, 28 F.Cas. 226 (C.C. Mass. 1812)

Ware v. Hilton, 3 U.S. (3 Dall.) 199 (1796)

Wolff v. Oxholm, 6 M & S 92, 105 ER 1177 (1817)

Wright v. Nutt, 1 H. Black's Rep. 149 (1789)

BIBLIOGRAPHICAL ESSAY

The foundation of this project is the trial transcripts from the three cases that make up the study: D. F. Murphy, *Full Report of the Trial of William Smith for Piracy As One of the Crew of the Confederate Privateer* Jeff Davis (Philadelphia: King & Baird, Printers, 1861), A. F. Warburton, stenographer, *Trial of the Officers and Crew of the Privateer* Savannah, *On the Charge of Piracy* (New York: Baker & Godwin, Printers, 1861), and J. Woodruff, phonographic reporter, *The Sequestration Cases before the Honorable Judge A. G. Magrath* (Charleston, S.C.: n.p., 1861). Collectively they comprise more than 500 pages of trial transcript and argument. They exist only in their original form, and I am indebted to the University of Georgia Law Library and the Center for American History at the University of Texas for making these materials available to me.

Newspapers provided a key component to understanding not only the trials themselves but also the social and political contexts in which they occurred. The main papers for this study were the *New York Times*, the *Philadelphia Inquirer*, the *Charleston Mercury*, *Harper's Weekly*, the *Boston Daily Evening Transcript*, and the *Richmond Dispatch*.

The Official Records of the Union and Confederate Armies in the War of the Rebellion (O.R.), 128 vols. (Washington D.C.: Government Printing, 1880–1900) and *The Official Records of the Union and Confederate Navies in the War of the Rebellion (O.N.R.)*, 30 vols. (Washington D.C.: Government Printing Office, 1894–1922) provided invaluable primary source material for both the piracy cases and issues of Union and Confederate confiscation. In addition to the *O.R.* and the *O.N.R.*, two other published primary sources provided invaluable material for this study. *The Southern Historical Society Papers*, 52 vols. (Richmond, Va.: Wooster, Ohio, Bell & Howard, 1879–) chronicled the evolution of the sequestration laws and gave some insight into the debates on the subject. *Confederate Imprints, 1861–1865* (microfilm) (New Haven, Conn.: Research Publications, 1974) provided a diverse collection of primary documents, including the sequestration laws themselves; broadsides and advertisements issued by Confederate receivers; correspondence from such key participants as Judge William Hill Pinckney in Texas, whose grand jury charge on sequestration was among the collection; and a lengthy treatise by a correspondent identified only as "Nemo."

General information on the Civil War used as context came from Brooks Simpson, *America's Civil War* (Wheeling, Ill.: Harlan Davidson, Inc., 1996), James McPherson, *Battle Cry of Freedom* (New York: Oxford University Press, 1988), and Russell F. Weigley, *A Great Civil War: A Military and Political History* (Bloomington: Indiana University Press, 2000).

For background on privateering and its use in the Civil War, I relied on Donald A. Petrie, *The Prize Game: Lawful Looting on the High Seas in the Days of the Fighting Sail* (Annapolis, Md.: Naval Institute Press, 1999), Stuart L. Bernath, *Squall across the Atlantic: American Civil War Prize Cases and Diplomacy* (Berkeley and Los Angeles: University of California Press, 1970), and an older work, William Morrison Robinson Jr., *The Confederate Privateers* (New Haven, Conn.: Yale University Press, 1928). I found Joseph-James Ahren's "Prize Rules: Civil War Prize Procedures in the Philadelphia Prize Court," *American Neptune* 58, no. 4 (1998): 343–352, helpful in providing not only background on how federal courts dealt with the issues of taking prizes in the context of a civil war but also insight into one of the judges, John Cadwalader. Although the *Prize Cases* were officially reported, I gained valuable insight into how the piracy cases may have shaped the debate and arguments as presented to the Supreme Court by reviewing William Evarts's oral arguments before the Supreme Court in Philip B. Kurland and Gerhard Casper, eds., *Landmark Briefs and Arguments of the Supreme Court of the United States: Constitutional Law* (Arlington, Va.: University Publications, 1975). I also found an excellent analysis of how the decision created Confederate belligerent rights in Ludwell H. Johnson, "Abraham Lincoln and the Development of Presidential War Making Powers: Prize Cases (1863) Revisited," *Civil War History* 35, no. 3 (1989): 208–224.

Although little existed in the way of secondary material on sequestration, I found William C. Davis, *Look Away, Look Away: A History of the Confederate States of America* (New York: Free Press, 2002) helpful. In the absence of any monographic material on the subject, I benefited from an array of periodical literature on sequestration and confiscation. Sarah V. Kalinoski, "Sequestration, Confiscation and the 'Tory' in the Vermont Revolution," *Vermont History* 45, no. 4 (1977): 236–246, put sequestration in the context of the American historical experience and allowed me to draw comparisons between America's first and second "revolutions." The notion that sequestration was part of a broader war on property and how that war was waged in both the North and the South was fleshed out in Silvan R. Siddali, "'The Sport of Folly and the Prize of Treason': Confederate Property Seizures and the Northern Homefront," *Civil War History* 47, no.4 (2001): 310–333, and Brian R. Dirck, "Posterity's Blush: Civil Liberties, Property Rights, and Property Confiscation in the Confederacy," *Civil War History* 48, no. 3 (2002): 237–256. J. Cutler Andrews, "The Southern Telegraph Company, 1861–1865: A Chapter in the History of Wartime Communication," *Journal of Southern History* 30, no. 3 (1963): 319–344, provided an excellent insight into the interconnected nature of prewar American business and the efforts of both Northerners and Southerners to mitigate the effects of Confederate sequestration. Two articles on Texas Confederate federal judge William Pinckney Hill provided insight into how sequestration operated and the concerns voiced by those charged with its operation: Nowlin Randolph, "Judge William Pinckney Hill Aids the Confederate War Effort," *Southwest Historical Quarterly* 16, no. 1 (1912): 14–28, and Brian Dirck, "'Administer in Much Discretion': William Pinckney Hill and the Confederate Grand Jury in Galveston, Texas, 1861–62," *Houston Review: History and Culture of the Gulf Coast* 13, no. 1 (1991): 21–34. Sequestration did not discriminate based on gender, and Drew Gilpin Faust, *Mothers of Invention: Women of the Slaveholding South in the American Civil War* (New York: Vintage Books, 1996) provided background on women's status in the antebellum South.

For background and secondary material on the Confederate legal system and civil rights issues, I looked to Mark Neely, *Southern Rights: Political Prisoners and the Myth of Confederate Constitutionalism* (Charlottesville: University of Virginia Press, 1999), and William Morrison Robinson Jr., *Justices in Grey: A History of the Judicial System of the Confederate States of America* (Cambridge, Mass.: Harvard University Press, 1941).

International law lay at the center of both the piracy cases and the sequestration trials. For sources and background on the state of international law in 1861, I relied on several general works on the subject: J. E. S. Fawcett, *The Law of Nations* (New York: Basic Books, 1968), Gerhard Von Glahn, *Law among Nations* (New York Macmillan, 1968), and Charles G. Fenwick, *International Law* (New York: Appleton-Century Crofts, 1965). For an analysis of how broad concepts of international law were applied in the United States prior to the American Civil War, I used Daniel George Lang, *Foreign Policy in the Early Republic: The Law of Nations and the Balance of Power* (Baton Rouge: Louisiana State University Press, 1985). Because the work of Emerich de Vattel appeared as a prominent part of the arguments on both sides in all three trials, I consulted his *The Law of Nations; or, Principles of the Law of Nature Applied to the Conduct and Affairs of Nations and Sovereigns: A Work Tending to Display the True Interest of Powers* (Northampton, Mass.: Thomas M. Pomroy for S.& E. Butler, 1805).

One of the difficulties inherent in studying nineteenth-century legal history is the lack of the comprehensive case reporting we grew accustomed to in the twentieth century. I was fortunate to find Salmon P. Chase's postwar sequestration cases in Bradley T. Johnson, *Reports of Cases Decided by Chief Justice Chase in the Circuit Court of the United States Fourth Circuit, 1865–1869*, rev. and corr. Chief Justice Chase, new introduction by Ferne B. Hyman and Harold Hyman (New York: DaCapo Press, 1972). In instances where cases were not officially reported, I owe a debt of gratitude to the Library of Congress, where I found the entire transcript of the *David*

Collins case in *"The Chesapeake": The Case of David Collins, et al. Prisoners Arrested under the Imperial Act, 6 & VIC, CAP. 76, On a charge of Piracy, Investigated before Humphery T. Gilbert, Esq. Police Magistrate of the City of St. John, and Arguments on the Return to the Writ of Habeas Corpus, before His Honor, Mr. Justice Ritchie, Compiled from Original Documents* (Saint John, New Brunswick, Nova Scotia: J. A. Macmillan, Publishers, 1864).

People and their stories are what distinguish constitutional history from the study of constitutional law. Insight into the parties, lawyers, and judges who debated and decided these cases came from a variety of sources in addition to those previously mentioned. Among the more important for the sequestration cases was the South Carolina Historical Society in Charleston, where I found the paper collections of James Petigru, Nelson Mitchell, William Whaley, and Edward McGrady. Isaac Hayne's and Charles Richardson Miles's papers were housed at South Caroliniana Library on the campus of the University of South Carolina. I gained a clearer understanding of the social status of some of the litigants through James Garner Patey, *The Whaley Family and Its Charleston Connections* (Spartanburg, S.C.: Reprint Co., 1992). In addition to primary documents, I found secondary sources on Petigru, McGrady, and Judge Andrew Magrath. One short article contained material on both Petigru and Magrath: Brian Dirck, "Confederate States of America v. James Petigru (1862)," *Proteus: A Journal of Ideas* (n.d., 12–14). The most helpful work on Petigru was William H. Pease and Jane H. Pease, *James Petigru: Southern Conservative, Southern Dissenter* (Columbia: University of South Carolina Press, 2002). Lyon G. Tyler, "Drawing the Color Line in the Episcopal Diocese of South Carolina, 1876 to 1890: The Role of Edward McGrady, Father and Son," *South Carolina Historical Magazine* 9, no. 2 (1990): 107–124, provided insight into the elder McGrady both before and after the war. David Heidler and Jeanne Heidler provided a current thumbnail sketch of Magrath in *The Encyclopedia of the American Civil War*, 5 vols. (Santa Barbara, Calif.: ABC-CLIO, 2000), 3:1240, which helped me understand the contemporary newspaper comments on his activities. Manisha Sinha, *The Counterrevolution of Slavery* (Chapel Hill: University of North Carolina Press, 2000), detailed Magrath's antebellum judicial career. John B. Edmunds, "South Carolina," in *The Confederate Governors*, ed. W. Buck Years (Athens: University of Georgia Press, 1985), 162–184, chronicled South Carolina governors throughout the war, including Magrath and his term.

For background material on the players in the *Savannah* trial I owe an immeasurable debt to John D. Gordon III, "The Trial of the Officers and Crew of the Schooner 'Savannah,'" *Yearbook: Supreme Court Historical Society* (New York: Second Circuit Historical Committee, 1983), 31–45. The article gave me valuable insight into pretrial matters and background on Baker,

Harleston, Sullivan, Lord, Brady, and both Judge Shipman and Justice Nelson. It also led me to D. McAdam, ed., *A History of the Bench and Bar of New York* (New York: n.p., 1897). For some background on Jeremiah Larocque and insight into how the defendants afforded such a prominent defense team, I relied on "America's Successful Men of Affairs: An Encyclopedia of Contemporaneous Biography, Volume 1," *Cosmopolitan*, 1888, and Obituary of Samuel L. M. Barlow, *New York Times*, July 11, 1889. I found I. Edwards Clark, "A Great Advocate: James T. Brady," *Galaxy* 7 (January–July 1869): 716, an excellent source of background material on James Brady.

For personal background information on the litigants in the *Jeff Davis* trial, I relied on John Hill Martin, *Martin's Bench and Bar of Philadelphia* (Philadelphia: Rees Welsh & Co., 1888) and Elis P. Oberholtzer, *Philadelphia: A History of the City and Its People, a Record of 225 Years* (Philadelphia: S. J. Clarke Publishing, n.d.). Using these two sources as a starting place, I was able to identify most of the litigants through newspapers or other sources. I found information on J. Hubley Ashton through a biographical sketch attached to a reminiscence he wrote of Lincoln in 1864 and reprinted as J. Hubley Ashton, "Lincolniana: A Glimpse of Lincoln in 1864," *Journal of the Illinois State Historical Society* 69, no.1 (1976): 67–69. The easiest figure to research was William Kelley. There were several unpublished theses and dissertations, but the most useful source for my purposes was Ira V. Brown, "William D. Kelley and Radical Reconstruction," *Pennsylvania Magazine of History and Biography* 85, no. 3 (1961): 316–329. At the other extreme, Nathaniel Harrison proved the most difficult. However, using *Martin's Bench and Bar*, I was able to track him in Lynda Lasswell Crist, Mary Seaton Dix, and Kenneth H. Williams, eds., *Papers of Jefferson Davis* (Baton Rouge: Louisiana State University Press, 1995) and the *O.R.*, and through the help of the Mercer County, West Virginia, Historical Society, I learned a great deal about who he was. I found short but useful sketches of Justices Robert Grier and Samuel Nelson in Kermit Hall, ed., *The Oxford Companion to the Supreme Court of the United States* (New York: Oxford University Press, 1992).

The political affiliations of the parties in part defined the competing sides in the piracy cases. For general background on antebellum politics, I relied on Michael F. Holt, *The Political Crisis of the 1850s* (New York: W. W. Norton & Co., 1983) and John Niven, *The Coming of the Civil War* (Wheeling, Ill: Harlan Davidson, Inc., 1990). The political affiliations of the participants came from the background material already cited.

Certain unpublished primary sources that exist only in their respective archival depositories cannot be omitted. In the Atlanta, Georgia, branch of the National Archives and Record Administration I found Record Group 21, wherein I discovered the sequestration court records for Alabama,

Georgia, and South Carolina. Within the twenty-nine boxes were stories, some of which appear in this book, of how sequestration affected people on a personal level. In addition these records provided a wealth of information on the details and scope of the Confederate sequestration process. In the Louisiana Department of Archives and History, I discovered the June 15, 1861, opinion letter from Louisiana Attorney General Thomas Semmes to the Merchants and Traders Bank of New Orleans. Almost two full months before the Alien Enemies Act, Semmes articulated what would become the Confederate position on U.S. citizens and their property rights. In so doing he would set the stage for the sequestration debate. To this material I added the December 7, 1863, Report of the Confederate Treasury found in the Documenting the American South Collection, University of North Carolina at Chapel Hill Libraries. That report added to the total picture by setting out revenue from sequestration for that year. Finally, in the Library of Congress, I found the James Mason Papers, which provided invaluable insight into the Confederacy's struggle for recognition.

{ *The Confederacy on Trial* }